Wiser. Hotter. Stronger.

LIVE COURAGEOUSLY THROUGH MENOPAUSE

Daniella Schoch

Praise

"Having worked closely with Daniella as both her mentor and coach, I've witnessed firsthand her exceptional gift for turning life's most disorienting moments into opportunities for profound growth. What sets her apart is her rare ability to guide people through the most challenging transitions with both fierce compassion and practical wisdom. In *Wiser. Hotter. Stronger.*, she's created something powerful—a roadmap that doesn't just acknowledge the struggle of menopause, but transforms it into a leadership awakening. She doesn't gloss over the challenges of the journey, but she shows women how to emerge from this pivotal life stage more powerful than they've ever been. This is mindset mastery at its finest."—**Zac Palmer, Sales & Persuasion Strategist**

Dedication

To the women who came before me and walk beside me: my mother, my godmother, my sister, and my niece—your love, your lessons, and your legacy live in these pages.

To my Inner Queen I finally learned to trust—thank you for your patience, for waiting through the doubt, the silence, the striving. I see you now.

To the men in my life—thank you for your presence on this path, seen and unseen.

And to all the women finding their way home to themselves—may these pages meet you exactly where you are and remind you: there is wisdom in you. Power in you. A Queen rising in you, too.

Cover Image: Dragoslav Andjelkovic
Editor: Krystal Hille
Published by: Hille House Publishing

ISBN: 978-1-7641985-2-3 (ebook)
ISBN: 978-1-7641985-3-0 (Paperback)

Disclaimer

The information contained in this book is for educational and inspirational purposes only and is not intended as medical advice. The author's intention is to refrain from providing medical diagnosis, treatment, or advice. If you are experiencing physical or mental health concerns, please consult with a qualified healthcare professional.

The exercises, practices, and techniques described in this book are based on the author's personal experience and professional work over twenty years as an art therapist and transformational coach. Many have been adapted and modified over time, drawing from general wisdom traditions, neuroscience and therapeutic practices. While many readers may find them helpful, individual results will vary. What works for one person may not work for another.

The author and publisher disclaim all responsibility for any liability, loss, or risk, personal or otherwise, which is incurred as a consequence, directly or indirectly, of the use and application of any of the contents of this book. The stories and examples shared are based on real experiences but have been modified to protect privacy and confidentiality. Any resemblance to specific individuals is coincidental.

By reading this book, you acknowledge that you are fully responsible for your own health, well-being, and life choices.

The Transformation Toolkit

To support your journey through the 5 pillars of transformation, I've created this collection of bonus resources to deepen your practice and accelerate your growth.

You may want to start with the *Sacred Space Setup Guide*—a practical guide to create your sanctuary for reflection, creativity, and Queen energy embodiment.

As you go along the book you'll find references to these additional tools:

- The Energy-Connection Audit Worksheet
- Beyond the Belief Barrier Worksheet
- Permission Slips for Creativity
- The Congruence Circles Worksheet
- The Ripple Effect Mind Map Template
- Your North Star Mapping Guide
- The Sacred Integration Visualization (Audio)

All this is free. Download your Transformation Toolkit at www.daniellaschoch.com/toolkit or by scanning this QR code:

SCAN ME

If you're looking for a clearer understanding of what's happening within your body—the *mechanics* and *mystery* of this transition—I've also created this wonderful guide: *The Big M Guide – (Almost) Everything You Need To Know About Menopause.*

It offers a grounded overview of the mechanics of menopause, the symptoms and hormonal shifts at play, along with practical lifestyle tips for nutrition, sleep, and energy that support your body during this transition.

Get The Big M here:

www.daniellaschoch.com/product/the-big-m-guide/

Together, *The Big M Guide* and *The Wiser. Hotter. Stronger. Transformation Toolkit* form the bridge between *understanding* menopause and *thriving* through it. Use them side by side to ground your transformation—in wisdom, self-trust, and everyday action.

Contents

Introduction

It's 3:00 a.m. I'm wide awake and hot, staring at the ceiling, wondering if I'll ever sleep through the night again. That was my unexpected introduction to perimenopause.

I didn't even realize it was perimenopause at first. I had this naive idea that menopause was all about hot flashes and a bit of crankiness for a few months—and then you're done. No hot flashes for me, so surely this couldn't be it, right?

Fast forward a few years: I'm standing on a beach in Mallorca, the sun warming my skin, and at fifty-four, feeling more alive—more myself—than I have in decades. I'm doing the same coaching work I'd done for years, but now on my own terms, guiding people through life transitions. The journey between these two moments?

That's what this book is about. It is for any woman who finds herself blindsided by menopause—confused, exhausted, and unsure of who she is becoming. There was so much I didn't know about menopause. I hadn't even really heard of perimenopause until it hit me. I didn't realise how many ways hormonal imbalances could manifest. And I definitely had no idea how hard those years would be before I finally reached menopause; not only on my body, but on my whole being: mind and spirit included.

After doing my own research on why I couldn't sleep through the night anymore, I finally realized: *Oh, that's a common symptom of menopause*. As I dug deeper, I uncovered a world of changes no one had prepared me for: food sensitivities, aches and pains in my bones, mood swings, anxiety, and feelings of depression that impacted my outlook on life as a middle-aged woman.

Then came another layer—something deeper. The grief of possibly never having children. It felt so final. So unexpected. Somewhere between the sleepless nights and the confusion, the self-doubt and the existential questions, I returned to what I knew best. I put on my curious coaching hat and asked myself the same question I ask my clients during big transitions: *Is there another way of looking at this?*

What if this wasn't just the end of a chapter, but the beginning of a whole new one? Maybe even the most exciting one yet?

I know what you might be thinking: *Exciting? Has she lost her mind, along with her estrogen?* But bear with me. Because what I've discovered—what I've lived—is that menopause can be a powerful turning point. It can be the catalyst for becoming the most authentic version of yourself.

In this book, I'll share what I've learned—through personal experience, through my work with women in transition, and years of study and practice. I'll walk you through how to navigate this chapter with grace and power, so that instead of enduring menopause, you emerge from it transformed.

Whether you're before it, in it, or beyond it, I'm here to help you rewrite your menopause story. To trade the old narrative of decline for one of awakening, evolution, and deep self-connection.

Reframing Menopause

So let's talk about menopause—"the change." It affects every woman, yet so many of us still approach it with fear, shame, confusion, or silence. This book aims to change that.

Menopause shouldn't be taboo. It's time we talk openly about all of it—its onset, its effects on our physical, emotional, and mental well-being, and what it can teach us about ourselves.

Yes, this phase can be intense. Many of us are juggling multiple responsibilities: our bodies are changing, our children may be leaving home, we might be caring for aging parents—all while questioning our own roles, dreams, and identity as we grow older. It can feel like a crisis, full of loss.

But if we shift our perspective, it can also become a gateway. A moment that holds tremendous opportunity, if we allow *the change* to change us.

As we let go of the biological purpose that has shaped so much of our lives—the potential to bear children—we enter a new space. A space where we finally get to choose, maybe for the first time in our lives: *Who do I want to be from this point onward?* That choice can be overwhelming, even intimidating. It's easy for old limitations and beliefs to resurface when we're standing at a crossroads.

But it can also be exhilarating. This is your time. Your opportunity to redefine who you are and how you want to live, on your own terms.

Menopause as a Unique Gift

Menopause, in many ways, is a gift—a gift uniquely given to women. Yes, men experience midlife transitions too, but rarely is it as clearly marked as it is for us. Our bodies draw a firm line and say: *This part is over. What comes next?*

Wiser. Hotter. Stronger. is your companion for this journey. It's not just about surviving menopause and stumbling into your next phase. It's about embracing this transition as an opening. An opportunity to grow beyond old limitations, rediscover your purpose, and step into the parts of you that have been waiting, quietly and patiently, for their time to shine.

This book will help you reframe menopause not as an ending, but as a sacred threshold—a powerful rite of passage into the most authentic, powerful version of yourself.

Maybe you're standing in front of the mirror, wondering who that woman is staring back at you. Maybe you're grappling with restless nights, mood swings, or a body that feels unfamiliar. Perhaps you're feeling invisible in a world obsessed with youth, or questioning your joy and direction in life.

You're not alone. So many of us arrive at this phase unprepared, isolated, and unsure. We're expected to juggle everything—hot flashes and board meetings, brain fog and family life—while culture whispers (or screams) that we're past our prime.

But I'm here to tell you that voice is wrong. And deep down, you know it.

You know there's more to you than your reproductive years. More fire in your belly. More wisdom in your bones. You are not done ... not by a long shot! You're just getting started.

Your Roadmap to Becoming Wiser. Hotter. Stronger.

Wiser. Hotter. Stronger. gives you a map to navigate this transition.

We'll explore the Heroine's Journey, embracing a uniquely feminine path to wholeness. As Maureen Murdock wrote, "Women find their way back to themselves not by moving up and out into the light like men, but by moving down into the depths of the ground of their being."

Rather than pretending menopause isn't happening—or trying to "fix" it—we'll embrace it as a natural, transformative part of the female experience; a call to come home to ourselves.

Here's how this book works: It's built around five pillars. Think of the first three as coming home to yourself—reconnecting with your body, remembering your wisdom, and getting back in touch with who you are at your core and what's really important to you at this stage of your life.

The last two invite you to look outward — to consider how you want to show up, make a difference, and share your gifts with the world in a way that feels deeply *you*.

- **Connection**: Reconnecting with your body, heart, and essence.
- **Clarity:** Cutting through conditioning to rediscover what matters most.
- **Creativity:** Tapping into new forms of self-expression and problem-solving.
- **Congruence:** Aligning your inner truth with how you show up in the world.
- **Contribution:** Giving from a place of purpose and authenticity.

Each chapter blends personal stories, practical exercises, and soulful reflections. Drawing on art therapy, self-mastery tools, and transformational coaching, this book offers a holistic and grounded approach to navigating this powerful transition.

And more than anything, it challenges the outdated narrative that menopause equals decline. Instead, it offers a new possibility: that this is your time of renewal, rediscovery, and unprecedented personal power.

As one of my clients said, "You make menopause sound like so much fun!"

Standing at the Threshold

At this stage in life, so many women find themselves standing at a threshold.

Take Maria, for example. She was considering stepping down from her leadership role, convinced she had "lost it." Through our work together, and the very tools you'll find in this book, she began to listen to her body and honor her new rhythms. Today, she's mentoring younger women and sharing her wisdom with strength and pride.

Then there's Sarah, who felt like a stranger in her own mind. She emerged from this work with renewed clarity about who she is, what she values, and what she wants next.

These stories aren't rare. I've witnessed these transformations time and again—in my clients, in myself, and in the collective shift awakening among women around the world.

Whether you're in your forties feeling the first whispers of change, in your fifties navigating the storm, or in your sixties seeking reinvention, this book is for you.

For the woman asking: *What's next?*

For the mother whose nest is emptying.

For the childfree woman ready to leave a different kind of legacy.

For the caregiver, learning to care for herself.

For the woman who's always put others first, finally ready to choose herself.

As a transformational coach, art therapist, panic healer, and leadership strategist with over two decades of experience, I've supported hundreds of women through major life transitions. But my deepest insights come from walking this path myself. This book is the culmination of everything I've learned—personally and professionally.

I wrote this book because I needed it. And I wrote it for you. For every woman who's ever stood in front of the mirror, not recognizing herself, and wondering, *Is this it?*

But more than that, I wrote it because I believe the world needs the wisdom, power, and authenticity of women like you and me. The world needs your fire—now more than ever.

This book is my contribution to unleashing that potential.

A Word on How to Use This Book

This book includes a variety of exercises—creative explorations, reflective journaling, and soulful practices designed to help you reconnect with your inner self. Most take just 10–15 minutes and require only a pen, paper, and a quiet moment.

You might read straight through the whole book and return to the exercises later, or pause and reflect as you go. Do what feels right.

But don't let the exercises slow you down. Let them support you as you flow with the empowering currents that carry you from pillar to pillar—allowing them to gently transform and uplift you as you progress.

And if you'd like personalized guidance on which pillar offers the most leverage for you right now—where to focus your energy for maximum transformation—you can book a Pillar Gap session with me at www.pillargapmap.org

Sometimes the clearest path forward starts with knowing exactly where you are.

Remember: you are exactly where you need to be.

Trust that. Take a deep breath.

Let's begin.

Chapter 1

When the Old Stories End

***"Owning our story and loving ourselves through that process is the bravest thing we'll ever do."* —Brené Brown**

"If you don't give me the time off, I'll go anyway. I'll just miss class for a week." That's what I told my headmaster.

I was sixteen. A high school student delivering what amounted to an ultimatum to the highest authority figure in my school. Looking back, I'm still not sure where I found the courage.

What could possibly have been so important to my teenage self? A concert? A boy? A shopping trip to Paris?

No. I wanted permission to miss school for a week so I could attend a seminar on esoteric psychology taught by Thorwald Dethlefsen, a visionary thinker whose work profoundly shaped my path. I'd already attended two of his seminars, both conveniently scheduled during midterm breaks. But Level III—the one I most wanted to attend—fell during regular school days. I feared it would be my only chance. I wasn't going to miss it. Not for anything—not even school.

A few weeks earlier, a classmate had been granted time off to complete Level III of his ski instructor certification.

"You gave time off for sports," I reasoned, steady and composed. "I want time off to develop my mind and my soul. Why should this be any less important?"

I still remember the look my headmaster gave me—a mixture of doubt, surprise, and maybe even a flicker of curiosity, as if he were seeing me for the first time. I left his office that day without an answer. But a few days later, word came: my request had been granted.

It was a bold move—and it paid off.

***

That seminar did turn out to be the last of its kind. It also lit a spark that would guide me for decades: a deep fascination with esoteric psychology and spiritual growth. That spark has never fully gone out, even if it flickered dimly during certain phases of my life.

What I learned that week extended far beyond the teachings themselves. I learned that stepping into discomfort—choosing courage over compliance—creates the space where growth happens. For better or worse, moments like these would come to shape who I am today.

And yet, it took me years to understand that my intuition and sensitivity were strengths, not liabilities to be hidden away.

Looking back now, through the lens of menopause, I can see the irony. The girl who once fearlessly challenged authority to honor her spiritual calling became a woman who, for a time, lost touch with that deeper self. I would spend years chasing society's definition of success—only to find myself, in midlife, coming full circle. Remembering the courage. Returning to my essence. Reclaiming the wisdom and authenticity I'd once possessed naturally.

The Fertility Path We Choose ... Or Not

Scroll through social media today, and you'll find a flood of content about menopause. There's advice on what to eat, which workouts will shrink the menopause belly, and a steady stream of memes that help us laugh through the tears about sleepless nights, brain fog, and night sweats. And then there's the "helpful" friend who's found the miracle tea or exotic supplement that promises to fix it all.

Today, we can find more information about how our changing hormones affect our health, our bones and brains, our emotional landscape, and how we experience overwhelm, anxiety, and depression. Much more than was available to our mothers.

But what we're still not talking about—at least not enough—is how the end of our fertility, the quiet retirement of our ovaries, touches something deeper: our identity, our sense of self.

To understand the end, we have to go back to the beginning.

Biologically, a girl becomes a woman when she gets her first period. But we know that growing into womanhood emotionally and psychologically is something entirely different. For many of us—including myself—it's a journey that continues well into midlife, through all the twists and turns in our relationship with fertility and femininity.

Like so many women my age, I've had a complicated experience with fertility—sometimes even ironic, looking back now. In my twenties, I spent most of my time actively trying *not* to get pregnant. Armed with contraception—and aside from the occasional scare thanks to a broken condom—I saw reproduction as something within my control, not something left to fate.

As I moved into my late twenties, pregnancy was the furthest thing from my mind. I had places to go, things to learn, and a whole world I was eager to explore. Children were a vague possibility, a "someday" thought—something to consider once I'd established my career and found the right partner.

My mother's generation had fought hard for those choices, and I wasn't about to squander them. Her message, though unspoken, was clear: Make sure you can stand on your own two feet. Never depend on a man for your livelihood. She had raised me to be strong and independent, to create my own security rather than seeking it from someone else.

So I did.

I threw myself into my studies, eventually completing a Master of Law degree. I didn't go on to do the bar exam or complete the necessary internships—much to the disappointment of my father, who had already prepared a nameplate that read "*Dr. Daniella Schoch, Attorney at Law.*"

Instead, I took a position at a bank and began building my career in the corporate world.

The Price of Success

As I navigated the corporate world, I quickly realized that traditionally masculine traits—perfectionism, compartmentalization, self-promotion, and hierarchical thinking—were what the system valued and rewarded. I felt that in order to compete and succeed, I needed to overwork and overcompensate while hiding my more feminine qualities. It became clear that ideas like *intuition* had no place in business meetings. So I gradually suppressed my natural tendencies toward sensitivity, creativity, and emotional intelligence, believing they would be seen as weaknesses rather than strengths.

And when I finally had a seat at the table, I realized the rules of the table weren't what I wanted or needed to feel fulfilled or alive.

The demands of my high-powered leadership development and project management role in the financial services industry left me feeling increasingly disconnected from my true self. To survive in that environment, I believed I had to buy into the narrative: *Eat or be eaten. Work long hours and neglect your life, your health, and your happiness. Play the game of politics. Keep your mouth shut when you spend hours crafting a presentation, only to have your boss take the credit and present your work as his own.*

I was caught in the hamster wheel of trying to prove myself.

And it didn't just affect my professional life. That disconnection began to spill over into my private life as I drifted further and further from the fullness of who I was. I stopped tending to the parts of me that had once brought joy and meaning—my curiosity about the mysterious and the numinous, my spiritual practices, and my creative rituals. No meditation. No incense. No journaling, reading, or listening to the kinds of books that had once lit me up: spirituality, psychology and personal development. I silenced the parts of myself that didn't fit into the world I was trying to succeed in.

Meanwhile, another script ran in the background—the societal one: *Have a boyfriend. Get married. Have kids.*

Somewhere in my early thirties, something shifted. I found myself in what looked like a stable relationship. I was reasonably established in my career. And suddenly, the topic of children wasn't just a hypothetical future—it became real. It was time to *consider.*

On top of that, came the well-meaning but loaded questions from relatives at every family gathering:

"So, when are you thinking about starting a family?"

"Oh, we're just taking some time to settle back in for now," I'd reply politely, fresh off a three-year assignment living and traveling in the U.S.—all the while acutely aware of the unspoken clock ticking in the background.

The thing about fertility that nobody prepares you for is how it becomes both a private journey and a public performance.

Everyone seems to feel entitled to weigh in on your reproductive choices—when you should have children, how many you should have, and heaven forbid you're even *considering* not having any at all. Meanwhile, you're navigating your own complex feelings and circumstances—often in silence.

For me, the path forward seemed relatively clear. My fiancé and I were talking about having children. We were on that track—the conventional one: build a career, find a partner, get married, have kids, maybe add the house and the dog. The fairy tale ending society had promised would fulfill me.

And then, life happened.

My fiancé was diagnosed with bipolar disorder, which eventually led to our breakup. After eight years together, I found myself single in my mid-thirties, coming out of a relationship that had taken a significant toll on my sense of self.

I needed time—time to heal, to rediscover who I was, to reclaim my power. Starting a new relationship wasn't my priority as I moved into my late thirties and early forties. *I still have time*, I told myself.

It's worth noting that before the breakup, I had discovered Pranic Healing—an energy healing modality that revived my connection to spirituality. In fact, this practice may have been the catalyst for the relationship ending. For the first time in years, I found myself in an environment where my sensitivity and intuitive gifts were seen not as liabilities, but as strengths. My ability to sense energy—something that had been dismissed or smiled at by adults since childhood—was now recognized as a skill that could be developed and used to support myself and others.

In the Pranic Healing community, these qualities weren't just accepted—they were celebrated and cultivated.

This practice became a sanctuary where I could finally be myself again, reconnecting with the spiritual dimensions of my nature that I had pushed aside for so long. While my love life and career remained in flux, this rediscovery of my spiritual self became my anchor—a foundation, something to hold onto as I prepared for what lay ahead.

And then life, with its own impeccable sense of timing, struck again—not once, not twice, but three times.

Three Accidents and a Funeral

When I was thirty-nine, I had three accidents within five months. The universe, it seemed, was determined to get my attention.

The first happened on a cold February morning. I was walking down the hill from my flat to catch the bus to work, dressed for success in my corporate uniform, when I slipped on a patch of ice. The fall dislocated my upper arm bone from my elbow joint, and the force of it springing back shattered the joint into pieces.

Emergency rooms were overflowing that day due to icy road conditions, so my surgery didn't happen until midnight. I went from being an independent career woman to someone who needed help with everything—dressing, showering, cooking, cleaning—overnight.

Okay, I thought, as I struggled to adapt to this sudden dependence. *I've been working too much, not taking care of myself. This is the universe's way of telling me to slow down.*

Message received. Or so I thought.

Just seven weeks later, while still recovering from the first accident, I stumbled into a pothole in a cobblestone square and flipped my foot. I knew immediately something was wrong, but I spent ten days hoping it would get better on its own before finally seeing a doctor. The diagnosis: a torn Achilles tendon requiring immediate surgery. If left untreated, the damage would be permanent.

Now I had a healing arm and a foot I couldn't put weight on. I couldn't use crutches or a wheelchair because of my arm. The only option was a physical rehabilitation center, where my planned three-week stay turned into six as the full weight of what was happening began to sink in.

It was there, in the quiet of the rehab center, that I began to confront something far more painful than the physical injuries: how profoundly unhappy I had been, not just in my body, but in my life and career. I didn't know it then, but my body was already trying to speak to me in more ways than one. Not just through injury, but through the deep fatigue, the emotional weight, the sense that something was out of alignment.

These signs weren't hormonal—not yet—but they were whispers of what was to come. A foreshadowing of how, later, my body would speak even more loudly during perimenopause, demanding that I listen.

A wise doctor encouraged me to try art therapy, something I'd heard of but never experienced. What began as a reluctant attempt to pass the time became a revelation.

On paper, I worked through things I had been struggling with internally: giving up control, going with the flow, finding my voice, daring to show my true self. The blank page became a practice ground for showing up differently.

It was also where I first began to face the inner forces that had undermined my confidence, ambition, clarity, and self-worth for years. The inner critic—sometimes appearing as a harsh ogre, sometimes as a wicked witch—reminded me of all the ways I wasn't enough. I had been caught in the myth of deficit thinking: *If only I work harder ... If only I were more perfect ... If only I achieved more ... then I'll be okay.*

I had been so focused on climbing the corporate ladder, on proving my worth through performance, that I'd lost touch with the sensitive, spiritual, creative person I once was. The girl who stood up to her headmaster to attend a seminar on esoteric psychology had disappeared—buried under spreadsheets, meetings, and 60-hour workweeks.

When I came back from rehab, I continued painting. I signed up for art classes several times a week. I truly believed I was making positive changes—bringing more balance into my life, focusing on what made me happy, learning to tap into my creativity. Slowly, I allowed myself to become visible in my unique expression. It was a major milestone.

But conditioning runs deep. And often, the first wake-up call simply brings *awareness* of what isn't working. Many of us need a second—or in my case, a third—wake-up call before we're ready to act on that awareness.

Looking back, it probably took being knocked over the head multiple times—literally—and being ripped out of my own hamster wheel to realize I couldn't just tweak around the edges. The changes I made were a start, but they weren't enough. Not bold enough. Not radical enough.

And as it turned out, the universe wasn't done with me yet.

The Turning Point: From Darkness to Dawn

The third accident was the most traumatic. It happened right in front of my own garage. My head got caught between the door of my car and the car itself. I smashed the window with my elbow and ended up with bleeding cuts on my temple and ear from the splintered glass. I experienced partial amnesia, wandering in a gray fog, trying to find my way out.

It felt like my own version of *Groundhog Day* as I kept asking my friends the same questions over and over: "How the hell did I get here?" And I didn't mean physically—I meant spiritually. Metaphorically.

It was then, lying in a hospital bed, disoriented and in pain, that I realized this wasn't just a string of bad luck. I wasn't living the life my soul had intended for me. I see it now as a profound awakening—a spiritual interruption. It was as if the universe was saying, "We tried the gentle approach, but you weren't listening. Now we need your full attention." It needed me to make a radical shift, not just take up art classes.

And then, as if the physical trauma weren't enough, my mother was diagnosed with cancer—and passed away just three months later.

Just like that, my entire life collapsed. Or perhaps—and this is the perspective I eventually came to—it was cleared away to make space for something new.

Two years after that final accident, I stood at the edge of the Grand Canyon, watching the sun rise. Surrounded by beauty and vastness, I reflected on the journey I had traveled to get there—on recovery, on losing my mother just six months earlier, on the many ways I had come undone.

As the sun warmed my face and the fog began to lift from the canyon below, tears welled in my eyes. I felt small and insignificant in the vastness of nature—and yet, at the same time, powerful and essential. Because what I did with this one precious, fragile life mattered.

It was up to me to manifest the divine intention for my life. I didn't want to reach the end and realize that fear—of being seen, of being different—had stopped me from expressing who I truly was and from sharing the gifts I was here to offer.

If not now, then when? What else was I waiting for?

I returned from that trip and handed in my resignation. It felt like an enormous relief. But soon, I was facing a new kind of challenge: I had no job. No real plan. I knew how I'd ended up where I didn't want to be—but I still didn't know where I wanted to go.

I didn't yet know who I was or who I wanted to become.

When a friend gently asked me, "What is your heart telling you?" I realized my heart was suspiciously quiet.

I had always believed I was more guided by my emotions than by logic. That my sensitivity was both a blessing and a curse. So why couldn't I hear what my heart was saying now? And what was that hum of unlived potential, not just career-wise, but biologically and emotionally, trying to tell me? Had I tuned in to others' expectations for so long that I had lost my connection to my own wisdom—my own inner voice?

In hindsight, I now realise that this disconnection wasn't only emotional—it was hormonal, spiritual. A veiling of the deep feminine essence I once trusted without hesitation.

As I began to shape a new life from the rubble of the old one, an unanswered question lingered quietly in the background. Not loud, not urgent—but persistent. Would I ever become a mother?

The Empty Doorframe of Fertility

Throughout all of this upheaval, the question of children remained quietly in the background. At first, I thought, *I'll heal, rebuild my life, and then focus on meeting the right partner and having a family.* I still believed I had time.

Looking back, I see how I held on to a vague idea that I would be a mother "someday." Perhaps a bit later in life—but still, someday. It felt possible. I never actively decided against having children. Life just kept presenting other priorities, other emergencies, other paths that demanded my immediate attention.

Maybe I never truly decided *for* having children either—at least not enough to make it a clear priority.

After recovering from my accidents and grieving my mother, I left my corporate job, completed my art therapy degree, and eventually, in my mid-forties, moved from my home country of Switzerland to the beautiful island of Mallorca, Spain, to start over completely.

It was there, at forty-six, that I met a man and started a relationship. We became intimate, and I realized we weren't being particularly careful about contraception. Suddenly, it hit me: *What if I get pregnant now? Is that even possible at my age? Do I still want it? How would that change my life? Am I ready for something* so *huge*? This moment of two hearts beating in my chest showed me I hadn't fully realised how deeply I had linked my identity to the potential of motherhood—until I began to feel it slipping away as I started a new chapter.

For the first time, I consciously confronted the reality that my fertility—something I had taken for granted, even tried to avoid in my younger years—was now a limited resource. The window that had once seemed wide open was closing.

Somehow, between difficult relationships, healing from trauma, rebuilding my life, and finding myself again, the years had passed. The path I had always assumed would include motherhood had led me somewhere else. No loud slamming door. No dramatic finality. Just a soft, unmistakable click I hadn't noticed until the silence settled in.

Becoming aware felt like both a loss and a relief. Like something in me had been waiting for this acknowledgment—not just from my body, but from my heart.

I remembered standing on a beach in Mallorca, hearing the soft lapping of the waves against the shore, watching the sunset on the horizon, where the sea meets the sky. It felt like a mirror—spacious enough to hold all of me: the grief, the beauty, the letting go.

And maybe that's what menopause invites us into. Not just an ending, but an expansion. A different kind of fertility. A new terrain of power, still largely unmapped.

I didn't yet have all the answers, but I was finally listening.

Because there's something they don't tell you about approaching menopause without having had children: there's a particular kind of grief that comes with it. A mourning for the path not taken, whether by choice or by circumstance.

And it's not just women without children who experience this. I've spoken with countless women—mothers, childfree by choice, women who wanted more children, women content with their family size—and discovered that the end of fertility represents a significant transition for all women. It's that door closing. That finite moment when a possibility is gone forever.

But it's not just grief for the children we didn't have. It's grief for an identity we've carried since puberty.

When fertility ends, we lose our status as childbearing women, even if only in theory. And society rarely acknowledges what is truly being lost. Even though we *know* we are more than our reproductive capacity, fertility has been inextricably linked to our value: our attractiveness as potential partners, our function in continuing the species, our place in the social order.

Our entire *raison d'être* as women has, in some way—explicitly or implicitly—been connected to bearing children. So when that capacity slips away, profound questions arise:

Who am I now?

What is my role?

What value do I bring?

These questions may sound outdated in a world where women contribute in countless ways beyond motherhood. But ancient associations linger. They hum beneath the surface of our collective consciousness, shaping how society views us and, more importantly, how we view ourselves.

The grief isn't just personal. It's existential.

While I was reckoning with that grief, the more severe symptoms of late perimenopause hit me at forty-nine: irregular periods, disrupted sleep, and weight gain around my midsection—despite maintaining the same lifestyle. My body and emotions aligned in a perfect storm as I faced the reality of my fertility's end.

Hot flashes weren't my main symptom, thankfully, but insomnia hit me hard. For nearly four years, I didn't sleep through the night.

The so-called "brain fog" was very real, though for me it felt less like fog and more like mental overload. My mind just didn't have the capacity it once did. I wasn't just forgetting things—although that happened too. I felt like I couldn't *process* anything. I had no headspace for the little stresses that once rolled off my back. My brain just ... stopped working the way I was used to. And of course, those blank moments always seemed to happen at the worst possible time, making me question my competence after years of priding myself on my sharp mind.

By fifty-three, I had officially entered menopause—twelve consecutive months without a period.

In hindsight, I can see that everything—from the relationship that ended, to the accidents that forced me to slow down and reconnect with my soul's purpose, from the grief of losing my mother, to my move to Mallorca—was preparing me for a deeper transformation.

And I knew I wasn't alone in that transformation.

In conversations with women from all walks of life, I discovered something universal: despite our vastly different paths, we all shared one single, unspoken moment—that quiet reckoning. That doorway each of us must pass through. The realization that our fertility is ending—ready or not.

Three Women, Three Paths, One Common Thread

My path to midlife and menopause might be uniquely mine, but that dawning realization—that fertility is ending—is something millions of women face in their own way.

Let me introduce you to two other women whose journeys, while different from mine, reveal how this transition touches us all.

Sophie became a mother in her early thirties. She birthed two beautiful children who were her whole world. She threw herself into motherhood with the same passion and dedication she had once brought to her career as a teacher.

By her mid-forties, as her children entered their teen years and began needing her less. Sophie started to feel the first stirrings of something unexpected. Her biological clock was ticking loudly again. Suddenly, there was a longing she hadn't anticipated—a realization that maybe, just maybe, she wanted another child.

"It hit me at my daughter's thirteenth birthday party," she told me. "I watched her blow out her candles and felt this wave of grief. Not just because she was growing up, but because I realized I might never hold a baby of my own again."

For Sophie, perimenopause brought not only physical symptoms—irregular periods, sleep disruption, mood swings—but also a confrontation with finality. The door to having another child was closing, and she hadn't consciously chosen to shut it. Time and biology were making the decision for her.

Marie's story took a different path.

She had focused on her career through her thirties, always assuming she'd have children "someday." When she met her partner at thirty-eight, they wasted no time trying to start a family—but conception didn't come easily. After two years of trying naturally, they turned to IVF.

"The injections, the appointments, the emotional rollercoaster—it consumed my life," Marie explained. "But then, at forty-three, our miracle happened."

Marie gave birth to a healthy daughter and entered motherhood with deep gratitude and joy. But as she approached her mid-forties, with a toddler demanding her energy and perimenopausal symptoms beginning to emerge, she found herself facing grief, too.

"Sometimes I look at my daughter playing and think, *you might be my only one*. I always pictured having at least two children. But at forty-six, with perimenopause in full swing, I'm running out of time."

These stories—Sophie's unexpected longing as her children became more independent, Marie's bittersweet joy mixed with the mourning of a second child—reflect different sides of the same experience.

Whether we've had children or not, whether we wanted them or not, the end of fertility represents a profound transition. It marks the closing of a door that has quietly shaped much of our adult lives, whether we walked through it or not.

The biological clock that ticked in the background of our decisions for decades suddenly winds down, and we're left facing the question: Who am I beyond this capacity to create life?

What we often miss is that perimenopause itself is the threshold, not just a hormonal shift but a rite of passage into a deeper self.

For me.

For Sophie.

For Marie.

For all of us.

There is a reckoning with time. We thought we had more. We thought the choices would remain ours. And then, suddenly, nature steps in and says: "Time's up."

This universal experience—the grief over lost possibilities, the fear of what comes next, the search for identity beyond fertility—is what unites us. It transcends our individual circumstances and creates a sisterhood of women navigating this threshold together.

But here's what I've discovered, what Sophie and Marie are discovering, and what I hope you will discover through this book:

There is life—vibrant, powerful, authentic life—on the other side of fertility.

A new archetype is waiting to emerge—not defined by our ability to nurture others, but by our wisdom. Our courage. Our self-sovereignty.

The Appearance of the Queen and the Path Forward

So what's on the other side of fertility? What's the compelling future that helps us let go and step into uncharted terrain?

I found my answer in the archetype of the Queen—a powerful figure that stands between the Mother archetype we're leaving behind and the Crone archetype we've yet to embody. The Queen is the sovereign woman, focused not on pleasing others but on her mission. She channels her energy into what matters most. She is ready to leave a legacy.

She's driven by purpose rather than performance. She carries the confidence that comes from lived experience. She no longer hangs her worth on external validation or chases certifications to prove her value. She simply *knows* she is worthy, capable, and powerful.

There's a particular liberation that emerges in this phase—a release from people-pleasing and the constant accommodation of others' needs at the expense of our own. We've spent decades caring for others, measuring our words, holding back our truth. Now, we reclaim our voice. Our time. Our priorities.

This transformation isn't always comfortable. During the time I struggled most with my disrupted cycles—when I felt the familiar build-up of tension, pressure, and emotional charge before my period, but the release that came with the flow of blood never arrived—it often felt like a breakdown. And yet, it also felt like a sacred dismantling—something ancient, hormonal, archetypal moving through me, preparing me for something I couldn't yet name.

For Sophie, it has meant confronting her identity beyond active motherhood and finding new ways to channel her nurturing energy.

For Marie, it has meant embracing the reality of her one-child family while navigating perimenopause with a young child in tow.

For me, it meant reckoning with the path not taken—the children never born—and finding purpose and power in other forms of creation.

But for all of us, this threshold marks not just an ending—it signals a powerful new beginning. A chance to redefine ourselves on our own terms. To reclaim parts of us we may have set aside. To discover parts of us we never even knew existed.

In every hero's journey, there comes a call to adventure—that moment when the ordinary world dissolves and transformation beckons.

Perimenopause is exactly this call for women. It announces, sometimes quietly, sometimes with unmistakable force, that life as we've known it is ending.

It isn't simply an invitation to survive a biological transition. It's a summons to return to the feminine, to reconnect with our authentic essence, and to discover our highest expression of feminine power.

After decades of adapting to a world that often undervalues feminine wisdom, perimenopause calls us home—to ourselves.

That's why the first step on this transformative journey is *Connection*—or more accurately, recognizing our disconnection and intentionally rebuilding that essential relationship with ourselves.

This reconnection becomes the foundation. The North Star. The very essence of the path forward.

Through my own experience and in working with hundreds of women navigating this transition, I've seen just how profound this reconnection can be. It is the bedrock upon which our entire transformation rests.

Without it, we remain adrift—searching for validation, seeking purpose in a world that too often fails to recognize our intrinsic worth.

So let us begin where we must: by coming home to ourselves. By realizing that even amid hot flashes and sleepless nights, in the chaos of changing roles and shifting identities, we can find our way back.

Back to the wisdom.

Back to the power.

Back to the truth that has always lived within us.

Forward into the next chapter that awaits us.

Chapter 2

Connection

The Recurring Fuel for Your Wiser, Hotter, Stronger Self

"Your vision will become clear only when you can look into your own heart. Who looks outside, dreams; who looks inside, awakens."
—C.G. Jung

I used to be brave when I was a kid—or rather, fearless, even long before the conversation with the school principal I described in Chapter 1; before I lost my connection to self and dimmed my feelings or words to make others comfortable.

During a holiday in Gran Canaria, my mom challenged my siblings and me to approach fishermen along the beach and ask them about their catch. The prize? A single ice cream—for the winner only. Being the youngest of three, I had already figured out that if I wanted something, I had to go for it. So I took the initiative, asked, and the fisherman let me peek into their bags filled with little crabs and mussels.

The ice cream that day tasted especially good.

***

Somewhere along the way, that version of me grew quiet. The emotional honesty, the natural confidence, the unshakeable sense of *this is who I am*—they faded gradually, buried under roles, responsibilities, and the slow, steady drip of social expectation.

It wasn't until my series of accidents that I began to realize how profoundly I had lost connection to the wishes and dreams in my heart. Those life-altering events forced me to pause and recognize that somewhere along the way, I had stopped trusting my inner voice. And if I wanted to follow my inner calling and go after what made my heart sing and my soul soar, I had to find my way back to myself, to honor the parts of me I once silenced. To stop softening my truth. To remember how it felt to be fully, freely myself.

This reconnection journey required me to master new levels of courage and do things that felt scary and uncomfortable—like moving to a new country (an island, nonetheless) in my mid-forties, on my own, to start over completely. I had to be brave enough to trust that everything life was throwing at me was serving a higher purpose, and commit to changing the very predictable (and slightly boring) course I had set for my life.

Isn't it fascinating how perimenopause has a similar way of shaking us awake? One day, you're cruising along, thinking you've got it all figured out—or at least "under control." The next, you're a bundle of sweat, tears, and *who the hell am I?* moments. It's like your body is staging a revolt, demanding that you pay attention to where you are—right here, right now.

These disruptions—whether they come as life-altering accidents or perimenopausal hot flashes—arrive as profound messengers in our lives. They shake us awake, demanding that we pay attention to what we've been ignoring. They invite us to reconnect with ourselves on every level—our bodies, our hearts, and the deepest desires we may have set aside. When life knocks us off our familiar path, it often creates the space for something more authentic to emerge.

As part of a writing exercise, I was invited to have a written conversation with Connection—to treat it as if it were a living presence and simply ask what it wanted me to know, what it wanted me to share with you, the reader. In that quiet, contemplative space, Connection, it said, "I am the basis of everything." It felt true. Connection is our foundation, our pillar of safety and certainty. When we're truly connected to ourselves, we stand grounded—regardless of what storms life brings. Without this connection, we hang by a thin thread, blown in every direction by circumstances and life's challenges.

Once we're truly connected, that's when the magic unfolds. That's where we remember who we really are, what we truly want, and the incredible power we hold. That's where we become wiser, hotter, and stronger versions of ourselves.

Recognizing Disconnection As The First Step Towards Healing

"I don't recognize myself anymore."

That's what I hear over and over from women in menopause. And for many of us, the disconnection shows up in layers.

The first layer is often physical—suddenly noticing changes in your body that weren't there before. The weight that now stubbornly settles around your middle despite your unchanged diet. The unexpected chin hair that starts growing overnight. The lines that seem to have deepened when you weren't looking.

Then comes the brain fog and lack of headspace. Women who've built careers on their sharp thinking and reliable memory find themselves forgetting words mid-sentence or walking into rooms with no idea why. Tasks that once felt effortless now feel overwhelming, as if their brain is battling a hangover that won't go away, and wasn't even caused by drinking.

This isn't me. It's not always spoken, but it's there—in the sighs, the silence, the disorientation that creeps in when our reflection no longer feels familiar.

Perhaps the most profound layer is the existential one. It's the quiet voice that whispers, *I've done everything I was supposed to do... now what?* Or, *is this all there is?* It's looking at your life—the career you've built, the relationships you've nurtured, the path you've followed—and wondering if it truly reflects who you are.

This multilayered disconnection is often the first sign of transformation. But because we're so busy—so accustomed to pushing through discomfort—we often miss these early signals. We dismiss them as temporary fatigue or stress, not recognizing them for what they really are: invitations.

Discovering this disconnection in all its forms is the crucial first step toward transformation. Rather than pushing away these feelings or powering through them, consider them valuable signals worthy of your attention. Your body, mind, and spirit are communicating important truths—truths that become clear when we pause and listen.

And while hormonal shifts certainly contribute to these experiences, we can't lay all the blame at the feet of perimenopause. This stage of life often coincides with other major transitions: children leaving home, parents needing care, career plateaus or pivots. It's a perfect storm of change—inside and out. No wonder we feel adrift.

However, once we recognize this disconnection, we can begin the journey back to ourselves. The first step is simply to notice—without judgment—where you feel connected and where you don't. When you feel aligned, and when you feel anxious, afraid, or off-track.

This awareness becomes a map, gently showing you where reconnection is needed.

To help you create your own map, I'd like to share an exercise that has been transformative for many of the women I work with.

You'll find a downloadable worksheet for this in your Wiser. Hotter. Stronger. Transformation Toolkit at

www.daniellaschoch.com/toolkit

The Energy-Connection Audit Exercise

Purpose: *To discover which activities and relationships energize you and foster connection versus those that drain you and create disconnection.*
Allow at least: 5–10 *minutes daily for one week,* 20 *minutes for a weekly review.*
Materials: A *journal or notebook, colored pens (optional).*

Instructions:

1. ***Create a simple table in your journal with three columns:***
   - *Daily Activities & Relationships*
   - *Energy Impact (+/-)*
   - *Connection Level (1–10)*

2. ***For one week, take a few minutes each evening to record:***
   - *The significant activities and interactions of your day.*
   - *Whether each energized (+) or drained (-) you.*
   - *How connected to yourself did you feel during/after each (1 = completely disconnected, 10 = deeply connected).*

3. At the end of the week, set aside 20 minutes to review your entries and reflect:

- *Which activities consistently energize you and foster connection?*
- *Which relationships or responsibilities leave you feeling depleted and disconnected?*
- *What patterns or surprises do you notice?*
- *What one small change could you make to increase your energy and connection?*

Many of my clients discover that activities they thought were "not that bad" are actually major energy drains—or that certain relationships leave them feeling disconnected, not just from others, but from themselves.

***

When Rebecca completed the Energy Audit, she was surprised to realize that her weekly girls' night out—something she had been part of for years—consistently rated as energy-draining and disconnecting.

"I kept going because these were friends I'd known forever, and I thought I should enjoy it," she told me. "But my body was sending clear signals: tension headaches before each gathering, exhaustion the next day, and a knot in my stomach during conversations that had become more about gossip than genuine connection."

By suggesting a different format—meeting for a morning hike instead of drinks at noisy bars—Rebecca transformed the entire experience. The symptoms disappeared, replaced by a sense of replenished energy and connection that lasted well into the following day.

Perimenopause made her realize she simply couldn't afford to waste precious energy on activities that drained her. She had to become much more selective about where she directed her time and focus. And the more she prioritized what truly filled her cup, the more gracefully she could navigate the challenges of this transition.

As you map your energy and connection through the Energy Audit, you'll begin to notice how your body communicates with you. That heaviness before certain meetings. The energy surge during creative work. The ease you feel around specific people.

Your body often knows what supports or depletes you, long before your mind catches up.

This brings us to the next essential element of reconnection: developing a relationship with your body's innate wisdom.

The Wisdom Within Your Body

True connection doesn't begin with others. It begins here: within your own skin. And during perimenopause, that connection deepens, sometimes painfully, as your body insists on being heard.

Our bodies—yes, even the ones throwing hot flashes our way or suddenly deciding that sleep is optional—are among our most powerful allies in this transition. Beneath the discomfort and disruption lies something more enduring: wisdom. Our bodies have always held profound intelligence about our needs, our experiences, our trauma and unhealed wounds. And in midlife, this wisdom grows louder, demanding our attention in ways we can no longer ignore.

For many of us, the relationship with our body has long been a complicated one, marked by frustration, criticism, dismissal, or denial. In my twenties and thirties, I pushed through exhaustion, numbed pain, skipped meals, pulled all-nighters, and treated my cycles as inconvenient—when all I really wanted was to rest and allow the purification to unfold naturally, on all levels. Like so many women of my generation, I learned to override my body's signals to keep functioning, meet deadlines, show up for others, and stay in control. We were conditioned to see our bodies as unpredictable or untrustworthy, something to manage, perfect, or push through.

But perimenopause doesn't let us bypass anymore.

The familiar shortcuts stop working. The habits we used to get away with—too much caffeine, too little sleep, stress without boundaries—suddenly backfire. Our bodies grow less tolerant, more vocal. What once felt like subtle nudges becomes a full-body protest. It may feel like betrayal, but in truth, it's a sacred recalibration. Perimenopause is the body's way of asking, *Are you listening yet?*

For me, it started with sleep. Or more precisely, the absence of it. I began waking up night after night, restless, wired, and desperate for rest. That sleeplessness led me down a path of research and trial: adjusting my diet, cutting out sugar and alcohol, experimenting with natural remedies, shifting how I moved and worked. But deeper than the protocols, I began listening. Really listening.

And what I heard surprised me. My body wasn't just begging for sleep, it was asking for tenderness. Simplicity. Truth. Congruence. My body had its own voice, one I'd drowned out with overachievement and external noise for years. The more I slowed down, the more I began to hear: *Not this. Let go of that. Yes to this.*

One of my clients, also struggling with insomnia, discovered her truth in a surprising way. By paying closer attention to her body's signals, tightness in her chest before bed, a lingering anxiety she couldn't explain, she realized that her nervous system never fully relaxed while sharing a bed with her partner. That wasn't easy to bring up with him, but when she did, they found a solution. She began sleeping separately, and almost instantly, her sleep improved, and so did their intimacy. Her body had known what she needed long before her mind could articulate it.

Our bodies speak to us in subtle languages: tension and ease, energy and depletion, comfort and contraction. This conversation becomes more important than ever during perimenopause. We are being invited into a deeper dialogue, a reconnection with the wisdom that has been within us all along.

This reconnection with your body is more than symptom management. It's a spiritual partnership. When you treat your body not as a problem to fix but as an ally to honor, you open a channel that nourishes every other dimension of connection: emotional, sexual, intuitive, and sacred. You build trust within yourself, and that trust ripples outward into your relationships, your choices, and your sense of purpose.

You don't have to get it perfect. You just have to begin. Take a moment each day. Place a hand on your heart. Say: "Thank you. Thank you for carrying me. For adapting, even when I haven't been gentle. For speaking to me, even when I didn't want to listen.

Then ask: *What do you need right now?*

It could be more sleep. More greens. A walk. Stillness. Maybe it's water—simple, clear, life-giving. Or a pause before that third coffee. Over time, you begin to develop a felt sense of your body's language. You start to notice the difference between true hunger and emotional hunger. Between exhaustion and avoidance. Between what depletes you and what replenishes you.

And when you give your body what it truly needs, not what it's been conditioned to crave, it responds. There's a softening. An exhale. A quiet "yes."

This practice of presence is a practice of gratitude—but it's also a practice of non-violence: choosing presence over pressure, honoring instead of overriding. It's an invitation to shift from the autopilot of the saboteur, who demands, punishes, and pushes, to the wisdom of the inner Sage, who listens, trusts, and responds.

You don't have to do it perfectly. Just honestly. Notice what your body is asking for, and when you can, offer it. Your body doesn't need perfection—it needs partnership. And these simple acts of presence? They can be revolutionary.

Reconnecting with Your Inner Essence

While our bodies provide tangible signals and insights that are essential to the menopausal journey, there's another dimension of connection—one that lives beyond the physical. It's the connection to our emotions, our minds, our hearts, and our essence. I call it the connection to your inner self—a deeper wisdom that, together with your bodily knowing, can guide you toward a fuller understanding of who you are.

This deeper form of connection works through the heart and intuition, rather than the mind. The heart is the gateway to yourself, to others, and your higher essence.

I remember the moment I realized how disconnected I'd become from my own inner self. After my accidents, my coach asked me a simple question: "What do you want for your life?" I was shocked to discover that, while I could give plenty of socially acceptable answers, I couldn't identify a single desire that felt truly mine. I could easily list what I didn't want, but when it came to articulating my own dreams, my heart remained suspiciously quiet.

This disconnection from our hearts and inner essence often leads to a sense of being lost, a kind of emptiness that becomes especially apparent during life transitions. You might wake up one day, realize the kids are grown, the career goals have been achieved, and yet you feel a quiet dissatisfaction. The successes you once longed for no longer bring the joy you expected.

One of my clients described it this way: "For twenty years, I was the center of our home. Every day had a purpose: making breakfast, helping with homework, managing schedules, supporting the kids through the emotional ups and downs of growing up. Now, no one needs me to get up early. There's no one waiting for me to take care of them." While sleeping in felt luxurious at first, a well-earned break, she soon realized something was missing. This realization sparked her journey to explore and expand to reconnect with a deeper sense of purpose.

Disconnection is the root of much pain in our lives and in the world. As human beings, we intuitively understand the importance of connection; our brains are literally wired for it. But in seeking connection with others, we often forget the most essential relationship of all: the one we have with ourselves.

When we disconnect from our bodies, we miss vital cues about our well-being. When we disconnect from our emotions, we lose access to our intuitive guidance system. When we disconnect from our inner essence, we deprive ourselves of the nourishment our soul requires to thrive.

Connection to self is the basis of everything. It is a pillar of inner safety, security, and strength. It nourishes us from within and provides a vitality that no external success, relationship, or possession can replicate. It also offers something even more powerful: direction—a compass for navigating life with clarity and confidence.

The connection to your inner wisdom becomes your North Star. Your heart remembers the sacred wishes and quiet dreams that have patiently waited—through the years of building a career, raising a family, or healing life's wounds. Beyond society's "shoulds," your authentic desires have been quietly holding space, waiting to be rediscovered.

This connection lays the foundation for the clarity we'll explore in the next chapter. Without it, any attempt to define the path forward is built on shifting sand. Reconnection is the bedrock upon which true clarity can emerge.

The liminal space between letting go of who we've been and stepping into who we are becoming can feel disorienting—but it serves a profound purpose. It's a time of possibility, of curiosity and exploration. A moment when anything is possible, and we get to try on new roles, new expressions, and new desires.

Any form of creative expression—something we'll explore more deeply in Chapter 4—offers a powerful playground for navigating this uncertain space. Creativity becomes one of our most potent tools for reconnecting with our true selves during this transformative time.

Having once lost my own connection to desire, I started to notice how often my clients experienced the same. Many dismissed their old wishes as foolish or indulgent dreams from a more naive time. I could feel the grief in those abandoned hopes—dreams that never got to breathe.

So I created a simple exercise to bring those wishes back into the light.

The Sacred Wish Ritual Exercise

Purpose: *To reclaim and honor your authentic desires that may have been set aside or dismissed over the years.*

Allow at least: 10–15 *minutes of uninterrupted time.*

Materials: *A candle, Incense or essential oils (optional), small pieces of paper, a pen, and a beautiful container (box, jar, or bowl).*

Instructions:

1. **Create a sacred space in your home**—*a quiet corner where you won't be disturbed. Light a candle, and, if you wish, some incense or use essential oils to create a meditative atmosphere. To learn more about how to create a sacred space in your own home, please go to www.daniellaschoch.com/toolkit and download the free guide.*

2. **Sit comfortably and take a few deep breaths,** *focusing first on your body and then on your heart center. Breathe in and out through your heart for a few cycles.*

3. **Take a small piece of paper and write down a wish or desire that you have.** *Don't judge or censor yourself—it could be anything from "I want to travel to Japan," to "I want to learn to paint," or "I want more time alone."*

4. **Hold the paper to your heart** *and say aloud: "I honor and validate this desire as a sacred part of who I am."*

5. **Place the paper in your container.**

6. **Close the ritual by saying:** *"These desires are valid and worthy, regardless of others' opinions or my own judgments."*

Repeat this process daily for a week or weekly for a month, until you feel yourself connecting with deeper, more authentic desires.

***

Let's look at Lisa's story. Let's take Lisa's story. She discovered through this ritual a long-buried desire to sing—something she had been told as a child she had no talent for. After completing the Sacred Wish Ritual, she found the courage to take voice lessons. "It wasn't about becoming a professional singer," she told me. "It was about reclaiming a part of myself that brought me joy, regardless of what anyone else thought of my voice."

As you collect your wishes, you may begin to notice patterns—desires that echo through the years or themes that keep resurfacing. These are the golden breadcrumbs that lead you back to your most authentic self. They help you hear the voice of your inner Sage—the part of you that knows what truly nourishes your soul.

What's most humbling about this process is that we're not only reconnecting with ourselves to feel more fulfilled (though that's important!)—we're also stepping into a deeper realization of the wisdom and gifts we've accumulated. We are being invited to share them in new ways.

Embodying the Queen And A New Kind of Power

As we begin to honour our inner truths and reclaim our long-silenced desires, we naturally step into a new phase of becoming. The Queen archetype emerges—not to control, but to serve, to lead, and to leave a legacy. She is the woman who has walked through fire, gathered her wisdom, and is now ready to rule her realm with both grace and grit.

For millennia, a woman's primary purpose was seen as bearing children. Whether we're consciously aware of it or not, this idea is deeply imprinted in our collective subconscious, and it's ingrained in our physiology and nervous system. So when our fertility comes to an end, it can trigger a profound crisis in how we see ourselves and the roles we play. If we're no longer mothers, or potential mothers, then who are we?

As we deepen our connection to our bodies and hearts, a new opening appears: the chance to explore our place within the larger cycles of life. I want to touch on this briefly, because the spiritual dimension of connection could fill a book of its own.

In my work with women from all walks of life, I've seen how reconnecting with our inner essence becomes especially meaningful in midlife. As the clarity of the Sage begins to crystallize within us, we feel an ancient invitation rising. We begin to sense the emergence of the Queen: the deeply initiated, powerful visionary who radiates strength, compassion, wisdom, and vulnerability. She is the sovereign who has come home to a power she has always carried, now refined by lived experience.

For many women, including myself, perimenopause becomes the portal into this Queen energy. It's a sacred initiation. A time not just for letting go, but for stepping up. For growing, contributing, and building a legacy. By now, you've gathered a lifetime of experience, navigated countless seasons, and cultivated deep reserves of empathy, clarity, and patience. Now is the moment to live and lead from that wholeness, to offer your gifts in a way that feels authentic and aligned.

The Queen understands that real power comes not from striving, but from rooted presence. She is attuned to both the smaller rhythms of her daily life and the larger, cosmic cycles of transformation. She doesn't shame herself for moments of disconnection. She holds them with grace. She knows they are not detours, but part of the spiral path.

She also understands that leadership is not about perfection—it's about presence. About choosing again and again to return to what matters most.

And here's the beautiful truth: this chapter of life is not a descent into irrelevance. It's an emergence into sovereignty. You get to choose who you want to become beyond your reproductive role. You've earned the freedom and the power to lead your life on your own terms.

You've done the work. Now it's time to root into your power and share your gifts in the way only you can.

To help you deepen this sense of grounded sovereignty and align with the cyclical wisdom of nature, try this visualization practice.

The Sovereign Tree Visualization Exercise

Purpose: *To help you embody the grounded wisdom, strength, resilience, and legacy of your inner Queen by aligning with the natural cycles of life and your own sovereign essence.*
Material: *Your journal.*
Allow at least: *10–15 minutes uninterrupted time, including 5 minutes of journaling time.*

Instructions:

1. **Find a quiet, comfortable space where you won't be disturbed.** *You may want to use soft background music if you prefer.*

2. **Close your eyes and take several deep, steady breaths.** *Let your body settle. Feel your feet grounded and your heart open.*

3. **Imagine a beautiful ancient tree.** *This tree has witnessed count-*

less seasons. Its roots run deep into the earth, and its branches reach expansively toward the sky. It feels strong, wise, and deeply familiar—like an external mirror of your own inner sovereignty.

4. Imagine approaching the tree *and placing your hand on its trunk. Feel a connection forming between you and the tree.*

5. Now, visualize yourself becoming this tree.

- *Your feet become roots: stretching deeply into the nourishing earth, anchoring you in strength, memory, and ancestral wisdom.*
- *Your spine becomes the trunk: resilient and steady, carrying the truth of all you've lived.*
- *Your arms become branches: reaching outward to nurture, uplift, and offer your unique gifts to the world.*
- *Your heart becomes the center: holding compassion, clarity, and quiet power.*

6. Move through the seasons.

- *Feel yourself in spring: budding with new life and possibilities.*
- *Shift into summer: radiant, abundant, fully leafed and vibrant.*
- *Move through autumn: your leaves changing color, letting go of what no longer serves, releasing with grace.*
- *Enter winter: bare but wise, resilient, conserving energy, preparing for the next cycle.*

7. Notice what each season evokes in you. *How do these cycles mirror your own journey through perimenopause? Where are you now in your personal season?*

8. *Now, imagine drawing up wisdom.*

- *From your roots: what wisdom rises from the earth, your lineage, your body?*
- *From your branches: what vision flows down from the sky, your intuition, your soul?*

9. *Begin to transition gently from the tree back into your human form.* *Carry with you the messages and sensations you received. Let them settle in your heart.*

10. *Harvest the gifts:* *open your eyes and take a few moments to write down anything that stood out.*

Consider:

- *What season are you in right now, internally?*
- *What message did your roots and branches offer you?*
- *How does this image of sovereign rootedness speak to your next chapter?*

This exercise can help you see your current transition as part of a natural, beautiful cycle. Just as the tree doesn't mourn the falling of its leaves but prepares for new growth, you, too, are simply entering a new season of life, one rich with potential and wisdom. The Queen within you is like the tree: rooted in her power, she extends her branches to nurture others, and plants seeds of legacy that will outlast her. May the insights you receive remind you not only of the strength you carry but of the lasting impact you are here to make.

***

Joanne came to me feeling overwhelmed by perimenopause and uncertain about her future. After the Wisdom Tree Visualization, she told me, "When I became the tree in autumn, watching my leaves fall, I initially felt sadness. But then I realized the sadness lifted when I understood that the tree was simply entering a necessary phase of release before renewal. When I asked for wisdom from my roots, I heard: 'You've spent decades nurturing others; this is your time to nourish yourself.' From my branches came another message: Your worth isn't in what you produce, but in your very existence.'"

Three months later, Joanne told me this visualization had transformed her perspective on perimenopause. "I no longer see this transition as a loss," she said. "Instead, I recognize it as my autumn—a necessary release of what no longer serves me before entering a new season."

Embracing these spiritual connections and life cycles can bring a profound sense of peace and purpose. It helps us see beyond the immediate challenges of perimenopause to the greater journey we're on. We begin to understand that our worth isn't tied to our fertility or our ability to care for others, but to the unique essence we bring to the world.

This journey of spiritual connection is deeply personal and may express itself in many different ways. The key is to find what resonates with you—what helps you feel connected to something larger than yourself.

Deepening this spiritual connection becomes a source of strength and resilience as you navigate the changes of perimenopause. This perspective can help you reframe hot flashes as power surges, see mood swings as invitations to emotional honesty, and view physical changes as signs of your body's wisdom and adaptability.

As we wrap up this exploration of connection, it's important to recognize that this isn't a one-and-done process. Just as perimenopause itself is a journey with its ups and downs, so too is the experience of connection and reconnection.

Think of it as cycles within cycles. There's the overarching transition of perimenopause, moving us from our reproductive years to post-menopause. But within that, there are smaller, ever-shifting cycles of hormones, emotions, energy, and awareness. Understanding these cycles can be incredibly liberating. It helps us recognize that moments of disconnection are not failures, but natural parts of the journey. With awareness, we can develop practices that return us to connection more quickly and easily each time.

Expecting a state of constant, blissful connection isn't always realistic (wouldn't that be nice, though?). What's more valuable is becoming more skillful at navigating the cycles—learning to find your way back to yourself, again and again.

In my own journey toward embodying the Queen energy, I've found that simple daily practices help maintain a sense of connection, even through the most challenging moments:

- **Morning check-in:** A brief body scan and emotional check-in to begin the day.
- **Mindful moments:** Short pauses for breath and presence scattered throughout the day.
- **Evening reflection:** A quiet time to acknowledge moments of connection and disconnection.
- **Gratitude practice:** A regular acknowledgment of what truly matters.

Every time you choose to reconnect—with your body, your heart, your inner essence, or the greater rhythms of life—you're navigating perimenopause more consciously. You're actively participating in your own evolution and stepping more fully into the wise, powerful, and strong woman you're becoming.

And that is a beautiful thing to witness.

Coming Full Circle

As we complete this journey through the realm of connection, I find myself thinking about that fearless little girl on the beach in Gran Canaria—the one who approached strangers without hesitation, trusted her instincts, and knew exactly what she wanted. On my healing journey, I've reconnected with her and the unwavering trust in her desires and yearnings she embodied.

What I've discovered is this: that part of us never truly leaves. It simply gets buried under years of conditioning, expectations, and responsibilities.

The work we've done in this chapter isn't about becoming someone new. It's about remembering who we've always been. That brave, connected child still lives within each of us, waiting to be acknowledged and honored. Through the practices we've explored, we begin to return to that original state of trust and courage—this time guided by the wisdom we've gathered along the way.

We've also met the Queen within us—the woman who integrates that childlike trust with mature clarity. She understands that the heart is the gateway: to ourselves, to others, and to our higher essence. She knows that *directed awareness*—choosing to focus on what truly matters—is the unshakable foundation from which her power flows.

As the veil of disconnection lifts, we begin to see ourselves and our potential with fresh eyes. And this is where *Clarity* begins to emerge—naturally, from *Connection*. That doesn't mean we suddenly have all the answers. But we're learning to ask better questions—ones that open new pathways, stir our imagination, and pull us forward, instead of keeping us trapped in old patterns.

And the ice cream that awaits us now? It's even sweeter than the one I won on that beach all those years ago. It tastes like coming home to ourselves—crowned not with sprinkles, but with the Queen's wisdom that transforms everything it touches.

As we step into the next phase of our journey together, we carry this connection with us.

It is the foundation upon which everything else will be built.

You're not on this journey alone. If you'd like personalized guidance on which pillar to focus on for maximum transformational leverage right now, I'm here to help. Book a complimentary Pillar Gap session at www.pillargapmap.org.

Chapter 3

Clarity

The Star That Pulls Us Forward

"We are all in the gutter. But some of us are looking at the stars."
—Oscar Wilde

"I used to be so sure of everything," says Emily, a 49-year-old marketing executive and mother of two, tucking a strand of hair behind her ear as she fidgets with her coffee cup. "My career path, my relationships, my goals—they all felt crystal clear. Now? I'm stumbling through fog."

"One minute I'm confident, the next I'm questioning every decision I've ever made. Is this what perimenopause does? Steals your clarity along with your sleep? I barely recognize myself."

I nod—not just in recognition, but in solidarity. I've heard this before—so many women who once trusted themselves, now feeling lost and without clear direction.

"What scares you more?" I ask gently. "The fog ... or what it might mean?"

Her eyes meet mine—I see fear but also relief. "Both. I had a presentation last week where my mind went completely blank. I was so embarrassed. I've had moments of forgetfulness before, but now it's louder. Like ... I'm losing my edge. Am I losing me?"

"I hear how frightening that is," I say. "Many women describe it just like you have—a sense of mental overwhelm that feels like failure. A 'menopause moment' that feels like weakness. But what if it's not just hormonal fog, but confusion about what you want from life?

I pause. "What if this isn't failure ... but a message? What do you think it's trying to tell you?"

She thinks about this for a moment. "Maybe ... it's a wake-up call. A signal to slow down. To question. To start listening again."

"And if you did?" I ask. "If you listen to the call instead of resisting it ... who might you become?"

Her voice is quiet but steady: "Someone wiser. Stronger. More ... me.

***

This chapter is an invitation to reconnect with your inner compass, challenge what's no longer true, and begin rewriting the story of who you're here to become.

When I had a conversation with Clarity through the flow-state writing exercise, the first thing it said to me was: "I bring peace, calmness, and focus."

And I felt it, not as a grand revelation, but like an exhale I didn't know I'd been holding.

The confusion we experience during menopause—or any life transition, for that matter—which we so often interpret as a disturbance, isn't a flaw in our thinking. It's not something to hide or be ashamed of. It's the beginning of a deeper conversation, an invitation into the parts of ourselves we've ignored, overridden, or forgotten.

Like Connection, Clarity reveals itself in layers.

There's cognitive clarity: the mental sharpness that hormonal shifts can cloud. Emotional clarity: understanding our true feelings beneath the mood swings and heightened sensitivity. And then there's existential clarity: the kind that whispers, "Where do I go from here now that so many paths are open?"

All three dimensions of clarity can be disrupted during perimenopause, but separating them in this order often leads to the most profound transformation.

For the purpose of this chapter, let's focus on the third, existential clarity, and explore it as a *transformational elixir*. Like a rare tonic that works on every level—mind, heart, and spirit—clarity doesn't just sharpen our thinking; it shifts our perception. It cuts through the haze of expectation and noise, revealing what's true, what's essential, and what's been waiting beneath the surface all along.

When we reach a certain point in life—and it's often midlife—we grow tired of the self we've constructed through decades of meeting expectations, fitting in, holding things together, putting others first, or measuring our worth against yardsticks we never chose.

We grow tired of the conditions we've put on our self-love.

Feeling exhausted, confused, and frustrated is a gateway to transformation. As one of my mentors, Tony Robbins, often says, confusion is a sign you're about to grow or have a breakthrough.

Instead of fighting the lack of direction that comes with a major life transition, we can choose to see it as an essential step in our evolution. An invitation to slow down, to get quiet, to question more, and to listen longer.

Clarity dissolves illusions. It clears away the debris of outdated roles, silences the noise of "shoulds," and reconnects us with the quiet voice in our hearts. It reveals the subtle dissonance between how we're living and who we've become. It shows us where we've been performing, rather than aligning and reacting, and choosing instead. Once we see clearly, we can't unsee.

That's the power of it.

Clarity doesn't always arrive all at once. It can't be forced. But even a single beam of it can transform everything.

It's not always comfortable. But it's always catalytic.

In this chapter, we'll begin to dust off the lens through which we view ourselves and the world. We'll untangle the values, beliefs, and stories that have been clouding our vision, so we can turn toward the light of a truer identity waiting to emerge. We'll venture into the wilderness of the subconscious mind, using the connection we've already established to illuminate what lies beneath, and gently challenge (almost) everything you might have taken to be true.

You may encounter moments of uncertainty or a void that feels paralyzing. But as we unravel the threads of conditioning, you may discover more than just a few laugh lines. You may also stumble upon a long-buried dream that's been patiently waiting its turn.

My intention is to help you see yourself, your experiences, and your potential with fresh eyes. Finding a new perspective, opening your horizon and recognizing that the view from midlife, while different, can be breathtakingly beautiful when you know where to look.

And that clarity will reveal itself when we least expect it.

Embracing the Wilderness

I call this next part of the journey *embracing the wilderness* because that's exactly what it feels like.

It's the moment you step off the map and into uncharted territory when you experience all the discomfort and uncertainty that comes with it. The wilderness is uncharted territory; there's no predefined plan or societal inspiration for how to navigate this stage of life.

The roles that once defined us begin to dissolve. The rules we lived by no longer make sense. Life no longer moves in predictable patterns. Instead, we're pulled into something messier, more tender, and profoundly "in-between."

That's the wilderness.

It's not chaos.

It's not failure.

It's the fertile, confusing terrain between what was and what's not yet clear.

We don't talk enough about this space. There's plenty of guidance for how to build a career, raise a family, or grow a business. But there's little guidance for this phase of descent into the unknown that often comes with midlife. No one gives you a roadmap for how to become a wise woman.

And yet, this in-between is where transformation happens.

In our younger years, the world handed us a script of what a successful life "should" look like. But as that script begins to fray, we're left with a blank page. And while that blankness can feel terrifying, it also holds immense creative power—because we get to choose how to fill it (which is what we'll do in the next chapter on creativity).

But for now, we're standing in this space. A sacred space. It's where your next self begins to form—not by force, but by emergence.

One of the most important lessons of the wilderness is learning to sit with uncertainty and discomfort. Our natural instinct is to avoid discomfort and to quickly seek solutions or distractions. The temptation is to find "something"—anything—to focus on and direct our energy toward, whether it's serving us and others well or not.

We must learn to sit with the discomfort of uncertainty instead of rushing to fill the void with busyness or a purpose that doesn't fit anymore. Many women, not yet clear on who they're becoming, find themselves sliding back into familiar dynamics: focusing too much on their grown children's lives, overgiving, and seeking validation through service that doesn't truly nourish them.

It's understandable. In the absence of clarity, we crave purpose.

But these reactive moves are often *mirages in the wilderness*. They look like oases of meaning, but quietly pull us further from our authentic path.

I saw this with my client Rachel, a successful HR director who had built her identity around being indispensable—to her team at work, to her now-adult children, and her wide circle of friends.

As perimenopause coincided with a company restructuring, she found herself panicking about her relevance. "I started volunteering for every project, even ones I didn't care about," she admitted. "I'm answering emails at midnight, jumping in to solve problems for my kids they can handle themselves, and saying yes to social obligations that drain me. I'm exhausted, but terrified of what happens if I stop." Rachel's frantic pace was keeping her busy, so she didn't have to face the question of who she might be if others didn't constantly need her.

Speaking of messages about women in midlife, we absorbed growing up: Did you know the women in *The Golden Girls* were all in their fifties? At the time, the show was quite groundbreaking—portraying single, independent women supporting each other through life after children, divorce, and aging, when few stories centered on midlife women at all.

But watching it now, it's striking how much has changed. Their clothing, hairstyles, and conversations often made them seem decades older than today's vibrant, purpose-driven women in midlife. The storylines revolved around loss and limitation more than reinvention and desire. And while the show broke barriers, it still reflected a cultural expectation that women in their fifties should wind down, not start over.

That old narrative is dissolving. Increasingly, women in midlife are opting for visibility and embracing reinvention. The reality is that today, women in their fifties are vital, purposeful, and just hitting their stride with decades of productive life ahead of them. This is where the Queen archetype we've been exploring rises to meet us.

The Queen doesn't fade. She's just getting started! And she doesn't fear the wilderness. She *expects* it. She knows that transition is part of her rite of passage. She meets the unknown not with frantic answers, but with curiosity, presence, and power.

She's prepared. Her toolbox includes discernment, boundaries, inner authority, self-trust, vision, and a growing ability to choose alignment over approval.

In my own life—and in the lives of the women I work with—I've witnessed a profound shift toward legacy and impact. The Queen no longer asks, *How can I be needed?* Instead, she asks, *What do I stand for? What do I want to leave behind?* Her clarity emerges by giving up control and being willing to let go of what no longer fits.

There's a quiet, radical power in being able to say: "I don't know."

After I left my corporate job, everyone asked, "So what's next?" And for once, I didn't make something up to sound impressive. I simply said, "I don't know—yet." At first, it felt terrifying. People looked at me with concern, even pity. But in time, it became one of the most liberating things I'd ever done. I gave myself permission not to have the answers. And in doing so, I made space for something new to arise.

This is self-actualization in its truest form; not the self-indulgent pursuit it's sometimes mischaracterized as, but the alignment of our inner truth with our outer expression. The Queen knows that congruence between values and actions is non-negotiable. She's unwilling to compartmentalize or compromise any longer. The inner has to match the outer.

Each moment of uncertainty pushes us to question our assumptions and consider possibilities we've never explored. This inner questioning often manifests externally in ways that might surprise those around us—and sometimes even ourselves.

These transformative decisions often emerge from countless moments of discomfort— signals we've been receiving but perhaps ignoring until perimenopause amplifies their volume. What looks like a sudden upheaval to others often represents the final step in a long internal journey toward authenticity.

It might show up as a decision to leave a job, sell the family home, end a relationship, or travel solo for the first time. To others, these choices might look impulsive or drastic. But they usually reflect a deeper, not yet tangible clarity that has been building beneath the surface.

I experienced it myself when I left Switzerland for Mallorca. To outsiders, it may have looked like a dramatic leap. Some thought I was running away. But I knew the truth: I was running *toward* something. Toward myself.

These bold moves don't always come from complete certainty. Often, they arise from a simple, powerful recognition that the status quo no longer fits and that we're willing to step into the unknown. After years of making careful, measured decisions, there can be profound liberation in saying, "This isn't working anymore, and I'm brave enough to try something different."

That's the Queen in action.

She disrupts what no longer serves. She doesn't wait for perfect clarity to act—she listens deeply and moves when the soul says "now."

When we stop fighting the fog and dare to admit, *I'm not sure where I'm going, but I trust myself to find out*, we open the door to new information, insight, and possibility, and invite transformational experiences that will guide us toward a deeper understanding of ourselves.

Discomfort is *part* of the path. How do we walk it? By practicing presence.

Clarity doesn't emerge because we chase it. It arises when we stop, breathe, and listen long enough to let the fog clear on its own. One of the Queen's most powerful tools is her ability to be with herself. To feel what she feels. To pause, notice, breathe. Presence through the senses, tuning into smell, sound, texture, and light, pulls us out of mental noise and into our bodies.

From there, intuition can speak. Insight can land. No fixing, no rushing. Just listening.

Letting the wilderness do its work. Letting yourself transform.

To start finding your way through the wilderness, you don't need a map—you need a moment of quiet attention. *The Wilderness Walk* is a simple yet powerful exercise that helps you connect with your inner guidance, even when the path ahead isn't clear.

The Wilderness Walk Exercise

Purpose: *To practice being present in uncertainty and connect with your intuition through nature, helping you develop comfort with the "wilderness" state that leads to clarity.*
Allow at least: 30–45 *minutes.*
Material: *Comfortable clothes and walking shoes, water and light snacks, a journal and pen (for later).* Optional: *weather-appropriate gear (hat, sunscreen, light jacket).*
Note: *If you have mobility limitations, you can adapt the exercise to be seated in a natural setting, like a park, where you can hear, see, and smell different things.*

Instructions:

1. **Choose a natural setting**, *like a forest, park, or beach, where you can walk safely and undisturbed. Leave behind your electronic devices.*

2. **Arrival and centering:** *Take five deep breaths, focusing on body sensations and your surroundings.*

3. **Mindful walking:** *Begin with a* 15–20 *minute walk. If you have more time, you can extend it to* 45–60 *minutes. Walk slowly and pay attention to your body moving, your steps, and your breath. Observe your surroundings without categorizing or labeling what you see.*

4. **Sensory exploration:** *Find a spot to pause. Spend two minutes focused on each sense:*
   - *Sight: What colors, shapes, movements do you notice?*
   - *Sound: What do you hear near and far?*
   - *Smell: What scents reach you?*

- *Touch: Feel the texture of something natural—a leaf, bark, stone, or sand.*
- *Taste: Notice the taste in your mouth or in the air.*

5. Reflect: *Return to your starting point and ask yourself:*

- *"What is unclear in my life right now?"*
- *Notice any thoughts and feelings that arise without judgment.*

6. Gratitude and return: *Stand tall. Take a few deep breaths. Express gratitude for this time and experience. Walk back slowly.*

When you return home, spend ten minutes journaling about the experience and any insights that emerged. Notice connections between what you observed in nature and what might be unfolding in your life. Often, the patterns we see in the natural world reflect our inner landscape in surprising ways.

***

I practice this exercise regularly, especially during times of uncertainty. During one particularly memorable wilderness walk along the cliffs of Mallorca, I was drawn to the ancient olive trees that have stood there for centuries—twisted and gnarled, yet still bearing fruit.

As I reflected on my conflicting desires—to push forward with launching another program versus honoring my need for rest and introspection—those trees offered profound wisdom. They didn't produce fruit on anyone else's schedule; they followed natural seasons of productivity, balanced by essential periods of dormancy. Their strength came from this rhythm—not from constant output.

I realized I'd been caught in a pattern of continuous striving, without allowing the necessary fallow periods that would clarify what work I truly wanted to offer. The clarity I needed wasn't about how to do more, faster—but about honoring my natural cycles and recognizing that rest is a prerequisite to productivity.

That insight transformed not just how I structured my work, but how I defined success itself.

It also revealed how deeply I'd been operating from inherited beliefs about worth being tied to productivity—conditioning that no longer served the woman I was becoming.

Unraveling the Threads of Conditioning

As we navigate the wilderness of perimenopause, one of the most important inner tasks is to *unravel the threads of conditioning* that have shaped our perspectives and behaviors over time. This process matters because it helps us identify which beliefs still serve us—and which may be limiting our growth.

Conditioning refers to the beliefs, expectations, and patterns we've collected throughout our lives. These influences come from many sources: family, society, culture, friends, partners, and even our children. Together, they form the intricate web of what we believe to be true.

When you begin to look more closely, you may find that many of these beliefs were formed early in life, at a time when we lacked the capacity to fully understand events. As children, we are natural meaning-makers and create what I call meaning-monsters—stories we tell ourselves that seem true at the time, but are often distorted by our limited perspective. We assign significance to experiences based on our limited understanding. A five-year-old whose father leaves might decide, "I'm not worthy of love," or "People always leave." These early beliefs, while untrue, often remain buried in the subconscious and continue to shape our choices and perceptions decades later.

To understand how our inner landscape is shaped and begin unraveling this inner web, it helps to understand the difference between *beliefs* and *values*.

Values are the emotional states or experiences we seek and consistently prioritise. They shape our decisions and form the fundamental personal rules we live by in pursuit of fulfilment and meaning.

Beliefs are thoughts we hold with certainty over time. They evoke a feeling of certainty about what something means. For example: "Somebody ignores my message. That means I'm not important, I don't matter." It could also mean that the person is busy or their battery is down. Most people are unaware of how deeply their beliefs influence their lives. Beliefs carry emotion, and emotion leads to action.

The fascinating interplay between values and beliefs becomes especially important during perimenopause: outdated beliefs can prevent us from living in alignment with our deepest values, while clarifying our values can help us recognize and challenge limiting beliefs that no longer serve us. By examining both, we create a more coherent inner compass for this next phase of life.

Whether you hold negative or positive beliefs about yourself—your health, and your worth as a woman in menopause or your own abilities—those beliefs shape the path you walk.

Common limiting beliefs I hear from women in perimenopause include:

- I'm becoming invisible and irrelevant.
- My best years are behind me.
- It's selfish to focus on myself at this stage.

- I'm too old to start something new.
- My body is betraying me.

You're not stuck with the beliefs you inherited or created years ago. Beliefs can be changed, especially when we're willing to examine and question them.

Think of a limiting belief like a table: it stands on four legs made of experiences, perceptions, and selective memories. Our job is to weaken those legs. Each new piece of evidence, each question we ask, and each alternative perspective we consider chips away at the belief's foundation until it no longer holds.

For example, a woman might say, "I'm too old to start a business." But what if the opposite were true? What if you were the *perfect* age because only now do you have the experience, wisdom, and resilience to make it successful?

That's what happened with my client, Elaine. At fifty-seven, she felt she'd missed her window. Despite her decades of expertise in sustainable fashion, she believed she was "past her prime." But through our work together, we challenged that story and gathered evidence to the contrary. Elaine realized her experience was precisely what made her valuable. Within a year, she had more clients than she could handle and was preparing to build a team.

We live in an era filled with examples of women defying outdated narratives. Entrepreneurs launching ventures in their fifties. Models starting their careers in their seventies. Actresses thriving well into their eighties. These women remind us that possibility doesn't diminish with age—it expands.

Now let's talk about *values*. They are the standards we have for how we want to live our lives. They shape our decisions and guide our behavior. A value might be "integrity," "growth," or "success." And just like beliefs, values can shift.

In perimenopause, many women begin to reassess the values they've lived by. Values that once served, such as achievement, caretaking, or perfection, may start to feel misaligned. In their place, new values such as authenticity, spaciousness, or legacy may emerge.

That doesn't mean you're rejecting who you were. In the chapter about contribution, we'll look at how you can honor the life you've lived. You're updating your inner compass to reflect who you are becoming.

To gently explore the beliefs, expectations, and patterns that may be limiting the expression of your authentic self—or obscuring your true desires—I often suggest the following exercise.

Aligning Your Values Exercise

Purpose: *To identify the values that matter most to you at this stage of life and begin aligning your beliefs and behaviors with what you truly care about now.*
Allow at least: *40 minutes.*
Materials needed: *a journal or notebook, a pen, and a comprehensive values list.*
Note: *This is a powerful exercise to do with someone else: a coach, trusted friend, or colleague. It can offer a valuable perspective and reflection.*

Instructions:

1. Start with a list. *Download your value's list in the Transformation Toolkit at www.daniellaschoch.com/toolkit.*

As Brené Brown notes in her Dare to Lead *work, "Living into our values means that we do more than profess our values; we practice them. We walk our talk—we are clear about what we believe and hold important, and we take care that our intentions, words, thoughts, and behaviors align with those beliefs."*

This is what we're after here!

2. Circle what resonates. *Read through the list and* circle up to ten values *that resonate most strongly with you right now, in this season of life.*

3. Narrow it down. *Now comes the challenging part: narrowing your list to just* two absolute core values. *Most of us feel torn choosing between ten and fifteen—but stay with it.*

If you're unsure which value to choose, use the comparison method:

Ask yourself, "If I had to choose between these two values, which matters more to me right now?" If you do this exercise with someone, have them ask you this question and use them as a sounding board.

Keep comparing until you've identified your top two.

4. Reflect. *Once you've chosen your top two core values, take time to reflect on the following questions.*

For each value, ask:

- *What does this value specifically mean to me? (Create your own definition.) Example: If "Freedom" is a core value, what does freedom mean to you?*
- *How do I know when I'm living this value? What does it look like in action?*
- *On a scale of 1–10, how well am I currently living this value?*
- *What beliefs might be limiting my full expression of this value?*

- *What small action could I take today or this week to better honor this value?*
- *How might my expression of this value evolve in this next phase of life?*

Write your answers in your journal.

5. Create a values statement. *Craft a short statement that reflects your two core values.*

6. Anchor it in your life. *Post your values statement somewhere you'll see it daily.*

For the next week, reflect each evening on:

- *Moments when you acted in alignment with your values*
- *Moments when you strayed from them*

Notice how it feels—physically and emotionally—when you're living in versus out of alignment with your core values.

Consider revisiting this exercise annually during perimenopause, as your values may shift more than once during this transitional time.

***

When I did this exercise during my own perimenopausal transition, I discovered that my two core values were *courage* and *joy*. What hit me was how out of alignment I'd been—especially with joy. I began to see how both were essential companions on the perimenopausal path: *courage* to meet the unknown with openness, and *joy* to keep me tethered to what uplifts my spirit and reminds me of who I truly am, even when everything else is shifting.

I was taking courageous action, but rarely acknowledging it or allowing myself to celebrate it as meaningful. For years, I'd been slamming my head against the same wall, trapped in the belief that I wasn't "good enough." That belief left me diminished and depressed, blind to my own capability.

A perfect example: for four years, I managed the full renovation of an old townhouse I'd bought in Mallorca. It was a massive project—completely disrupted by COVID—where we stripped the building down to its bones. We replaced beams and floors, built ceilings, installed plumbing and electrics, created two new bathrooms (plus two half-baths), designed a kitchen, and added a staircase to the attic. When my architect fell short, I took over: managing the budget, coordinating workers, and making every decision. It was a full-time job in itself.

Yet I dismissed it as done "on the side," while simultaneously working, earning coaching certifications, rebuilding my business from scratch, developing and launching new programs, creating websites ... all while perimenopause robbed me of sleep and left me exhausted.

The values exercise was a wake-up call. It showed me how deeply I'd been minimizing my own accomplishments. I realized I had been demonstrating a lot of courage already: starting over in a new country, managing complex projects, building a business, without giving myself credit.

What I needed next was a different kind of courage: the courage to set boundaries, to say no to misaligned opportunities, to charge what I was worth, and to share my voice even when I feared judgment.

Recognizing what I had accomplished in the renovation gave me a new level of confidence—not just in my resilience, but in my capacity to lead, make decisions, and deliver in my professional work as well.

Perimenopause became an invitation to stop playing small. My body was amplifying a message my soul had been whispering for years: I was done with self-sabotage and ready to make a real impact.

That clarity changed everything. I stopped pushing so relentlessly and started honoring my need for rest. I saw my overwork patterns for what they were and began setting firmer boundaries. Most importantly, I began acknowledging myself, pausing to say, "Well done," instead of rushing to the next task. The byproduct of this courage was authenticity.

No one around me knew about my struggles—because I didn't share them. I was always the one who had it together, even when I was lying awake at night in tears. Real courage meant not just handling external challenges, but also being honest about my internal ones.

And joy? It meant allowing myself to celebrate my wins instead of minimizing them.

This shift created the foundation for a life that feels both braver and more joyful. A life where I finally give myself credit for what I've achieved, while making space for both *vulnerability* and *celebration.*

Mapping Your Inner Stars: From Values to Limiting Beliefs

Now that you've identified your core values—your guiding stars—it's time to address what's been blocking their light.

Remember Emily from the beginning of this chapter? Her experience of confusion and "stumbling through fog" wasn't just about hormonal shifts. The clouds that obscure our path during perimenopause are often made of *limiting beliefs* or thought patterns that no longer serve the woman we're becoming.

In this transitional season, we're invited to lift our gaze from the familiar ground of roles and responsibilities and look to the stars, to the brilliance of our inner essence and the values that have always lived within us. For years, maybe even decades, we've defined ourselves by external identities: mother, partner, professional. Our sense of worth has been tethered to productivity, appearance, caretaking, and achievement.

This is why limiting beliefs hit so hard during perimenopause. When a woman tells me, "I feel invisible," or "I'm scared I have no value anymore," she's naming the painful collision between old definitions of worth and a truth that's just beginning to rise. It's as if the world expects us to quietly fade into the background, just as we're finally ready to step into our full power.

As you may have noticed during the values exercise, identifying what matters most often sheds light on the beliefs standing in the way. When I named courage and joy as core values, it became clear how the belief "I'm not good enough" had been dimming both for years.

Beliefs don't appear out of nowhere in adulthood. Most were formed in childhood—even the most "perfect" ones—as we tried to make sense of the world with a young mind and a hungry heart. Often, they were survival stories, created in moments when love, connection, or safety felt uncertain.

But survival stories are not soul stories. And they are not the whole truth.

These beliefs feel solid because of the energy we've poured into them over time. Hormonal shifts during perimenopause can heighten emotional sensitivity, making old patterns and limiting beliefs feel sharper or more pronounced. In this way, the body becomes a messenger, amplifying what needs our attention and inviting us to do the deeper inner work. As we explored in Chapter 2, this is part of the body's wisdom: It often speaks the truth before the mind can make sense of it.

The limiting story becomes familiar, automatic, and goes unquestioned. But your body is already sensing the dissonance. Now, with your values as a new compass, and the Queen energy rising in you, you have the tools to respond differently. She's no longer here to replay the old story. She's here to rewrite it.

This is what clarity makes possible.

When you know what stars you're navigating by, it becomes easier to recognize what clouds are blocking your view.

Let's begin to clear the sky with this powerful exercise.

I know this work can feel big, so I've created a worksheet to help you move through it with ease.

You'll find it at www.daniellaschoch.com/toolkit.

Beyond the Belief Barrier Exercise

Purpose: *To identify and transform key limiting beliefs that may be blocking the expression of your authentic self and obscuring clarity during perimenopause.*

Allow at least: *30–45 minutes of uninterrupted time. Give yourself space to reflect deeply—this is not a quick fix, but an opening into powerful self-awareness.*

Materials needed: *Your journal or notebook, a pen you enjoy writing* *with, and ideally a quiet space, a candle or comforting object nearby, and a timer if you'd like to pace yourself.*

Instructions:

1. Identify a core limiting belief: *Let's begin with three of the most common limiting beliefs I hear from women in perimenopause. Which one resonates most strongly with you right now?*

- *"I'm not enough" (not accomplished, attractive, smart, or worthy enough."*
- *"I'm invisible" (unseen, unheard, my contributions don't matter).*
- *"I'm alone" (unsupported, disconnected, without true allies).*
- *In your journal, write down how this belief currently shows up in your life. Be specific.*

Example:

"I feel invisible because people don't seek or value my opinion the way they used to."

If you're unsure, reflect on your biggest frustrations or irritations. They often reveal underlying beliefs.

Here are a few patterns to help spark insight:

- *You constantly overperform to receive the same recognition others get with ease (I'm not enough).*
- *You ignore or suppress your own needs, prioritizing others to the point of disappearing yourself (I'm invisible).*
- *You rarely ask for support—or ask in ways that push others away, for example, through complaint, resentment, or vague hints. (I'm alone).*

2. Explore how this belief affects you: *Use the following questions as journaling prompts:*

- *How do I act when I believe this is true?*
- *What do I avoid doing because of this belief?*
- *How might I be unconsciously creating evidence that supports it?*
- *Please be gentle with yourself. These beliefs often feel like facts—and they are usually layered with emotion. This isn't about blame; it's about bringing curiosity and compassion to patterns that may no longer serve you.*

Example:

"I held back in that project meeting last week. I didn't share my opinion because I believed it wouldn't matter. But maybe that wasn't true—maybe that was my belief speaking, not reality."

3. Notice the impact on others: *How might this belief-based behavior influence how others respond to you?*

- *If you never assert your needs, people may unintentionally overlook you.*
- *If you overgive, others may expect you to keep doing more for less.*
- *If you struggle to ask for help clearly, people may feel unsure how to support you—or may stop trying.*

4. Reflect:

- *How might others' reactions reinforce your original belief?*
- *How has this created a self-confirming cycle in your life?*

5. Challenge the belief: *Try on different perspectives:*

- *If your best friend believed this about herself, what would you say to her?*
- *What three experiences from your life contradict this belief?*
- *Who were you before you first formed this belief?*
- *How would you act differently if you no longer believed this?*

6. Rewrite the story. *Create a new empowering belief that directly counters the old one. Examples:*

- *"I am here to be seen and heard. My voice matters—now more than ever."*
- *"My existence has value. I am a blessing to the people in my life."*
- *"I was not born to be alone. I am capable of creating deep and meaningful connections."*

7. Take one brave step. *Design one small action this week that supports your new belief. It could be as simple as speaking up in a meeting, asking for help, setting a boundary, or celebrating yourself out loud.*

8. Find evidence for the new belief. *Even if you don't fully believe it yet, find three examples from your life that show this new belief might be true.*

- *Find a successful public figure who has defied your limiting beliefs*
- *Look at one of your role models and think about which limiting belief she or he had to break through*

- *Ask a trusted friend to help you find experiences from your own life when you accomplished something that you've not celebrated or acknowledged*

The more evidence you collect—the more you strengthen the legs of the new table you're building—the stronger it gets and the new empowering belief becomes part of you. Strengthening your clarity, confidence, and self-trust.

Each day for one week, deliberately act from your new belief in a small way. Notice any shifts in how others respond to you. Journal about these experiences, building evidence that supports your new empowering belief.

This work can stir up a lot. If you find yourself wanting to talk through what you've discovered—or feeling stuck on how to move forward—let's connect. Book a complimentary Pillar Gap session with me at www.pillargapmap.org.

***

When I did this work myself, I discovered that *I'm not enough* was the belief that had limited me the most. By examining how I constantly diminished my accomplishments and withheld my opinions, I began to recognize this belief in action. The turning point came when I realized that what had once protected me was now exhausting me.

Creating my new belief statement—"My accumulated wisdom and authentic voice create meaningful impact"—felt awkward at first, like wearing someone else's clothes. But as I gathered evidence to support it, from client transformations, heartfelt feedback I'd dismissed, and the real-world changes I'd helped create, the new belief began to feel more natural. More like mine.

What surprised me most was how quickly my behavior shifted once I challenged the old story. I stopped habitually downplaying my achievements. I became more direct in my communication. I set clearer boundaries around my time and energy. With each conscious decision I made, my old belief lost more and more of its grip.

As we complete this chapter on Clarity, we've embraced the wilderness of uncertainty and begun to untangle the conditioning that once blurred our inner vision. We've identified our core values and started practicing them. We've faced and softened limiting beliefs around being "not enough," "invisible," or "alone," and replaced them with empowering truths that honor our intrinsic worth.

Oscar Wilde's quote at the beginning of this chapter, "We are all in the gutter. But some of us are looking at the stars," captures the essence of clarity during perimenopause: the power to choose our perspective, even in the midst of profound change. We may not see the full path ahead—but we are learning to trust ourselves. We're developing the discernment to question old stories, and the courage to write new ones.

Once we've cleared the fog and reconnected to what matters most, the natural next step is expression.

If clarity helps us identify our values and purpose, creativity gives us the means to *experiment*, *express*, and bring them into form.

In the next chapter, we'll explore *Creativity* not just as artistic expression, but as a tool for *self-revelation and integration.* Whether through brushstrokes, journaling, or movement, creativity gives the subconscious a voice—bypassing the mind's defenses and illuminating truths we haven't yet found words for.

Chapter 4

Creativity

From Descent to Expression

"Art is restoration: the idea is to repair the damages that are inflicted in life, to make something that is fragmented, whole."
—Louise Bourgeois

Erica arrived early for our weekly free painting group. Over a steaming cup of tea, she confided, "I keep painting palm trees," she said, half laughing, half exasperated. "I don't know why, but it's been months now. I'm so sick of it! Today, I swear—I'm definitely *not* painting a palm tree."

I smiled. "Maybe the palm trees aren't done with you yet?"

She rolled her eyes but grinned. "Well, they'll have to be. I'm over it."

The session unfolded as usual, each woman quietly working on her own piece. There was that hum in the room I love: the sound of creativity unfolding in the group.

During our closing share, Erica held up her painting. "I don't know what this is," she said hesitantly. But before she could say more, another participant across the circle squinted, tilted her head, and said, "Hey, Erica ... when you turn it upside down ..." Erica flipped the canvas. "... it looks like a palm tree!"

Sure enough—there it was. Yes, the colors were unusual, the shape abstract, but the symbol had found its way in again.

Intrigued by the recurring appearance of this image, Erica asked me for a one-on-one session. As we gently explored her connection to palm trees, a memory began to surface.

"I hadn't thought about this in years," she said quietly. "My husband and I used to talk about retiring in the Caribbean ... lying under palm trees, drinking rum. It was our dream."

"But now, after the divorce, that's gone. And the kids are grown. That dream just kind of ... disappeared."

That moment opened the floodgates. Through tears and conversation, Erica began to process the grief she'd been holding, not just for her marriage, not just for the fact that she no longer felt needed, but for the life she had imagined. A life that had quietly disappeared without proper mourning.

Over the next few creative sessions, we dove deeper into what needed to be seen. She painted the loss. She sculpted the ache. And slowly, she began to reclaim a new vision for her life and herself.

And interestingly, once Erica fully acknowledged her grief, the palm trees stopped appearing.

***

Erica's story beautifully demonstrates how creativity can bypass our conscious barriers, allowing the subconscious to speak truths we've been unable—or unwilling—to voice. In the process of creating, we begin to give form to our innermost emotions, fears, and aspirations, helping us reconnect and discover new aspects of ourselves. That in itself can be healing.

Creativity is always about the endeavor, the journey rather than the outcome. It's about allowing and listening.

When we release our attachment to the result, our own expectations and the need to create something that others deem "good" or "pretty," we start a conversation with the parts of ourselves that live just beneath the surface: sometimes raw, sometimes radiant, always real.

Creativity challenges us to let go of the mind's control. In my work as an art therapist, I've seen how easily we can filter or shape what we say to others and ourselves. But creative expression, like painting or sculpting, bypasses the logical mind that wants to "manage the message." What we create is honest, pure and unique. There's a direct channel from heart to hands, and our intuition and subconscious mind use it to speak to us.

Creativity creates. And when we give space for its expression, it reveals what the mind cannot.

In this book so far, we've reconnected to the body and begun to reclaim clarity by identifying what matters most. We've questioned old roles, rewritten limiting beliefs, and started stepping into more authentic alignment.

Now, creativity invites us to go deeper, to give voice to what has no words yet, to explore the space beyond logic and into essence. This is what creativity does: it leads us into the wilderness of what we've buried, then gives us the tools to return with something new.

This is the work of innermost expression, and it takes courage.

The courage to make a mark before we know where it's going.

The courage to face what emerges in the process.

The courage to roam, not perform.

If you're reading this while navigating brain fog and mental exhaustion, exploring something new, like creativity, is literally the last thing on your mind. I hear you. But here's something

I've learned: creativity doesn't need your sharp memory or your ability to multitask that perimenopause has disrupted. In fact, softening of our analytical minds can open doorways to intuition and expression that may have been previously dimmed by our need to be competent, efficient, and perfect.

When you can't remember where you put your glasses (because yes, now you need those too!), perhaps you can feel your way into a painting. When you can't articulate what you're going through, perhaps you can put it on paper.

And if you're thinking *I don't have time for this*—especially when you're already overwhelmed by everything life and perimenopause have thrown at you, let me assure you that you don't need a big setup or a studio. Even five minutes with your hands in clay, pen on paper, or colors on a page can shift something. I don't want you to feel like you have to add yet another item to your to-do list. You're just giving yourself a different way to unwind and express what you're already experiencing.

All creativity needs is your willingness to feel, to explore, to let something unknown emerge. And perimenopause, for all its challenges, has given you unprecedented access to the raw material of creation: intense feeling, questions about identity, and freedom from who you used to be.

In this chapter, we'll explore how creativity becomes your tool for self-revelation and integration, especially during perimenopause. We'll look at three key aspects of its power: how creativity serves as a tool for descent into our inner worlds, its role as an emotional processor—especially for uncomfortable and difficult emotions—and its ability to unlock new forms of expression.

Before we dive into the creative practices ahead, I want you to give yourself permission. Real, tangible permission.

I've created a set of Permission Slips for Creativity that you can download and print from your Transformation Toolkit at www.daniellaschoch.com/toolkit. Post them where you'll see them, and let them remind you: creativity isn't about doing it right. It's about showing up."

Creativity as a Tool for Descent

In the perimenopausal journey, many women experience what I call *the descent*—a turning inward that can feel like a fog settling over your inner landscape. Your mind feels dull, your energy is unpredictable, and your very sense of self is unstable. To the outside world, it can look like burnout, depression, or withdrawal. To the woman living it, it can feel like an unraveling.

Your inner judge will tell you that this is a failure, a departure from your usual tendency to please and look after everybody else. But what if the loosening of your logical grip is actually opening space for a different kind of knowing to emerge?

When we no longer know who we are, when the roles that once defined us feel ill-fitting, when we look in the mirror and see a stranger, and everything feels uncertain, we become open to discovering who we might become. This dissolution of familiar identity is a creative opportunity.

In the Heroine's Journey, descent is a necessary initiation. It's the moment we stop pleasing and performing, and instead turn inward and start to gather the lost pieces of ourselves. It's a sacred pause for shedding old skin and growing deeper into who we're meant to become. And in this process, creativity becomes one of our most powerful tools to navigate the unknown territory where we surrender to mystery and learn to trust what arises.

Unlike logic or language, creativity doesn't demand explanation. It doesn't require a plan. It simply asks us to show up—with our hands, our senses, our presence—and let something come through. That's why, in my work with clients, I often invite tactile forms of creation like finger painting, collage, or clay work. Working with your hands brings you back into your body, centering and grounding you. It makes you *feel*.

Sarah, a successful entrepreneur, suddenly found herself unable to work. It's not that she didn't want to. It's that she simply couldn't perform the way she had before. Instead, she began spending hours in her garden, hands deep in the earth. To outsiders, it looked like she was having a breakdown. Her family worried; they'd never seen her like this before. But in truth, she was reconnecting with the primal need to sink her hands into earth, to breathe in the scent of soil, to remember the simple pleasure of touch that her busy mind had long forgotten how to access.

This urge to "return to basics" is common during the descent, especially as our bodies change in ways that feel foreign: weight shifting to places it's never been before, energy fluctuating like weather we can't predict, even our skin feeling different under our own touch. When our physical selves feel unfamiliar, creativity offers a bridge back into partnership with our bodies.

The purpose of Sarah's gardening wasn't to create a perfect landscape. She needed to feel the soil between her fingers, follow the rhythm of planting, harvesting, nurturing, and surrender to the slow pace of watching things grow. The time spent with the earth, its cycles and silence, and the patience it required became her way back to herself. It was a necessary retreat that helped her re-root her soul.

When you work with your hands—whether in soil, clay, or paint—you reclaim your physical self and all it's in the process of becoming. Whatever you feel drawn to during this time, follow that pull. Let the exercises in this chapter inspire you. Your descent doesn't need to make sense to anyone else. It's not for them.

And if you feel resistance to creating, if your inner judge is telling you it's "pointless" or "indulgent," know that this is normal too. Many of us have internalized the belief that unless something is useful, beautiful, or impressive, it's not worth doing. That, unless we can call it "art," it doesn't count.

But creativity doesn't exist to impress. It exists to reveal. In my work as an art therapist, I've witnessed this again and again: when we let go of the need to get it "right," something more honest and whole begins to emerge.

That is the gift of descent: the chance to meet yourself without the mask of your saboteurs and by going inward to give voice to your truth. And truth, when expressed honestly, is always enough.

Let's start with a practice to help you descend gently—one mark, one image, one truth at a time.

The Intuitive Collage Exercise

Purpose: *To gently access your subconscious and uncover hidden thoughts, desires, or feelings through spontaneous visual imagery.*
Allow at least: *30–45 minutes of uninterrupted time.*
Materials: *a large piece of paper or cardboard, glue stick or tape, scissors, and a stack of old magazines. Optional: journal or notebook for reflection.*

Instructions:

1. **Prepare your space.** *Set aside time when you won't be disturbed.*

Create a cozy, non-judgmental environment—with tea, music, and candlelight, for example.

2. Begin without a plan. *Flip through the magazines without looking for anything specific. Let your hands and your intuition guide you. Cut out any images, words, colors, or patterns that catch your attention. If something stirs a reaction—curiosity, warmth, even discomfort—clip it out. Don't overthink it.*

3. Let the story emerge. *Once you've gathered a good stack of cutouts, begin arranging them on your paper. Let the images speak to each other. There's no right or wrong way to do this. Trust the placement that feels most satisfying or curious to you.*

4. Commit to the creation. *When it feels good, glue the pieces down. Sit with the finished collage for a few moments. Let your gaze soften.*

5. Reflect. *What story does your collage tell?*

- *Are there patterns, themes, or symbols that surprise you?*
- *What feelings arise as you look at it?*

6. Journal (optional, but powerful). *Write a few reflections on what emerged.*

- *What did you notice?*
- *What felt unexpected?*
- *What message might your subconscious be offering you?*

The beauty of this exercise lies in its simplicity. It doesn't require any artistic skill, just an open heart and a curious mind. And because you're working with images you found, it can feel less intimidating than facing a blank canvas. And yet, what emerges often holds un-

expected insight. The collage becomes a mirror, reflecting emotional truths you may not have words for yet.

***

I once had a client whose collage turned into an underwater wonderland: shades of blue, coral, dolphins, silence. When we talked about it afterward, it turned out she used to be an avid scuba diver—something she had abandoned years ago when life got "too busy." Her collage was her subconscious whispering, *Remember how alive you felt underwater*?

Within a month, she'd taken a refresher course and booked a dive trip. That one intuitive, creative act rekindled a passion she didn't even know she'd lost.

That's the power of letting creativity lead the way. It reveals what your soul remembers—even when your mind forgets.

Approach your collage with the mindset that you're not trying to create a masterpiece for others to admire. You're creating a visual representation of your inner landscape, meant for your eyes only. And when the pressure of perfectionism lifts, something far more meaningful can rise in its place: authenticity, emotional truth, and self-recognition.

If you feel like you're in the middle of your own messy descent, let me also assure you that you won't stay in the depths forever. This phase of the menopausal and midlife transition is about retrieving wisdom from your innermost self and bringing it back to the surface. Creativity is your diving gear—helping you to go deep while keeping you connected to the world above.

Curiously enough, through this process, we're reconnecting with the ultimate feminine power: the power to create. Whether it's tending a garden, shaping clay, or arranging images in a collage, you are giving life to something new. Your capacity to create and nurture extends far beyond your reproductive years.

And that leads us to the next truth about creativity: *It helps us process our emotions.*

Creativity gives emotion a safe place to land, be expressed, and move through that might otherwise remain stuck or hidden.

Creativity as an Emotional Processor

You know those moments when emotions crash over you like a tidal wave, leaving you gasping and disoriented? Those sudden tears over a commercial? The rage that erupts from nowhere over small things? The grief that hits while you're folding laundry?

Yep. Perimenopause is full of those.

Believe me when I say: you're not suddenly becoming a "mean girl." It's your emotional system recalibrating as estrogen fluctuates, and that's exactly what creativity is designed to hold. Your hormones aren't betraying you; they're giving you unprecedented access to feeling: raw, unfiltered, sometimes shocking. All that intensity, all those contradictions? Creativity speaks fluent "emotion." It can translate what logic cannot explain and give form to what has no words.

The beautiful thing is that creativity can be both your life raft *and* your surfboard through these emotional storms.

When I was deep in my own perimenopausal descent, I often woke up at 3 a.m., buzzing with an energy I couldn't name. After months of waking up and lying there, frustrated by yet another sleepless night, battling my racing thoughts or scrolling my phone in defeat, I started to get up; to read, to watch TV, and eventually to paint. No still lifes for sure, nothing demanding or meaningful, just abstract doodles and explorations of color. Something to occupy my hands and my mind. And it helped. My nervous system started to calm down, and I was able to go back to bed earlier than before. Even though most of those paintings aren't very pretty, I've kept them because they're real. And because they look like my insides felt ... pretty chaotic.

If you're reading while you're awake yourself, with your mind going to weird little places that only seem available in the middle of the night—I'm here with you. Perimenopause messes with our sleep in ways that can feel cruel and random. And fighting it often makes it worse. Sometimes the kindest thing we can do is stop struggling with our bodies and give that restless energy somewhere to go.

And that's exactly what creativity does: It gives you an outlet for your energy and a form to the formless. Nameless worry and anxiety become a sculpture you can touch. Inexplicable anger becomes a dance you can move through. Profound sadness becomes a melody you can hear.

It doesn't make the emotions go away, but it *does* make them tangible. And once they're tangible, you can start to understand them. This is where the alchemy begins. As you pour your raw, unfiltered emotions into your creative practice, you're expressing them and by doing so, already transforming them. That painting might start as pure rage, but as you work, you might find pockets of tenderness, sparks of joy, depths of strength you never knew you had.

The key is to focus on the act of creating, allowing your emotions to move freely and take shape in the physical world, giving them a safe place to land.

This process can be especially powerful in perimenopause, where the emotional terrain can feel unpredictable or overwhelming. So much of what rises doesn't live neatly in the mind. It lives in the body: in the flutter of anxiety in your chest, in the restless energy of nameless apprehension, and the worry that loops endlessly through your mind. These emotions don't just want to be "figured out" logically (because there might be no logic to them). They ask to be felt, honored, moved.

That's where creativity steps in as an outlet for all the contradictions. Hope and heartbreak. Frustration and curiosity. Tenderness and full-blown *fuck-this-shit* energy.

Creativity can hold it all.

A brushstroke can hold your fury. A torn page can carry your anger. A melody, a movement, a splash of paint—all of them become vessels for what you don't yet have words for.

But sometimes ... words *are* what want to come.

Not polished prose. Not a journal entry with tidy conclusions. But a single sentence. A quiet poem. A string of eleven words that crack you open just a little.

Writing, in its raw and somewhat not-so-intimidating form, can offer just as much release as painting or sculpture. You don't have to be a poet. You don't have to be profound. You simply have to turn inward—and let it out.

That's why I love the next practice. It's simple. It's powerful. And it lets emotion find shape through language—quickly, honestly, and without pressure.

Here's how to do it.

The Elfchen (or Elevenie) Poem Exercise

Purpose: *To process and distill emotions into a concise, intuitive form using a poetic structure similar to a haiku—gentle, fast, and revealing.*

Allow at least: 5 *minutes.*

Materials: *Pen and paper or a digital writing tool, a quiet space for reflection.*

Instructions:

1. Find stillness. *Settle into a quiet space where you can reflect without interruption. Take a few slow, grounding breaths.*

2. Tune in. *Ask yourself: What's going on inside of you right now? Notice what's present in your body or heart. Choose one emotion that feels strongest or most ready to be explored.*

3. Write your Elfchen. *Follow the five-line structure below to shape your feeling into language. The description of the world is just a gentle suggestion to get you started.*

- **Line 1:** *One word – Name the emotion*
- **Line 2:** *Two words – Describe the emotion*
- **Line 3:** *Three words – How does it affect you?*
- **Line 4:** *Four words – What does it teach you?*
- **Line 5:** *One word – A concluding thought or image*

Don't overthink it. Be present and let the words flow. Don't worry about being poetic or profound. You can be deep, humorous, cynical, sarcastic, or completely irreverent here. The beauty lies in honest expression, whatever that looks like for you.

4. Read it aloud. *Once you've written your Elfchen, gently speak it out aloud to yourself. Notice how it feels in your mouth, in your body, in your heart.*

5. ***Reflect:***
   - *What surprised you?*
   - *How did it feel to distill the emotion into so few words?*
   - *Did a new perspective, layer, or insight emerge?*

Here's an example of one of my Elfchens:

Longing.
Heart aches.
Reaching for connection.
Reminding me I'm alive.
Hope.

And a slightly different one:

Creativity.
Eludes me.
*What the f***ck?*
At least I'm honest.
Progress.

Try writing one a day for a week. Don't edit. Don't judge. Just let the words come. It's a quick, focused tool for emotional processing, and it's accessible even if you don't consider yourself very versed with words. You can share them with someone, but you don't have to. The act of creating them is what matters.

***

I love the Elfchen because it's so simple. I can experiment with different words until something clicks. And the constraint of structure can offer more freedom than a blank page ever could.

I've kept a small notebook just for Elfchens. Over time, it's become like an emotional journal—each tiny poem capturing a snapshot of my inner world. It's fascinating to look back and see how certain themes recur, evolve, or resolve.

You might want to keep your own: write them, date them, and revisit them later. You'll be surprised by what your own words reveal when you read them in hindsight.

Speaking of judgment, even great artists face it for not being "artsy" or technically elaborate enough, yet their emotional honesty is exactly what makes their work so powerful.

Take Jackson Pollock, for instance. Pollock became famous for his "drip paintings," pouring and splattering paint onto large canvases laid flat on the floor. His method was revolutionary, focused on movement, patterns, and subconscious expression. His paintings are often dismissed as "just splashes of paint," the kind anyone could make. But when I stood before one for the first time, I was completely mesmerized. There's a rhythm and a pulse in the chaos that follows a secret order.

Creativity is not about copying nature—it's about expressing a galaxy of inner workings that can't always be put into words. It's available to all of us. When we follow our own rhythm and inner pulse, we're tapping into the same creative intelligence Pollock used. We don't need to understand it; we just need to feel it and eventually, hopefully, learn to trust it.

Then there's Rothko, known for his large *Color Field* paintings, floating rectangles of hazy luminous color. He layered thin washes of pigment over months to create depth and emotional resonance. He poured his soul into those canvases. If you've only ever seen his work on small-scale postcards (which, by the way, I love!), it's easy to dismiss his work as "just blocks of color." Until, again, you stand in front of one.

When I visited The Museum of Modern Art (MoMA) in New York and stood face-to-face with a towering Rothko, it filled my entire field of vision with color that reverberated and enveloped me. Looking at it, I felt it all: the joy, the grief, the existential ache of "Why are we here?", the stillness, the presence. His paintings feel like a portal into the depths of the human experience.

Again, your creative practice works the same way. When you layer color, when you let emotion guide your brush, when you focus on feeling, you're working with the same principles. And your five-minute painting can carry just as much emotional truth as Rothko's months-long masterpieces.

These artists remind us that it doesn't matter if people "get" what you do. What matters is the space you allow for something unnamed to rise to the surface and discover something about yourselves you didn't expect; to speak truths we didn't know we needed to say, to unlock new ways of expressing who we're becoming.

That willingness to let something unnamed rise to the surface becomes especially important as, for many women, accessing that authenticity means confronting emotions we've been taught to suppress entirely.

Creativity as Medicine for Anger, Rage, and the Witches' Wound

I'd like to add another layer to how we can use creativity, one that expands beyond menopause. It has to do with the courage to acknowledge and process the "forbidden feelings" we're rarely encouraged to name out loud: anger and rage.

No matter our personal background, most of us struggle to navigate these emotions. As women, we've been conditioned, explicitly and implicitly, to be nice, polite, quiet, agreeable, composed, and pleasing. To swallow our discomfort, smooth over tension, and smile through the sting. Anger, rage, and even assertiveness have been seen as disruptive or "too much." Women who express these emotions are often labeled hysterical, dramatic, or difficult—coded language that reinforces centuries of silencing.

So we tuck those feelings away. Deep into our bodies, into the tissues of our being, where they don't disrupt the peace, but quietly corrode our inner world.

By midlife, the facade of always being "nice" begins to crack. You might feel something else rise instead: anger, sharp, unexpected, even frightening. It's the heat under your skin. The clench in your jaw. The lump in your throat when someone dismisses you—again.

We carry it in our bodies. But we also inherit it. Through the stories of our mothers and grandmothers. Through centuries of women being silenced, controlled, shamed, and disempowered. Through the fear of taking up too much space and being told we were irrational, crazy, or wrong when we dared to speak truth.

Persecuted for being healers, seers and custodians of ancient knowledge: wise, intuitive, different. For being women.

This is what some call the *witches' wound*, and it's not metaphorical. It's cellular. Studies in epigenetics show trauma can be passed down through generations. The flinch when we speak up for ourselves, the guilt when we want to say no, the shame that surfaces simply for wanting more.

And beneath the shame? Rage. Grief. Fury. A deep, embodied knowing that something was taken from us: time, voice, safety, power. Because deep down, we know we deserve better.

You deserve to be seen. To be heard. To matter.

And still, we're told to smile. To be grateful. To "calm down."

Negative emotions don't disappear by being ignored. They ferment. They stagnate. They take root in our beliefs, our relationships. Scientific research shows that they lodge in the body and suppress our immune system. They dysregulate your hormones, and over time, they can contribute to severe or chronic illness. The body always keeps score, and eventually, it speaks.

Recently, my own body spoke. During a routine skin check, a mole was removed from my right arm. Eight days later, I received the results: it was malignant. Skin cancer. Just like that, the big C had entered the room.

At first, I didn't connect this to anger or rage. But in a therapy session, old wounds resurfaced—especially around my father. He wasn't a bad man. But he was absent, critical, emotionally distant. A man of his generation. A product of his own upbringing. Still, I carried the imprint: I never felt truly seen. Not for who I truly was. And I held on to the resentment of feeling small and unworthy as a child.

After my parents separated when I was seven, I only saw him every few weeks, always on his terms. He never created space for us in his life—literally or emotionally. And decades later, when he finally wanted to spend more time with me, I felt cynical. *Now you want to show up? Now you care? Well, tough luck! What goes around comes around.* And worse, I noticed something I didn't want to admit: part of me wanted him to feel what I'd felt, for him to hurt the way I had. That wasn't just anger. That was rage.

And it had been living in my body all this time.

Naming it was a release. But rage needs more than just acknowledgment; it needs motion. It needs a voice. It needs somewhere to go.

That's when creativity became something of a lifesaver.

It is the sacred container. The ritual fire. The alchemist's tool that takes what could poison us—all of those difficult, uncomfortable, and shocking emotions—and transforms them into something meaningful. Into truth.

We can scream on paper. Pound our fists into clay. Rip up old paintings. Write letters we'll never send. And through it, we stay safe. No one gets hurt. Not us. Not our kids. Not our bodies. But the rage moves. It breathes. It releases.

Whatever you create, you don't need to like it. You don't even need to keep it. But you do need to let it out.

Let your rage speak in color. Let it wail in sound. Let it slice through the page. Let it be seen, finally. Not to shame it. Not to fear it. But to honor it—as the part of you that remembers injustice. That knows your worth. That refuses to be silent any longer.

We must learn to turn toward our anger with open eyes and an open page, inviting our feelings to be expressed and witnessed. The next practice is one of my favorites for this very reason. It gives your rage and all of your difficult emotions a safe place to land, and a powerful way to be released.

Releasing Rage on the Page Exercise

Purpose: *To give voice to your rage safely, allowing it to move through your body and onto paper where it can be witnessed, honored, and ultimately transformed.*
Materials: *Large sheets of paper (A3 or larger), red, black, and orange markers/paint, timer, private space, Optional: fireproof bowl and matches.*
Time: *20–30 minutes.*

Instructions:

1. **The Summons (5 minutes)**
    - *Sit with your materials. Close your eyes and breathe deeply.*
    - *Place one hand on your heart, the other on any tight or activated part of your body.*
    - *Ask gently: What am I angry about? What am I tired of carrying?*
    - *Don't overthink—just listen. Whatever comes up is valid.*

2. **The Release (15 minutes)**
    - *Set your timer for 15 minutes.*
    - *Write a letter to whoever or whatever you're angry with. Try your non-dominant hand to bypass your inner critic.*
    - *Say everything you've never said. Everything you've swallowed. Everything that's burned in your chest.*
    - *If words aren't enough, draw your rage. Scribble, slash, layer color over color.*
    - *Make sound if needed. Growl, sob, yell. Your rage has a voice.*
    - *No editing, no censoring, no making it pretty. This is your rage, your release, your rules.*

3. **The Witness (5 minutes)**
    - *When the timer rings, put your pen down.*
    - *Look at what you've created—not to judge, but to witness.*
    - *Place your hands on the page and say aloud: "I see you. I hear you. You matter."*
    - *Notice your body. Has anything shifted? Softened? Released?*

4. **The Choice (5 minutes)**
    - **Choose** *how to complete the ritual:*

- **Keep it:** *Store privately for future reference.*
- **Burn it:** *Watch it transform into smoke and ash.*
- **Bury it:** *Return it to the earth.*
- **Rip it up:** *Sometimes, physical destruction is most satisfying.*

Remember, this isn't about being "cured" of anger—it's about giving it motion and space. Intense emotions may rise; that's normal. You might feel tired afterward. Your anger deserves a voice.

Not everyone can access their rage the first time. And that's okay.

***

I once worked with a client named Suzanne who had buried her anger so deeply that she couldn't feel it. When we did this exercise together the first time, she looked at me and said, "I don't think I'm angry. Just tired. Numb, maybe."

But numbness is often what protects us when the real feelings feel too dangerous to name.

So we did it again. And again. Gently. With patience. We created a safe space where her anger didn't need to justify itself. And one day—it came. Quietly at first. Then, like a storm. She filled pages. She sobbed. She laughed through her tears and said, "I had no idea how much I was holding."

That session changed something for her. Not just emotionally, but physically. She said she felt ten pounds lighter. Her voice became steadier. Her boundaries firmer.

Anger, when acknowledged, becomes energy. It becomes the strength to say no. The clarity to walk away. The power to protect what matters most.

If it doesn't come right away, don't force it. Come back. Try again. Let the fire find you in its own time.

And when it does, let it move you forward.

Unlocking New Forms of Creative Expression

What I also learned from witnessing many perimenopausal descents is that they have a way of shattering every box you've ever put yourself in. Including your ideas about who you are and what you're *good at* creatively.

I had a client—let's call her Lisa—who had always seen herself as "not the creative type." Numbers were her thing. She thrived in spreadsheets, strategy, and systems. But as she descended into this phase, she needed a way to calm her mind during bouts of insomnia and increased anxiety. She was so desperate that she was open to trying anything that could help.

So, I introduced her to the practice of Zentangle[1] : a simple form of drawing on a small piece of paper composed of repetitive patterns. It seemed like a low-pressure way to "do something creative" each day. Just five minutes. No big blank canvas. No expectations. Even though Lisa was sceptical at first, it quickly became her favorite thing to do, a kind of moving meditation. She started doing a Zentangle every morning with her coffee and started to have fun with it, exploring new patterns and finding inspiration.

What surprised her most wasn't just the soothing effect it had on her nervous system, but also how much *clearer* she began to feel. Her thoughts were more spacious, her emotions less volatile. And

1. Zentangle® is a simple, meditative drawing method that uses repetitive patterns—called "tangles"—to create structured, often beautiful designs. It was created by Rick Roberts and Maria Thomas as a way to promote focus, relaxation, and creativity. The best part? Anyone can do it. You don't need to know how to draw. All it takes is a pen, a piece of paper, and a few minutes of mindful attention. Learn more at https://zentangle.com or search "Zentangle patterns" online for inspiration.

soon, she was having ideas that felt fresh and inspired; creativity, not in spite of her structure-loving brain, but because she'd finally allowed herself to play.

Creativity in this phase helps us process what has been and helps us imagine what's next. It's not only a way down into our depths, but a way outward into possibility.

Expression becomes expansion.

This becomes especially important as society begins to overlook women of a certain age. We navigate our fears about becoming invisible: worrying that our voices won't carry the same weight in boardrooms, feeling that dread when we think about dating apps (and who are we going to match with now?), and concerned that society might treat us as if our most vital years are behind us. When the world tries to tell us we're past our prime, creativity offers us a different kind of visibility. Not the kind that depends on others' approval or fits into someone else's narrow definition of valuable, but the kind that emerges from authentic self-expression.

When you create, you make yourself visible to yourself first. You discover that your worth isn't tied to your fertility, your productivity, or your ability to turn heads. You become visible as a creator, as someone with something unique to offer. And that shifts everything, not just how you see yourself, but how you show up in the world.

This is an invitation to try on forms of creativity that feel unfamiliar. Love to write? Pick up a lump of clay and see what your hands want to create. Love music? Try painting ... with music!

Let your hands, your voice, your body choose—not your inner critic.

If a voice in your head is saying *I'm too old to start something new*, *I've missed my chance*, or *What's the point now*? What if you're finally old enough? Old enough to create without needing anyone's permission. Old enough to experiment without it reflecting on your competence. Old enough to fail spectacularly and call it research. Old enough to please yourself first.

Let's exchange mastery for mystery. Begin again, like a child—with curiosity, courage, and zero concern for perfection. Give yourself permission to mess up, to start over, and follow the thread of joy wherever it leads.

The teenager in you who was told she couldn't sing might finally discover her voice. The woman who always colored inside the lines (because that's what good girls do) might revel in the freedom of mess-making. The perfectionist might finally create something imperfect and beautiful. This isn't your consolation prize for growing older—this is your reward for surviving long enough to stop caring what anyone else thinks.

This mindset can be incredibly liberating, especially as we navigate the changes and challenges of perimenopause. Because after the shedding comes the shaping. After the fire comes the form. And creativity is how we begin to touch the edges of the life that's waiting for us.

Here's a simple exercise to help you unlock new forms of creative expression.

Storytelling With Your Senses Exercise

Purpose: *To awaken your senses and explore fresh ways of expressing your inner and outer world by focusing deeply on one sensory lens at a time.*

Allow at least: 5–10 *minutes daily for a week.*

Materials needed: No *materials required—but a pen and journal can help you capture insights afterward.*

Instructions:

1. **Choose a quiet moment** *in your day—somewhere you can be present without distraction.*

2. **Pick one sense** *to focus on: sight, sound, smell, taste, or touch. Let it be random, or follow your curiosity.*

3. **For the next 5–10 minutes**, *tune in deeply to that one sense. Let it take the lead.*
   - *What do you see?*
   - *What do you hear?*
   - *What do you smell, taste, or feel against your skin?*
   - *Notice texture, rhythm, nuance. Let it surprise you.*

4. **Now, tell the story of that moment using only that sense.** *Describe what you noticed only through the chosen sense. For example:*
   - *If you focus on sound, describe your experience using only sounds: whispers, cracks, hums, rustles.*
   - *If you focus on smell, narrate it through scents: earthy, citrusy, sharp, musty.*

5. **Express it however you like:**
   - *Say it out loud*
   - *Write it in your journal*
   - *Whisper it to your cat.*
   - *Keep it simple. You're just capturing what you sense in the moment: messy, partial, perfectly imperfect. The form doesn't matter. The noticing does.*

6. ***Repeat daily for a week,*** *choosing a different sense each time. If you want, keep your entries and reflect on how your perception shifts with each lens.*

7. **Reflect:** *At the end of the week, reflect on the experience.*
   - *Which sense was most challenging?*
   - *Which revealed something new about your surroundings or yourself?*

This practice helps soften the dominance of logic and language and invites you to experience the world and yourself through your senses and awareness. It activates your so-called sage brain and helps you discover new creative metaphors, textures of memory, and subtle emotional undercurrents hiding in plain sight.

***

When I tried this practice for myself I quickly discovered that I liked to focus on the sound. I was shocked by the layers I'd been unconsciously filtering out. My own breath, the gentle hum of the refrigerator, distant traffic, a dog barking and even the crowing of a rooster in the fields behind my house. It made me realize how much of life I experience on autopilot, missing the rich sensory world that's constantly available to us.

After we've moved through the grief, the rage, the unraveling, this is what begins to stir: playful emergence, surprising expression, and the courage to create again.

And just like that, play opens the door to presence.

Remember, your creative practice is a form of self-care. The time you spend painting, writing, dancing, or engaging in any form of creative expression is time invested in your well-being.

Create a sacred space for your creativity: a corner of your room or a pocket of time in your day. Protect it fiercely. And protect your creative privacy, too. Your creative work—and everything else in your life—deserves the conscious choice of who you want to share it with. Some paintings are meant for your eyes only. Some poems are private conversations with your soul. Not everything needs to be shared, critiqued, or understood by others.

Also, your creative energy, like our hormones, will ebb and flow. When energy runs high, dive into projects with gusto. When it wanes, give yourself permission to rest, gather inspiration, or engage in gentler forms of creativity. Fallow periods aren't wasted time—they're necessary renewal.

And yes, creativity takes courage. Courage to begin without knowing where it's going. Courage to face what emerges. Courage to follow curiosity instead of certainty. As you've seen through the exercises in this chapter, the goal isn't mastery or perfection; it's presence. Creative expression invites you to show up, mess and all, and reclaim the parts of yourself you may have left behind.

Remember Erica and her palm trees that we met at the beginning of the chapter? What began as a frustrating compulsion became a portal for healing. Each palm tree she painted held a piece of the life she'd imagined, the grief she hadn't yet named, making way for the future she could still create, even if it looked different from what she once envisioned.

The paintings, poems, or dances that you create may be beautiful, and they might touch and inspire others. And that's wonderful. But don't go into your creative process with that in mind. Allow creativity to ignite something in your brain and your soul that's different. You may notice how it begins to ripple outward. You might even approach a challenge at work with a new perspective, or discover deeper ways to connect with those you love.

All of the exercises in this chapter are invitations. You've stepped into the creative process to meet yourself fully, fiercely, and honestly. You've learned to value process over product, expression over perfection, and truth over performance. And in doing so, you've unlocked a different kind of power: the kind that comes from no longer pretending to be fine and daring to become whole instead.

You've descended into your inner depths with courage.

Now, we rise.

And build on these inner truths.

In the next chapter, we meet *Congruence.* You are now asked: Does your outer life reflect this inner truth? Are your choices, your relationships, and your voice congruent with the woman you're reclaiming?

Chapter 5

Congruence

Aligning Your Inner Truth with Outer Expression

"When I dare to be powerful—to use my strength in the service of my vision—it becomes less and less important whether I am afraid."

—Audre Lorde

I went to a women's gathering on a day I probably should have stayed home.

I was exhausted. Another sleepless night had left my nerves frayed and my energy drained, but still, I pulled myself together. I showered, washed my hair, and put on some makeup. I looked in the mirror and thought, *Okay ... I can do this.* I felt relatively okay—until I got there.

The moment I walked in, one of the women came up to me, her energy pouring out in a monologue of stress and frustration. I listened, nodded, held space. I waited for her to pause, to ask how I was. She didn't.

The second woman approached with the same urgency: more venting, more unloading. Again, no check-in. Just an assumption that I had capacity.

Then the third woman walked by me, smiled and said, "Oh, you look great. You always do!"

And something in me cracked.

I didn't know whether I wanted to scream or cry—maybe both. But I could feel the anger rising, not just at them, but at something deeper: at the role I had always played, the way I had learned to hold space for others while quietly abandoning myself.

For most of my life, I'd felt torn between two selves: the powerful, self-reliant woman who had it all together, and the sensitive, intuitive soul who longed for softness, for connection, for support.

How could I be both? How could I stay strong while admitting I was hurting? These parts of me had always felt like opposites—two poles that refused to meet.

But that day, they collided.

When we gathered for the opening circle, I couldn't hold it in.

I burst out: "I'm *not* fine. Nobody here has asked me how I am. I'm miserable. I'm tired. I'm lonely. I'm worried. And I'm *so* sick of everyone assuming I'm okay just because I know how to cope."

There was a stunned silence. And then a strange, beautiful relief.

Because in that moment, I saw the truth: it wasn't just that they hadn't asked. It was that I hadn't told.

I had kept playing the capable one. Wearing the mask. And my body, my hormones, my heart, had finally had enough.

Perimenopause stripped away my ability to keep up the illusion. I could no longer smile through the exhaustion or hide the anxiety, the sleeplessness, the emotional overwhelm. I couldn't "fake fine" anymore.

That day was a turning point. It taught me that congruence. *Real* congruence isn't about choosing one part of yourself over another. It's about allowing the full truth to rise.

To live as both strong *and* soft. Held together not by perfection, but by alignment.

***

Throughout our journey so far, we've done the vital inner work of connecting with ourselves, gaining clarity, awakening our creativity, and cultivating courage throughout. We've touched the authentic self beneath years of conditioning and expectation. And now, with congruence, we begin to move from awareness into embodiment—from inner knowing into outer action.

Congruence speaks both simply and profoundly: Live in alignment with what matters most. Let your words, actions, and choices reflect who you truly are.

You can think of congruence as the bridge between being and doing. Between sensing your truth and letting it shape how you show up in the world.

Let's pause here to clarify something important. Throughout this book, we've talked about *authenticity*—being true to your inner self, honoring your needs, emotions, desires, and inherent worth. We can define it as "the quality of being true and real or genuine ... despite external pressures." Authenticity is the compass that points you home.

But *congruence* is the path you walk. The Oxford Dictionary defines it as "the state of being in agreement or harmony." In mathematics, it refers to two figures that align exactly when superimposed—they match. In psychology, congruence describes a state in which your ideal self and your actual experiences are aligned—where you're being true to yourself across your roles, choices, and relationships.

We feel congruent when our inner world and outer expression are in sync. When what we *believe, feel, say, and do* reflect the same inner truth.

Congruence means living your authenticity—consistently, honestly, and courageously—in alignment with your deepest values and ideals.

Where authenticity means knowing your truth, congruence means expressing it—consistently, courageously, and in all areas of your life. It's your values in motion. It's the harmony between who you are inside and how you live outside. It's the willingness to adapt and adjust so that, when you superimpose both worlds, they still match.

This becomes especially important during perimenopause, when everything—our bodies, identities, roles, and rhythms—is shifting. Congruence calls us to move from resisting those changes to *responding* to them. To reshape our routines, relationships, and commitments so they reflect who we're becoming, not who we used to be.

For me, that meant integrating two parts of myself I had long believed were at odds: the powerful, self-reliant woman, and the sensitive, intuitive soul. Authenticity helped me name and accept both. But congruence? Congruence asked me to *live* both.

To ask for help while still standing strong. To express softness without giving up my fire. To create a life where I no longer had to choose between the two.

And yes, living this way requires courage. Congruence often asks us to set new boundaries, grieve old versions of self, and risk disappointing others to stay true to ourselves. There may be moments of loss when relationships, roles, or identities no longer fit. But what emerges is a deeper peace. A sense of wholeness that can't be faked or forced.

This chapter is about that wholeness.

We'll explore what congruence looks like in real life, not just in big decisions, but in the small, everyday choices that bring your life into deeper alignment. We'll reflect on what it means to live from your inner truth and evolving sense of self, and how that alignment can support your well-being, relationships, work, and purpose.

Perimenopause offers a powerful invitation: to become more integrated. To bring your whole self to the surface. To live from the inside out.

Let's explore how living in congruence can transform not just your menopausal journey, but your entire life.

Aligning Your Inner and Outer Worlds: Setting New Standards for Yourself

The first time I truly understood the power of alignment between my inner truth and outer expression came through an unexpected offer.

A potential client—impressed by my online presence and creative work—approached me about creating marketing content for her business. On the surface, it made perfect sense. I enjoyed writing. I was good at it. And the project promised steady, well-paid work.

Twenty years ago, I would have said yes without hesitation. Back then, I measured opportunities by how well they matched my skills, not how well they matched my soul.

But this time, something felt ... off.

It was subtle—just a tightness in my chest, a heaviness in my gut whenever I imagined doing the work. While I loved creating content to share *my own message* and connect with coaching clients, the idea of doing it for someone else's brand felt draining before I'd even begun.

Instead of pushing through or rationalizing it away, I paused. I listened. And underneath the discomfort, the truth became clear:

I could do this—but it would pull me off my path. It would siphon energy from the work that truly lit me up: guiding people through life transitions, supporting deep transformation, living and sharing my own message.

I said "no."

It wasn't a loud, defiant "no." It was quiet, firm, and clear. A *congruent* "no." A choice not to compromise my alignment for the sake of short-term gain.

Society holds countless expectations for women our age: how we should dress, behave, work, and live. These expectations vary across cultures and generations. In Mediterranean communities just two generations ago, widows in their fifties were often expected to wear black for the rest of their lives. Today, the expectations may look different: career milestones, homeownership, partnership, children. But the pressure to conform hasn't disappeared. It's simply changed form.

The problem is that when we try to live up to *external* standards that don't reflect our *internal* truth, we create a subtle but persistent dissonance. That dissonance often shows up in our bodies before it registers in our minds.

Anthropologist Angeles Arrien described this as "the gap between our knowing and our doing." It's the moment you say yes when you mean no. The heaviness that follows after agreeing to something that betrays your values. The slow, silent erosion that comes from abandoning yourself in the name of being agreeable, loved, or approved of.

We often experience this tension as a conflict between *authenticity* and *connection*. As children, we learn how essential connection is—literally for our survival. Disconnection could mean danger, even death. We carry that imprint into adulthood, often without realizing it, and often at the cost of our truth.

So we smile when we feel unseen.

We take care of others before checking in with ourselves.

We don't bring up the things that hurt us.

We avoid the hard truth.

We overdeliver, overperform, overextend—seeking approval through excellence, while ignoring the voice inside that quietly pleads, *I need rest.*

However, every time we abandon our authenticity to preserve connection with someone else, we weaken the most sacred connection of all: the one we have with ourselves.

That connection to our truth, our needs, our inner belonging is not only our right. It's our responsibility.

Congruence means learning to choose that inner connection first. It means honoring our body's signals, our intuitive clarity, our evolving truth, even when it might disappoint someone else, even when it feels unfamiliar.

Any time we sincerely want to make a change, the first thing we must do is raise our standards. Real transformation begins with a personal decision—not a plan or a goal, but a *new baseline for what you will and will not accept.*

Congruence means raising your standards to reflect who you truly are now, not the version of you that was shaped to please, perform, or prove.

You're not here to meet expectations. You're here to meet yourself, fully, honestly, and without apology.

And that begins with learning to trust the cues that live in your body, your energy, your emotional landscape. Just like I did when I turned down an offer that once would have tempted me—but that time, I chose alignment over my hyper-achiever.

To help you strengthen that same intuitive self-trust and begin mapping your own alignment, let's turn to the Congruence Compass, a simple yet powerful tool to help you identify where you're living in truth, and where something may be ready to shift.

The Congruence Circles Exercise

Purpose: *To map where you're in and out of alignment by visualizing where your time, attention, focus, energy, mental headspace and money actually go—and seeing if that reflects what truly matters to you. This exercise helps you become aware of the gap between what you say you value and where your energy really flows.*
Allow at least: 30–45 *minutes of uninterrupted time.*
Materials: *A large sheet of paper, journal, and (optional) colored pens or markers. You'll find a worksheet with an example and guided reflection prompts in your Transformation Toolkit at www.daniellaschoch.com/toolkit.*

Instructions:

1. **Draw your current reality:** *On your page, draw three circles—one for each major life area. Size each circle according to where your energy actually goes* RIGHT NOW *(not where you wish it went):*
    - *Physical Well-being (your body, health, rest, movement, nourishment, creative expression)*
    - *Relationships (partner, family, friends, community)*
    - *Work/Purpose (career, creative projects, contribution, calling)*

Be honest. If work consumes 70% of your energy, make that circle much larger than the others.

2. Tune in through the body: *Pause and look at what you've drawn. Close your eyes and bring this reality to mind. Let yourself feel into it, not think, but sense.*

- *Does your chest tighten or expand?*
- *Does your breath deepen or become shallow?*
- *Do your shoulders relax or tense?*
- *Do you feel energized, neutral, or drained?*

These bodily sensations are messages. They reveal what's aligned and what's not.

3. Reflect with honesty: *Now journal your responses to the following questions:*

- *What's your first reaction to seeing your circles? What surprises you?*
- *Which circle feels too small? Which feels too large?*
- *Does this allocation feel aligned with what truly matters to you?*
- *What societal expectations are you still trying to meet that don't resonate with your authentic self?*

Let your answers be messy, intuitive, and incomplete. You're not solving anything here—just listening deeply.

4. Draw your ideal circles: *Now draw three NEW circles showing your ideal allocation. What would feel aligned? What would honor all parts of you? Remember: your ideal doesn't have to be three equal circles. The goal isn't equality; it's alignment with your truth.*

5. *Identify what needs to shift:* *Look at both sets of circles—your current reality and your ideal. For each area where there's a gap, gently explore:*

- *What would need to change to move from current to ideal?*
- *What small step could I take this week to bring more congruence into this area?*
- *What old pattern or expectation am I ready to release?*

6. *Imagine what this shift would create:* *This is where the real power lives. Close your eyes and imagine you've made the shift. Your circles now reflect your ideal allocation. What has changed?*

- *How do you feel in your body when your energy is aligned this way?*
- *What becomes possible in your relationships?*
- *How does your work shift when it's balanced with the rest of your life?*
- *What becomes available to you that isn't available now?*
- *Six months from now, living in this alignment, what are you most grateful for?*

There is no perfect way of doing this. It's just a tool to help you make more aligned choices, one day at a time. Some days you'll feel fully congruent; others, you may drift. That's natural.

The power lies in noticing the drift and choosing to realign.

Keep your circles close. Revisit them when making big decisions or when that subtle feeling of "off" arises. Let them guide you back to choices that honor your truth and evolving needs during this transformational season.

***

When my client Elena first did this exercise, she was sure her misalignment would show up in her work quadrant—she'd been considering a career change for months. But when she tuned into her body, it was her *relationships* that gave her the strongest signal. Her chest tightened and her jaw clenched as she thought about a long-time friend who constantly drained her energy.

As she journaled, Elena realized she had been holding onto the friendship out of guilt and habit, not because it reflected the woman she was becoming. She had been saying yes to invitations that felt like obligations, nodding along to conversations that left her feeling unseen. Her Congruence Map showed a clear discrepancy between her inner truth and her outer actions.

That awareness alone was powerful—but what changed everything was the small step she took afterward. Instead of ghosting or creating drama, Elena chose a gentle, honest conversation. She let her friend know she was craving more space and wanted to shift the rhythm of their connection. It wasn't easy. But in the coming weeks she told me she felt a lightness in her body she hadn't felt in years.

"This was the first time I chose *me*," she said. "Not in a selfish way, but in a congruent way. I didn't abandon her. I just stopped abandoning myself."

Her words stayed with me. Because congruence isn't just about aligning your truth with your actions in the present—it also invites you to look back. To ask: *Where did I learn to abandon myself in the first place?*

Often, the answer leads us to one of our earliest relationships: the one with our mother.

Healing the Mother/Daughter Split

I sat at my mother's bedside, holding her frail hand as she began the slow process of leaving her body. I was struck by how much of her I saw in myself—not just in my features, but in my mannerisms, my strengths, and yes, even in the patterns I had spent years trying to break.

My mother had been a vibrant, creative woman. She sang opera. She was a gifted dancer. She had what people often called "healing hands"—the softest I've ever touched. And yet, only a few of her many talents and dreams came to full expression. Life had asked other things of her.

There comes a moment in this kind of goodbye when there is nothing left to do. Nothing to fix. Nothing even to say. I had said it all. What remained was presence—pure, quiet, loving presence. Sitting with her. Breathing with her. Just *being there.*

And in that stillness, something stirred in me. A quiet reckoning.

I began to wonder: *Where am I holding myself back?* Did I have talents and dreams I haven't fully expressed yet? And, if courage and joy are core values for me, which parts of my potential have I still not allowed to be fully seen?

It wasn't just about my mother—it was about *me.* About all the places within myself where something had gone quiet. Where I had tolerated misalignment. Where I had bent or shrunk or silenced myself in order to be loved, or to belong.

It was a moment to begin healing the grief of losing my mother, as well as the many unspoken threads between mother and daughter and every fracture of my own truth—every place I had become inconsistent with who I really was.

I took her hand and led her on an imaginary journey into my future. I wanted to show her that I'd be okay. More than okay, that

I'd be great again, after some time. As I showed her all the wonderful moments still to come, the beautiful life I would continue to create for myself, I could feel the echo of her unrealized dreams reverberating between us. I couldn't change her path, but in that moment, I made a quiet vow: to fully live mine. Not just for me, but for her too.

Losing my mother felt like losing an anchor, a primal lifeline to safety and unconditional love. Even as our roles had shifted over the years, and I had begun to care for her more, some part of me still trusted I could return to being mothered. That somewhere, somehow, there would be a warm hug, a cup of coffee, or a cheese sandwich waiting to make everything okay again.

Her death brought a profound truth into focus: I would need to mother myself now. To become my own anchor. To offer myself the tenderness, encouragement, and safety I had once instinctively looked for in her.

Many of us arrive at this threshold in midlife carrying the invisible imprints of our mothers, whether through loss, the reversal of roles as they age, or simply through the quiet unraveling of old dynamics. Something profound begins to shift in the mother-daughter bond. And something just as profound stirs within us.

In the mythology of the heroine's journey, this is a pivotal moment. It's when we begin to heal the split between mother and daughter within us. This is where we reclaim the mother. Not just the woman who raised us, but the archetypal energy she represents: nurturance, intuition, softness, sensuality, and fierce inner knowing. Qualities that may have been silenced in her, and thus in us.

This is also where the Queen begins to rise. Not the obedient daughter. Not the woman shaped by expectations. But the one who leads her life from the inside out. The one who knows what she values, what she will no longer tolerate, and what legacy she intends to leave behind.

To become congruent at this stage of life, we must examine the ways we've internalized our mother's voice—both her gifts and her wounds. We must ask: What parts of myself have I inherited unconsciously? What have I rejected in an effort to be different? And what am I ready to reclaim—letting go of both misplaced loyalty and rebellion, and standing instead in truth?

This healing is especially potent during perimenopause. And the timing is no coincidence.

Just as our bodies transition out of their childbearing years, we're invited to reimagine what it means to create, to nurture, and to care. Not as mothers in the traditional sense, but as women no longer defined by the role of mother, women guided instead by the wisdom, vision, and sovereignty of the Queen.

Whether or not we have children, we are still creators. We give birth to ideas, movements, healing, and change. We tend to the emotional and spiritual well-being of our communities, our relationships, and ourselves.

Have you ever noticed how, in many fairy tales and myths, the mother is missing? Replaced by a wicked stepmother or erased from the story entirely? That's because the psychological task of separating from the mother while still honoring what she gave us is so profound, it's often too complex to depict directly.

But that's the work we're called to now.

Healing this split and coming into full congruence in this area of your life isn't about rejecting your mother or erasing her influence. It's about conscious integration.

It's about recognizing where her unlived dreams may still echo in your own desires and which ones are truly yours. It's about acknowledging where you've rejected parts of yourself in an effort to be different from her. It's about learning how to hold both your independence *and* your connection to the maternal line, without collapsing into rebellion or self-abandonment.

This work is subtle, sacred, and deeply empowering. And like all true healing, it begins with a conversation.

To help you begin that dialogue, I've created a guided journaling process to explore the dynamic between the mother and daughter within you. This is your invitation to bring understanding, compassion, and coherence to that inner relationship—to listen, to integrate, and to lead from a place of wholeness.

The Mother–Daughter Dialogue Exercise

Purpose: *To begin healing the inner split between the parts of you shaped by your mother and create a sacred space for truth, tenderness, and reconciliation between the "inner daughter" and the "inner mother" within you.*

Allow at least: *30–45 minutes of uninterrupted time.*

Materials needed: *Journal or notebook, a pen, and (optional) a candle or nurturing object that helps you feel grounded.*

Instructions:

1. Create a sacred space: *Find a quiet, comfortable space where you won't be interrupted. Light a candle, wrap yourself in a soft blanket, or place your hands over your heart, whatever helps you settle into presence. You are preparing a space where truth can be spoken and heard with compassion.*

2. Meet your Inner Mother and Inner Daughter. *Close your eyes and take a few deep breaths. Now, imagine two versions of yourself sitting across from one another:*

- The Inner Daughter—*the part of you shaped by childhood, unmet needs, and the desire to be seen, loved, and safe.*
- The Inner Mother—*the part of you that offers care, wisdom, and protection (and may carry echoes of your actual mother).*
- *What do they look like?*
- *What is their posture, their energy, their tone?*
- *How do they feel toward one another in this moment?*

There is no right or wrong—just notice.

3. Begin the dialogue: *Open your journal and allow a written conversation to unfold between these two parts of you.* You *can write this as if scripting dialogue between two characters, letting each voice take turns.* Use *the following prompts to begin:*

- Inner Daughter: "What I've *always wanted you to know is …*"
- Inner Mother: "What I've *always wanted to tell you is …*"
- Inner Daughter: "The *way you've shaped me is …*"
- Inner Mother: "My *hopes and fears for you are …*"
- Inner Daughter: "I *feel angry/hurt/grateful to you because …*"
- Inner Mother: "I'm *proud of you because …*"

Let the conversation flow naturally and allow both voices to speak without interruption, analysis, or judgment.

4. Listen for understanding: As *the dialogue unfolds, notice any moments of tenderness, tension, or truth.*

- *What do these two parts need from each other?*

- *How can they begin to move toward understanding—not perfection, but mutual respect?*

5. Integration: *Invite both the Inner Mother and Inner Daughter to express a closing intention or commitment. You might write:*

- *"I will try to protect you without silencing you."*
- *"I will speak my truth even when I feel afraid."*
- *"I will remember we're on the same side."*

Quietly contemplate:

- *What does a healed relationship between these two parts look like?*
- *What does it feel like to lead from that wholeness?*

6. Reflect: *Once the dialogue feels complete, close your journal and rest your hands over your heart. Then ask yourself:*

- *What did I discover through this process?*
- *What patterns, wounds, or gifts became clearer?*
- *How might I carry this healing into my daily life?*

Let your answers arrive gently. You've just taken a powerful step toward wholeness.

***

Elise, a woman in her early fifties, came to me during a period of deep inner turmoil. She was burnt out from a high-powered corporate role in finance, yet every time we explored what she truly wanted next, she felt stuck.

For years, she had been quietly drawn to the mind-body connection. She often imagined herself becoming a kinesiologist, working hands-on with people to help them release pain and trauma through the body. But the idea always felt strangely ... off-limits.

"It just feels like I'd be giving up everything I worked so hard for," she'd say.

As a teenager, Elise had bristled every time her mother said, "You're so good with people. You'd be an incredible coach or healer." Her mother's certainty, always pushing, always sure, felt intrusive. So Elise did what many daughters do when the mother-daughter bond is entangled: she chose the opposite.

The path of logic. Numbers. Control.

When we finally explored her Inner Mother-Daughter dynamic, something cracked open. Through journaling, Elise realized how deeply that old rebellion had shaped her life. Her Inner Daughter finally admitted, "I didn't want what you wanted for me. And the Inner Mother, softened by time, replied: "I saw your gift. I just didn't know how to offer it without making it about me."

That moment brought tears and release.

Elise understood then that she hadn't been avoiding the dream because it wasn't hers, but because it felt too close to her mother's desire. And now, standing at this new threshold in life, she didn't need to resist it. She didn't need to rebel or prove anything. She could simply choose. For herself.

A year later, she enrolled in a kinesiology certification program. She hadn't walked away from her career overnight, but she had begun carving out space for her next chapter.

So often, we carry unconscious scripts that shape our choices long after they've stopped serving us. Sometimes we live out a dream that was never truly ours. Sometimes we abandon our truth simply because it echoes someone else's. And sometimes, we silence our desires to avoid repeating an old wound.

But healing the mother-daughter split doesn't mean becoming your mother. And it doesn't mean proving you're nothing like her either. It means standing in the truth of who you are now. It means choosing the life that's right for *you*—not because she wanted it, or didn't, but because it's yours.

The Mother-Daughter Dialogue creates space for a more congruent, integrated way of being. Through it, you might discover inherited gifts you've overlooked, like my mother's healing hands, or patterns you're ready to transform. You might find yourself ready to express talents that previous generations couldn't fully embody.

By reconciling the mother and daughter within you, you're laying the groundwork for a profound congruence—one that honors all aspects of your feminine nature, from the nurturing to the fierce, from the traditional to the trailblazing. This is the kind of congruence that can sustain and empower you through the transitions of perimenopause and beyond.

This is the liberation of congruence.

This is the liberation of congruence—the deep integration of the parts of you shaped by both inheritance and choice. By reconciling the mother and daughter within, you create a fertile ground for authentic self-expression and freedom from old patterns.

Healing this split is an ongoing dance between honouring where you come from and stepping fully into who you are meant to be. As you bring this inner harmony into your daily life, you begin to shape your future with clarity, courage, and compassion.

The next step invites you to translate this newfound congruence into tangible actions that reflect your truth. Your journey forward is not just about what you do—but about how deeply you live in alignment with your whole self.

Wisdom in Action and Aligning Your Future With Your Truth

Healing the mother-daughter split brings us back into alignment with our deeper truth. But congruence is not a final destination. It's a way of being, a daily practice of listening inward and acting outward, again and again.

Wisdom, after all, doesn't live in what we know. It lives in what we embody.

A friend once shared a piece of wisdom from her father that initially irritated me: "If you want a quick answer, it's 'no.'"

At first, I bristled. It felt unnecessarily negative, even cold. But as I navigated my journey toward congruence, I began to recognise its deeper truth.

Like many women, my default had always been "yes". "Yes" to helping move boxes, "yes" to creating content for someone else's business, "yes" to putting others' needs ahead of my own. Only later would the discord creep in, that subtle, familiar tension of having agreed to something that didn't align with my energy, my purpose, or my truth.

Over time, and still practicing every day, I began learning a new way: to pause. To check in with my body and that visceral feeling. To trust that first intuitive "yes" or "no" before logic, guilt, or people-pleasing could override it.

As one client told me, years after quietly observing my work: "I trust you because what you say and what you do align." Her words touched me deeply and reminded me: *people feel congruence*, just as clearly as they feel its absence.

But how do we cultivate this alignment consistently? How do we move from occasional moments of clarity to a sustained way of being? Through my own journey and work with hundreds of women, I've discovered that living your wisdom requires several key elements:

Congruence starts with the smallest promises you make to yourself. If you tell yourself you need rest, take it. If you claim creativity as a value, make space for it. Each time you honor these self-commitments, you strengthen your congruence muscle. This is how your "yes" becomes elevated, and your "no" becomes grounded.

Making Aligned Decisions

Now that we're learning to discern a true "yes" from a self-abandoning one, it's equally important to honor that inner clarity in real time, especially when it's inconvenient, unpopular, or easy to override.

During a healing seminar, the organizer mentioned someone was looking to share a room and asked if I might be open to it. I had intentionally booked a single room, so my instinct was immediate and clear: "no."

But then came the rationalizations: *It would be the smart thing to do—I'd save money. It would be kind—someone needs a roommate. Am I being selfish?*

Despite all that noise, I stayed with my original "no." And it turned out to be exactly right. The room layout would have made sharing deeply uncomfortable, and the fact that I was working through a bit of a cold made having a room to myself a true blessing.

That moment reminded me: our bodies often know the truth before our minds catch up. The key is to listen and to honor that wisdom without apology.

As we've discovered, perimenopause also often brings a shift in roles. Each role shift invites us to ask: *Who am I now—and how can I act in alignment with my present identity?* Perimenopause asks us to be our whole selves and lead from our evolving truth.

Congruence is where the inner alignment begins to shape your outer life. It's when your values show up in your calendar. When your words reflect your integrity. When even your smallest choices honor who you are becoming, not just who you've been.

This is the foundation of true leadership. Whether you lead a team, a family, a movement, or simply your healing journey, the way you walk through the world teaches others what's possible. Your energy speaks before you do.

And one of the boldest ways to lead?

Letting yourself be seen.

Showing up in your wholeness.

That requires vulnerability.

Sometimes the most courageous action isn't changing careers or leaving a relationship. It's saying, "I'm not okay." Or, "This matters to me." Or simply letting the mask drop and standing in your truth, even when it trembles.

Every time you let yourself be seen in your truth, you create space for someone else to do the same. That's leadership, too.

I once worked with a woman who had spent years hiding her intuitive gifts behind a polished corporate facade. She was brilliant, yes, but also deeply empathetic, emotionally attuned, and quietly spiritual. It wasn't until she began showing up as her *whole* self—*both* with clients, colleagues, and even in her LinkedIn posts—that she began to feel the deep satisfaction of living in alignment.

It wasn't about oversharing. It was about no longer hiding.

As we explore how our congruent choices ripple out into the world, I'm reminded that what starts as a simple decision to honor our truth can transform not just our own lives but also inspire others to live more authentically. Like dropping a pebble in a pond, each aligned choice sends waves of positive change through different areas of our lives.

To help you visualize how your congruence creates impact far beyond what you might imagine, I've created a real-life example mind map showing how one woman's aligned choices rippled through her entire life. You'll find it in your Transformation Toolkit at www.daniellaschoch.com/toolkit.

The Ripple Effect Exercise

Purpose: *To visualize and understand how living in personal congruence creates positive change across every area of your life.*
Allow at least: *45–60 minutes of uninterrupted time. While you might feel tempted to rush, allowing enough time to reflect on each area will reveal deeper insights and connections.*
Materials: *A large sheet of paper or poster board, colored markers or pencils, sticky notes (optional).*

Instructions:

1. Create your center point: *Draw a circle in the middle of your paper. Inside it, write "Congruent Self" or draw a symbol that represents your authentic, aligned self.*

2. Map your primary ripples: *Around your center circle, draw four larger circles, overlapping slightly. Label them:*

- *Health & Vitality*
- *Relationships*
- *Personal Growth*

- *Career/Business*

3. Add secondary ripples: *For each primary circle, draw 2–3 smaller circles branching outward. These represent more specific areas within each category. For example:*

- *Health & Vitality: Physical health, Emotional Well-Being, Energy Levels*
- *Relationships: Partnership, Family, Friendships*
- *Personal Growth: Self-awareness, Learning, Spirituality*
- *Career / Business: Work Satisfaction, Financial Stability, Professional Growth*

4. Reflect and capture insights: *In each circle (primary and secondary), reflect on:*

- *How living with more congruence has positively impacted—or could impact—this area.*
- *Specific changes you've noticed or anticipate.*
- *Actions you can take to deepen congruence.*

5. Show the connections: *Use arrows or lines to illustrate how these areas interconnect. For example, improved health might lead to more energy for professional growth, which could strengthen financial stability.*

6. Envision the future: *On the outer edges of your map, write or draw symbols that represent your vision for each area as you continue to live in alignment.*

7. Gratitude and affirmation. *Around the border of your map, write affirmations or expressions of gratitude for the ripple effects your congruence creates.*

8. *Reflect:*

- *Which area shows the most significant positive change as you've stepped into greater alignment?*
- *Are there any connections or ripple effects you hadn't considered before?*
- *How does seeing this visual representation make you feel about your journey toward congruence?*
- *What is one small action you can take today to strengthen alignment and create positive ripples?*

Be aware that this map is an evolving document. Revisit and update it regularly as you continue your journey through perimenopause and beyond, noticing new ripple effects and the evolving impact of your congruence.

***

The ripple effect of alignment extends far beyond your individual choices. When you begin to act from your authentic self, relationships deepen naturally. Work feels more purposeful. Even the smallest decisions start to carry a different energy—an integrity that others can feel.

One client, Julia, came to this exercise feeling sceptical. She described herself as "too busy to draw circles," but agreed to try it anyway. As she started mapping her ripples, she noticed something she hadn't seen before:

Nearly every positive change she desired in her health, career, and creativity traced back to one pattern—her habit of overcommitting and being the pleaser in her relationships.

When she looked at the arrows connecting her circles, it became obvious. Saying "yes" too quickly drained her energy. Especially saying "yes" to things she didn't really want to do—out of the fear of letting others down or not being loved—left little space for movement, rest, or reflection. She realized that until she learned to honor her own capacity and trust that she would belong no matter what, she would keep postponing the changes she most longed for.

Later, she told me, "Seeing it laid out in front of me made it undeniable. My people-pleasing wasn't just affecting me—it was touching everything I care about."

That single insight became a turning point. Julia began practicing saying "no" without apology. And asking herself, "What would please me?" Within a few months, she was sleeping better, had more energy for her creative work, and felt closer to the people she chose to spend time with.

That's the power of stepping back to see the bigger picture. When you name the ripples, you can finally change them.

To bring your journey of congruence to a close, think again of that ripple effect in a pond. Each small choice to live authentically, whether saying a hard "no" to misaligned opportunities or honoring your need for rest, sends waves of transformation through your life. These aren't just temporary changes; they become the foundation of your emerging identity as a wise, integrated woman.

Brendon Burchard expresses this beautifully when he says that the first belief needed for long-term success is: "I am congruent with the best of who I know I can be."

Through this chapter, you've discovered tools to embody that belief, from recognizing societal expectations that no longer serve you, to healing the mother-daughter split within, to making choices that honor your whole self.

Yet living congruently brings its unique challenges. As we align our outer expression with our inner truth, we often encounter resistance, both from within and from the world around us. This resistance presents another opportunity to build our mental and spiritual muscle and an invitation to our next level of growth.

Remember that moment when I stood in that women's circle and finally let the mask drop? When I said, "I'm not fine," and allowed myself to be seen? That moment was the beginning of something larger than my own healing. It was the spark of contribution: offering my truth in service of something beyond myself.

By showing up vulnerably, I gave permission to others to do the same. I eased the weight of pretending, and together, we created a space where honesty and real connection could flourish. That's how congruence became contribution.

In our final chapter, we'll explore this next frontier: *Contribution*. How your congruence can become not only a source of personal freedom but a gift you share with the world. We'll discover how your wisdom, once hidden or silenced, becomes a force for healing, leadership, and legacy.

Because true power means living in alignment and sharing that alignment with others, leaving something behind that matters.

You've done powerful work in this chapter—identifying gaps, healing splits, mapping ripples. If you'd like to talk through what you discovered or explore your next aligned steps together, book a complimentary Pillar Gap session at www.pillargapmap.org.

Chapter 6

Contribution

***"The meaning of life is to find your gift. The purpose of life is to give it away."* —Pablo Picasso**

"Can you come now?"

The message buzzed across my phone at 8:57 p.m. I stared at it sitting on the couch, blanket across my legs, soup long eaten, rain tapping softly on the windows. My trainers were still on—I'd stayed ready all day. Just in case.

My friend had asked me to help her move boxes. "I'll send the details later," she'd said that morning. So I waited. By lunchtime, I sent the first message asking when she might need me. No reply. So I sent another. And waited.

4:00 p.m. passed without a word. By 6:00 p.m., my stomach growled, so I started dinner. By 7:00 p.m., I was ready to wind down for the day. At the same time, my mind was rewriting her silence: maybe she'd changed her mind. Maybe she'd found someone else. Maybe I should send yet another message. But the flicker of annoyance had already started. By the time her message arrived, it was a flame.

I'd waited all day without any update. And now, cold, tired, and done, I was being asked to rally?

My evening was gone. My energy was spent. But immediately, a familiar voice, that was overriding my desire to just stay home, whispered: *You can't say "no" now. What's the big deal? This is what good friends do!*

Then something deeper stirred, something quieter—and stronger. Another voice said: *You've already given. You waited. You kept your whole day free. Now your body is saying "no." Can you honor that?*

I took a breath. Then sent a message that was kind but clear. I told her I'd waited, but it was late now, and I was winding down. I still wanted to help—but not tonight.

What followed was a tsunami of doubt. Was I being selfish? Petty? Overreacting?

But underneath the noise, there was stillness. A knowing. I hadn't let her down—I'd finally shown up for myself.

I also realized that this wasn't an emergency. I wasn't leaving my friend stranded on the highway with a broken tire. This was simply about convenience versus my well-being.

It may have seemed like a small act—to say "no" to a late-night favour. But in that moment, I was doing something revolutionary. I was breaking a pattern of self-abandonment in the name of being “nice.” And in doing so, I made space for something far deeper: giving and helping from the heart rather than from guilt or duty—true authentic contribution.

Not the kind that depletes you. The kind that expands you.

***

By now, you've likely begun building a kind of radical self-loyalty: a quiet, consistent commitment to appreciating and respecting your body, your needs, your desires, your truth—even when it's uncomfortable. That foundation makes everything else possible. Especially Contribution.

Because true contribution doesn't come from feeling like you have to, or trying to make people like you, or neglecting your own needs because "that's just what you've always done." It doesn't flow from living up to others' expectations or from the fear of disappointing someone. It comes from a well-tended inner garden. It flows from clarity and joy, not compulsion. From dedication, not depletion.

This kind of authentic giving requires a foundation—and that foundation is commitment.

Commitment is your promise to yourself. It's inward-facing: about your relationship with yourself. It's choosing to value your body's wisdom when it asks for rest, and maintaining your creative practice because it nourishes your soul. It means staying connected to your authentic desires even when they don't align with what others want from you. Commitment creates the container for everything else.

Contribution is what flows from that well-tended inner garden. It's outward-facing: about how you choose to share your gifts with the world. It's the act of giving or serving something greater than oneself, leading to ultimate fulfillment and a deeper sense of joy. What makes it different from the service you may have provided in the past is that it comes from a full cup, emerging from your authentic self.

For so many women in our generation, contribution has been synonymous with self-sacrifice: putting everyone else's needs first, taking on more than our share, saying "yes" to everything, even when our bodies and souls were screaming "no."

This phase of your life offers you the chance to reimagine what contribution means completely. You get to discover what happens when you contribute from a place of deep self-knowledge, authentic desire, and sustainable practice.

Your commitment to yourself becomes the bridge that allows your contribution to flow authentically into the world. When you've done the inner work—reconnected with your body's wisdom, clarified your values, aligned your life with your truth—contribution becomes inevitable. However, this time it's not the frantic, depleting contribution of earlier years. It's the generous, sustainable offering of a woman who has come home to herself.

Midlife invites us to shift our perspective: from overextending and overpromising to growing and giving because we can. From pleasing to offering. From proving to contributing.

In this chapter, I'll guide you through that transformation. We'll explore what it means to contribute from fullness, not depletion. To follow your body's wisdom as a sacred compass. To align your "yeses" with your deepest truth. To leave a legacy that doesn't exhaust you, but energizes everyone it touches.

I don't want you to think you need to do more. All you need to do is become more available to what truly wants to move through you—discovering the unique medicine you carry, and having the courage and clarity to offer it to the world.

The Dedication To Build Your Legacy

For much of our lives, we've been conditioned to equate contribution with obligation. We gave because we were supposed to. We pushed ourselves to show up, perform, produce, and please—often at the expense of our own well-being. We did it because we cared. Because we were capable. Because we wanted to be good mothers, good daughters, good partners, good leaders.

But perimenopause cracks open that illusion. The body, in its fierce wisdom, no longer lets us simply grit our teeth and power through. Fatigue, insomnia, anxiety, and restlessness invite us to reassess what we're giving our energy to—and why.

We are standing at a powerful threshold, called to balance the drive of the masculine—the part that takes action and gets things done—with the wisdom of the feminine—the part that listens, allows, leans back, magnetises, and trusts. This phase asks us to integrate our shadows and face our fears, to approach life, work, and purpose differently. We might not be doing less, but we do what feels true.

Contribution is a fundamental need of the soul, rooted in the growing awareness that we belong to something greater. Our spirit longs to grow and give. True fulfillment comes not only from what we experience but also from what we extend—the ways we uplift, heal, or inspire those around us.

As we sense this connection—whether we name it God, Life, Love, or the web of humanity—contribution becomes an impulse, a heartfelt urge to participate fully. Not to prove our worth, but to reflect the love, wisdom, and power within us. Even the smallest act, like offering a kind word, creating something beautiful, or sharing our story, can ripple outward in ways we may never fully see.

Now, we can step away from martyrdom and overextension. This is where contribution meets clarity—where devotion meets discernment. Wise women no longer ask, "What do others need from me?" but instead, "What is mine to give?"

This shift changes everything. It grants permission to channel your energy toward what truly matters—not because you should, but because your consciousness is calling you to do so. It's sacred. It's chosen.

You are ready to bring your purpose into form: to name your contribution, map your path forward, and make a living, breathing commitment to what you are here to create, heal, lead, or inspire. Not someday, but now.

Because everything you desire—clarity, vitality, fulfilment—lives on the other side of aligned action. Energy aligned with action is legacy in motion.

Understanding this shift from obligation to soul calling is one thing. Living it is another. The transformation begins with reclaiming something you may have given away without realising it: your power to choose.

You are invited not just to hear the call to offer your gifts, but to recognise that you get to decide how.

That's the quiet revolution of this phase. You're no longer here to say "yes" out of habit, fear of being disliked, or to avoid conflict. You're here to say "yes" because you choose to.

Contribution now transforms from performance into power—not power over others, but power rooted in self-awareness, discernment, and dedication.

Many women get tripped up here. We sense a deeper purpose, a desire to contribute, but still carry outdated rules about how that should look. We confuse busyness with impact. We mistake exhaustion for meaning.

Your contribution doesn't need to look like anyone else's. It doesn't need to be grand or public. It only needs to be yours—and it only needs to be true.

Here lies the reclamation. You get to decide: Where does your energy go? What deserves your purposeful commitment? Who receives the gift of your presence? How do you honour your own rhythms as you move forward?

For many, the path to midlife has been paved with invisible contracts: silent agreements to keep the peace, hold the family together, and show up—no matter the cost. These contracts were never formally signed, yet have governed choices for decades.

But every "yes" you say to something means a "no" to something else. The question is—are you aware of what you're saying "no" to?

Think about it. If I'd said "yes" to helping my friend move boxes late that rainy evening, I'd have been saying "no" to rest, nourishment, my body's rhythm, and vitality. Instead, I chose honesty and recognised my energy, prioritising my needs over expectations.

Here's the beautiful paradox: when we commit authentically—aligning our "yes" and "no" with our true values and energy—we often find we have more to give, not less.

You're not becoming selfish or uncaring—you're becoming intentional. Your energy, along with your time and money, is finite and sacred. Choosing how to spend it is one of the most powerful acts of self-sovereignty you can claim.

Your old conditioning might shout: You're being selfish. You're letting people down. Who do you think you are?

But the voice of your inner wise woman is rising too. She says: You have the right to choose. You get to direct your energy. You are allowed to offer your gifts in a way that honours you.

What once felt effortless now requires conscious choice. Your body asks you to become discerning about where your life force flows.

To help with this, I've created the Commitment Audit Exercise—a way to take an honest inventory of your commitments, honouring both the reality of your changing energy and your sovereignty over how it's spent.

The Commitment Audit Exercise

Purpose: *To take inventory of where your time and energy go and where your emotional and mental bandwidth is invested. The goal isn't to have a perfect picture but to get some clarity.*

You may want to revisit the "Aligning Your Values Exercise" from the Clarity Chapter on page 57. They'll serve as your inner compass as you assess where your energy belongs now—and what needs to shift.

Materials: *Journal and pens.*

Allow at least: 15 *minutes.*

Instructions:

1. Create a simple table with three columns:

- *Current Commitments*
- *Energy Impact (+/-)*
- *Alignment with Values (1-10)*

2. Begin by listing your current commitments: *personal, professional, social, and emotional. These can be big (your job, caregiving responsibilities) or small (weekly meetups, volunteering, even lingering "shoulds" you've been carrying).*

3. In the second column, *mark each one as either:*

- *(+) = it energizes you*
- *(−) = it drains you*

4. In the third column, *rate how well each commitment aligns with your current values, truth, and purpose: from 1 (not aligned) to 10 (fully aligned and meaningful).*

5. *Reflect on your findings by asking:*

- *Which commitments consistently drain you?*
- *Which ones light you up or feel deeply aligned?*
- *What patterns do you notice?*
- *What are you saying "yes" to that might be costing you more than you realized?*
- *Where are new boundaries needed?*
- *Are there any invisible contracts you're ready to rewrite?*

Remember, during this time, it's not just acceptable—it's essential—to renegotiate how and where you contribute. Maybe a daily 6 a.m. workout no longer values your energy, but you can commit to moving your body when it feels most alive. Perhaps you can't show up for every family emergency, but you can be clear and compassionate about when and how you're available.

***

My client, Sabine, was juggling full-time employment with managing teenagers and aging parents. Her Commitment Audit revealed a shocking truth: nearly every commitment drained her. "I've been showing up everywhere except in my own life," she realized. By stepping back from volunteer work and asking for family help, she reclaimed time for painting—something she hadn't done in a decade. That single creative act gave her more energy than all her previous commitments combined.

Sabine didn't stop giving; she gave differently. With boundaries. With purpose. And most importantly, with joy.

Inner authority—that's the key phrase in Sabine's transformation. It's what happens when we stop asking "What do they need from me?" and start asking "What is mine to give? And how do I channel that choice into authentic contribution?" With this, we are being called into the Queen's domain.

The Queen's Way Of Contributing

The Queen's energy is rooted in calm confidence and quiet strength. She moves through the world with intentional presence—grounded, sovereign, and fully herself. She chooses her contributions with discernment, knowing her worth, her limits, and her power.

Nina's story is another reflection of this energy in action.

She had spent years in the sailing world, supporting major events like the America's Cup through her expertise in fundraising and sponsorship. She loved everything about that environment—the people, the mentality, the energy. But after some challenging experiences, she stepped away, and a whole decade passed without her setting foot in the arena she once loved.

By the time she came to me for coaching, she felt unanchored. She was at a crossroads with the marketing and sponsorship agency she had built and wasn't sure where to go next. Her purpose felt distant, her passion dimmed. As we worked together to uncover her authentic contribution, a spark of that old fire began to flicker. "You know what?" she finally admitted. "I would actually love to work in sailing again."

That moment initiated a deeper integration: the courage to acknowledge her desire and the willingness to take action toward it. We focused on energy work to release the imprints of past trauma until Nina felt ready to return in a new way. This time, not driven by the past or the fear of missing out. This time, she would return on her terms: guided by intuition and sustained by wisdom.

This deeper work of contribution transforms that old impulse to deny ourselves the happiness of following our heart's desires and gives us things that no longer spark joy. Instead, we learn to give and serve from reverence: for what's real, what's aligned, what our souls are truly calling us toward. It's no longer about shoulds, duties, or proving our worth. It's about answering an inner summons.

As we enter this new phase of life, we're invited to integrate the divine feminine—the power that listens, senses, magnetizes—with the divine masculine, the energy that moves, builds, and brings things into form. It's not either/or. It's the dance between dedication and direction. Between being and doing. Between attunement and action. True contribution lives at the intersection of both.

From the connection we've cultivated since the beginning of this journey, we now ask: *What do we do with that connection?*

From the purpose we've started to sense, the North Star we've been moving toward, we begin to map a way forward. To come up with a plan to manifest that purpose. To build the muscle of willpower, we need to commit to the plan and make it a priority in our lives.

We can think of it as a dance between two realms of inner guidance: listening to intuition, embodying your values, healing yourself, embracing your rhythms, and resting when needed. And the outer expression: creating, leading, mentoring, parenting, writing, launching, or simply showing up, publicly or privately, in service of something greater.

Nina didn't rush back into her old world. First, she allowed herself to reconnect with her longing and admit that it mattered. That was feminine energy. Then she took clear, aligned action: reaching out to her old contacts, reconnecting with her passion, and stepping back in with purpose. That was masculine energy.

I've witnessed this integration in my own life and in the lives of women I work with. During perimenopause, something shifts that makes this kind of wholeness not just possible, but essential.

This is Queen energy.

She worships her own rhythms. She listens deeply. She chooses when and how to show up—not from urgency, but from sovereignty. She doesn't react, she responds. She doesn't hustle to earn her place. She knows she already belongs.

What I've learned about the Queen in her full expression and natural contribution is this: she's no longer driven by the need to prove, perform, or please. She's no longer pouring herself out for crumbs of approval. Instead, she becomes deliberate. Rooted. Radiant. Her energy is an offering. Her presence is medicine. Her choices carry weight because she knows how to say "no." Her commitment does not deplete her; it nourishes her because it's rooted in truth.

This is what becomes possible when we integrate both realms—when we hold our inner guidance in the highest esteem and express it through aligned action. Our contribution matters not because we're sacrificing ourselves, but because we're showing up from a place of mature devotion, not martyrdom; from overflow, not overextension.

While Nina's journey shows the power of integrating inner guidance with outer action, others like Anika experience a different challenge: knowing their calling inwardly but hesitating to express it fully in the world.

She had a gift for capturing the beauty of ordinary moments with her camera, yet her fear of visibility and self-doubt kept her from sharing it with the world. She'd convinced herself her contribution was too small and insignificant to matter. Through our work together, she was able to tap into her inner Queen and claim the worth of her contribution.

You might be wondering: How do I actually step into this Queen energy? What does it feel like from the inside?

The Queen knows that true contribution begins by stepping out of the frenzy of the autopilot mind and into presence—calling her mind back to the present, away from future worries and past failures. Connected to this moment, she can empathize, innovate, and see every challenge as an opportunity. She lets this present-moment clarity shape her next steps.

She might lean back and take a moment before she responds, and others might mistake her stillness for passivity. It's not. It's a gathering of power.

She listens so she can lead with grounded clarity, pausing to move with precision. The Queen doesn't scatter her energy or seek permission—she channels it and claims her alignment with courageous intent.

And then she acts from inner command.

To support you in experiencing this for yourself, I've created a special guided visualization called The Sacred Integration Journey. It's a practice designed to help you access your inner Queen—aligning both your sacred feminine and sacred masculine—so you can begin to sense what's truly ready to move through you now.

You can download it and listen to it here:

www.daniellaschoch.com/toolkit.

And return to it whenever you feel the pull inward.

Let this be your turning point. Let it be the moment you stop asking *if* you're ready and begin deciding *how* you will lead. Let it be the space where you reconnect, regather, and rise.

Because your contribution is a gift and the crown you've earned, and the world is ready to receive it.

Legacy as Living Contribution

Now that you're clear on the integration, how does this Queen energy translate into lasting impact and legacy?

How do the choices you make today create ripples that extend far beyond what you can see?

Everything you've clarified, courageously claimed, and reclaimed, your values, your energy, your truth, becomes the ground you now walk with intention. From here, we turn toward the impact of your presence. How your choices ripple. How your life becomes a living contribution, felt by others even in the smallest moments.

All the pieces come together here. In this final section, I invite you to integrate the journey you've taken across these pages and craft a vision for how you want to contribute moving forward, not in theory, but in action.

This can at times cause conflict, and I'm reminded of a client whose story beautifully illustrates this. She held a mid-level executive position and felt conflicted about not aspiring to C-level leadership—especially when such a role became available. She knew that if she applied, she would "actually, probably, most definitely get the job" (her words!). When she came to see me, she was struggling with the decision as she didn't know what to do.

"I don't want to be a top executive," she told me. "I'm actually quite happy where I am, doing what I love and having time for my hobbies. But I want to leave a legacy. And this might be my only chance to do it."

What she hadn't noticed was that she was already leaving one. During a team offsite soon after our conversation, she received feedback that couldn't have come at a better moment. Her genuine love for her work, her grounded leadership, and her daily dedication to her team created a ripple effect she had underestimated. Her colleagues told her how inspiring it was to work with someone who led with joy and presence, someone who was happy with who they were and championed others to excel. She didn't need to chase a bigger title. She only needed to recognize the power of who she already was.

Legacy, she realized, wasn't something out there in the future. It was something she lived into each day through every interaction, every decision, and every aligned "yes."

This experience also taught me that legacy doesn't always look like what we think it should. Legacy doesn't have to be monumental. It can be quiet. Devotional. Woven through the fabric of your days.

It's not always about grand achievements or having your name in lights. Sometimes it's about the consistent, everyday actions and conscious choices you make: in the way you build your business or write a book, in the way you support your aging parents or raise your children, care for your elders, mentor younger colleagues, or lead from within a team.

Each of these actions, when done with conscious commitment and authenticity, sends ripples far beyond what we can see.

It's showing up wholeheartedly when it matters most—with presence and heart. It's the way you hold others. The way you love. The truth you dare to speak. The courage you model.

It all matters.

However, here's where many women struggle: they want to leave a legacy, make a difference, and share their wisdom, but they get stuck in the idea phase—like Anika, who let her self-doubts get in the way. The gap between intention and action often comes down to fear: fear of visibility, fear of judgment, fear of not being "good enough."

What I've learned is that your commitment to living authentically, to sharing your wisdom, to embodying your truth permits others to do the same. Your dedication to your growth quietly inspires others to do the same. That means being honest with ourselves—especially in perimenopause—releasing the go-to coping mechanism that we need to push through with rigid consistency. Instead, learning to choose to invest in what truly matters and showing up for that with presence and care. Sometimes, that means doing less, but with more intention.

To contribute meaningfully now, you need clarity on where you actually want to go—a personal North Star. Not a finish line, but a steady guide that keeps you aligned with your deeper purpose. Everything you've uncovered in this journey feeds into that. Now, it's time to translate it into a clear, practical compass: your North Star Map.

This is it—the big one. The exercise that brings together everything you've discovered through your entire journey. It might feel like a lot at first glance, but if you follow my step-by-step guidance, you'll move through this with ease and flow. Each step builds naturally on the last, and before you know it, you'll be holding your North Star—clear, tangible, and ready to guide you forward.

I've created a comprehensive North Star Mapping Guide with dedicated reflection spaces for each step to make this process even smoother. Download it from your Transformation Toolkit at www.daniellaschoch.com/toolkit.

Your North Star Mapping Exercise

Purpose: *To gather everything you've discovered so far and shape it into a clear, visual guide for how you want to live, lead, and contribute in this next chapter. This is your personal compass—rooted in truth, aligned with your values, and designed to keep you oriented towards what matters most.*
Allow at least: 45–60 *minutes or* 10–15 *minutes for each step.*
Materials: *A large sheet of paper, pens, markers, or colored pencils, your journal or notebook, sticky notes, washi tape, or anything else that makes you feel creative and alive.*

Instructions:

1. Reflect on the journey: *Take a moment to pause and look back. Flip through your notes, journal entries, and highlights from this book. You can also simply close your eyes and ask:*

- *What feels most true for me now?*
- *What has shifted in the way I see myself?*
- *Which pillar was most transformational for me—and why?*

Let yourself treasure what has unfolded. No rush. No pressure. Just presence.

2. Gather the threads: *Begin mapping the essential elements that make up your living legacy—your personal constellation of meaning:*

- **Core Values:** *What do you stand for?*
- **Soul Gifts:** *What comes naturally to you? What do others consistently appreciate?*
- **Lived Wisdom:** *What life experiences have shaped you most?*
- **Callings:** *Where are you being pulled? What breaks your heart open or lights you up?*

- **Archetypal Energy:** *Which parts of you are most alive right now? The Queen? The Mother? The Sage?*

Think of this as your legacy foundation. No one else has lived what you've lived or carries your precise blend of insight, fire, and grace.

3. Name your North Star: *In a few words—or with an image—name the essence of your contribution: your North Star; a guiding light, not a destination.*

Examples:

- *"I inspire women to embrace their wisdom and power in midlife and beyond."*
- *"I create safe spaces for others to find their voice."*
- *"I live with radical kindness and light the way for others to do the same."*
- *"My life is a bridge between worlds—intuition and strategy, softness and strength."*

No need to overthink. Trust the simplicity. Your North Star is a lot about reconnecting with what already lives within you.

4. Plot your contribution pathways: *From each legacy area created in #2, draw 2–3 lines outward. Along each line, list aligned actions you can take to bring that legacy to life. These can be simple, sustainable gestures or larger creative expressions.*

Examples for creativity:

- *Start a poetry journal.*
- *Share one insight on social media each week.*
- *Host a creative circle with friends.*

- *Keep it real. Keep it doable. Keep it true.*

5. *Map the expression:* *Explore how this contribution wants to move through you:*

- *What projects, relationships, or decisions are most aligned with this essence?*
- *What's ready to be released so you can move with more congruence?*
- *What simple action could help you walk in alignment with your North Star—today?*

Use whatever form helps you see the connections: constellation, ripple map, flowchart, spiderweb. Make it yours.

6. Anticipate the obstacles: *Draw a small "Challenge Box" at the bottom of your page. Inside it, name the recurring roadblocks that might arise:*

- *Self-doubt*
- *Fatigue*
- *Time constraints*
- *Fear of visibility*

Next to each one, write a compassionate strategy. For example:

- *"When self-doubt arises, I'll reconnect to my values."*
- *"When I'm tired, I'll rest instead of quitting."*
- *"I'll remind myself: small is still sacred."*

7. *Anchor your visibility:* *Legacy needs to be seen to create ripples. List 1–3 ways you will allow yourself to be visible in your contribution:*

- *Sharing your work online.*

- *Speaking up in a meeting.*
- *Asking to lead a project.*
- *Hosting a small gathering.*

Then, next to each one, write a soft affirmation:

- *"It's safe for me to be seen."*
- *"My story has power."*
- *"I don't need to be perfect—just present."*

8. Declare your commitment: *Close your map with a statement that seals your intention. Something simple, bold, and sacred.*

Example:

"I commit to cherishing my contribution—to moving forward with alignment, letting my presence be felt, my voice be heard, and my wisdom be shared."

Sign it. Date it. This is your soul's agreement.

9. Create a consistency checklist and weekly review: *In your journal, draw a weekly chart with your legacy areas and chosen actions.*

- *Each day, check off the actions you've taken.*
- *At the end of the week, reflect: What worked? What needs adjustment?*

Celebrate even the smallest win. Consistency isn't rigidity but devotion to what matters.

As with all the exercises I shared in this book, it's progress over perfection. Life will throw curveballs, energy will fluctuate, and consistency may look different from week to week. That's the reality of life. The true power lies in returning to your commitment again and again. Every time you realign with your North Star, no matter how quietly, you send ripples of authenticity into the world. And that matters more than you know.

***

Helena came to me in the midst of what she called "a midlife confusion." She had spent the last twenty years building a career in nonprofit management, raising two children, and quietly holding her family and team together. She was respected, capable, and utterly exhausted.

"I've been doing what I'm good at," she told me, "but I don't know if it's what I'm *meant* to do anymore. And I don't even know how to begin figuring that out."

Together, we worked through a version of what became this North Star Mapping exercise. When Helena began identifying her core values, her eyes lit up. "Beauty," she said, surprised. "I've forgotten how much I need beauty—creating it, noticing it, being surrounded by it."

Her soul gifts included empathy, storytelling, and humor. She was funny! Her lived wisdom encompassed years of navigating difficult family dynamics and finding harmony in complex teams. When we mapped her callings, a clear thread emerged: she longed to create spaces for others to reconnect with themselves.

Her North Star became: *I create spaces of beauty, honesty, and restoration where women can come home to themselves.*

From there, her contribution pathways began to take shape. Not a career overhaul, but a realignment. She started by hosting playful, restorative Sunday gatherings in her garden, a space for reflection and conversation. She said "no" to one draining board position and "yes" to a photography class she'd put off for years.

The ripple effect was immediate. Her energy shifted. Her voice became more confident. She no longer felt like she was running on empty because she wasn't. She was giving from a place of alignment, joy, and congruence.

"This map," she told me, holding up her scribbled North Star page, "is a lifeline. It reminded me who I am and gave me a way to walk it."

Helena's transformation shows that when you align your contribution with your authentic self, the impact ripples far beyond what you can see. In her process to make a greater contribution, she didn't overhaul her entire life. She just reconnected with what lit her up and let that be her guiding principle for the choices she made.

This is the shift from performing contribution to embodying it. From giving because you should to giving because you choose to. From depleting yourself to expanding yourself and others in the process.

As we close this exploration of authentic contribution, take a moment to feel what's shifted. You now understand that true contribution doesn't come from obligation or the need to prove yourself. It flows from that well-tended inner garden we've been cultivating, the commitment to yourself you've been building and the urge to share from a place of joy and authenticity.

If you take nothing else from this chapter, let it be this: Contribution is the act of giving or offering something—your time, energy, ideas, or resources—to your loved ones, your community and the world. It's about becoming a force for good. It's a meaningful expression of your gifts, experiences, and values in service of something greater than yourself. And doing what matters with heart, with presence and with purpose.

This is the truth no one told us in our striving years: You grow *so that* you can give. Not to prove your value—but because you've come to know it. When you give from that place, that's where the real joy lives. The real power. The real fulfillment.

Contribution isn't just about philanthropy or legacy. It's about showing up—right now—with who you are and what you have. It's the decision to let your growth become useful. To let what you've lived, learned, and overcome serve something beyond yourself.

Find something that tugs at your heart—a cause, a community, a conversation waiting to happen. Maybe it's animal welfare, human rights or environmental protection. If you had to start a foundation or charitable organization, what would its focus be? What are *you* passionate about?

Offer your time, your energy, your story. Support it financially if that feels aligned. Volunteer if that lights you up. Mentor someone, start a circle, write the words you wish someone had given you.

Just don't stay in the waiting room of good intentions.

So start now. Be a force for good in your corner of the world.

As you step into contributing from your essence, you are helping others. But you're also completing your own transformation.

You have something the world needs. Let that be the compass that guides you forward.

Afterglow

The Queen Emerges

"There must be those among whom we can sit down and weep and still be counted as warriors." —Adrienne Rich

The kitchen is quiet at 3.00 a.m. I sit at my table, scrolling thro ugh my phone, trying to distract myself from another sleepless night. In this moment, a memory surfaces—my mother, decades ago, sitting in this same liminal space between night and dawn, flipping through magazines. Now I understand she wasn't just passing time through a sleepless night; she was navigating her own journey through perimenopause and insomnia, alone in the quiet dark.

I never talked to my mother about menopause. When she was going through it, I was too young to understand the significance of those midnight vigils. Like many women of her generation, she handled it silently, eventually turning to HRT (Hormone Replacement Therapy) and continuing with estrogen into her sixties. But I'm not sure it helped her much—not in the ways that matter most.

Now, sitting in my own midnight kitchen, I wish I could have that conversation with her. I'd tell her about all the things she could try to make the transition into menopause easier on her body. About the power she had to adapt her nutrition and lifestyle to this phase of her life. I'd tell her she wasn't broken. That her body was wise.

That her soul was in the midst of a powerful initiation. Most of all, I'd want her to know she wasn't alone.

We don't have to be.

As we stand at this threshold of completion, perhaps the most important question arises: How do we take everything we've learned—about ourselves, our power, our wisdom—and bring it fully into the world?

How do we break the cycle of shame and create new traditions that honor this profound life transition?

Like my mother and I, generations of women have navigated this change behind closed doors, in silence, in fear, in isolation. It's a pattern we've inherited—but we don't have to continue it.

Think about it: we celebrate so many life transitions. Baby showers to welcome motherhood. Weddings to mark partnerships. Retirement parties to honor decades of work. But one of our most profound transformations—the emergence of the Wise Woman—often passes without acknowledgement.

It's time for that to change.

And change is happening.

Living the New Paradigm

I see it every day in my work with women.

Where our mothers may have whispered about hot flashes and quietly filled prescriptions, we are speaking more boldly about the physical, emotional, and spiritual dimensions of this transition. We are questioning the old narratives of decline and discovering something else: this can be a time of unprecedented clarity, power, and purpose.

Remember the research from *The Menopause Brain* that we discussed earlier? About the discovery that our brains rewire themselves during menopause, recover and often improve afterwards? Yes, there's disorientation, but what emerges on the other side is often more aligned and authentic than before.

I see this new paradigm alive in women like Evelyn. I coached her five years ago during her perimenopausal transition. When we reconnected recently, I was struck by the quiet power she now emanates.

"The noise in my head has finally quieted," she said. "All those years of second-guessing myself, tiptoeing around others—what a waste! I know who I am now. I know what I'm here to do."

Evelyn realized that the very symptoms she had resisted—sleeplessness, emotional surges, relentless questioning—were a refining fire. They stripped away what wasn't essential and revealed her truest self.

Today, she runs a successful consulting practice on her own terms. She works with clients aligned with her values. She builds in time for rest and playfulness. She says no without guilt. "The most surprising thing," she told me, "is how much more impact I have now that I'm not trying so hard to make one."

Women like Evelyn and all the women mentioned in this book are creating new pathways for others to follow. They're rewriting the story, showing us what's possible when we embrace this season of life.

They don't have perfect lives. They haven't escaped struggle. But what they have discovered is something rare and real: a way of living rooted in self-mastery, self-love and self-trust. A life led from essence, not ego, a rhythm defined by wholeness, not hustle.

They know that their value is in who they are. They've reclaimed their time, their energy, and their voice. They've stopped apologizing. And they've started leading in their businesses, in their homes, in how they embody presence, alignment, and joy.

This is what conscious living beyond menopause can become.

And for many, it's just the beginning.

But perhaps most importantly, these women aren't keeping their transformation to themselves. They're creating new ways to celebrate this passage—both for themselves and the women coming after them.

This is how cultural change happens—one story, one conversation, one celebration at a time.

We are reclaiming what it means to be an empowered woman in midlife. We are naming her. Honoring her. The Queen.

Creating New Traditions

Something shifts when we stop enduring this transition in isolation and begin marking it—with reverence, ritual, and realignment.

This impulse is what gave birth to *The Larger Life Lab*—a space I created for heart-inspired women seeking something more. Some are navigating menopause. Others are stepping into new leadership. All are hearing the call of a "larger life"—and choosing not to ignore it.

And by larger, I don't mean louder or more complicated—quite the opposite. A larger life means more simplicity, more honesty, more agency, more freedom.

The Lab is a living container—part sanctuary, part launchpad—where transformation is witnessed, celebrated, and supported. We gather for body wisdom practices and energetic reconnections. We rewire limiting beliefs. We celebrate micro-wins and moon cycles. We rest and rise, grieve and grow, laugh and lead.

We're not waiting for culture to give us a ceremony. We're creating our own.

We move together—from breakdown to breakthrough, from confusion to congruence.

We think we're healing ourselves, but we're healing forward and backward at once.

Our daughters watch us rise. Our mothers witness us standing where they could not.

The choices we make in this season of life have the power to reshape the whole lineage.

One woman's awakening becomes another's permission slip.

And just like that, a new legacy begins.

The Ripple Effect

Each woman who navigates this transition consciously—who refuses to shrink into invisibility, who tells the truth about her experience—becomes a giant on whose shoulders others will stand.

What feels like a personal shift often becomes a quiet reordering of the field.

The ripple might start with something small: a boundary drawn, a truth spoken aloud, a quiet, internal decision to stop apologizing for the change and start honoring it.

It shows up in how we parent, how we lead, how we love, how we listen. It shifts what we tolerate, what we model and what we make space for in others.

For some, it's a solo retreat. For others, a weekend with close friends—sharing stories, holding ceremonies, marking what's been and what's becoming. Some gather across generations to create new rituals. No one way is right.

Here in Mallorca, I created *The Wise Woman Weekend*—a blend of reflection, celebration, and deep connection.

If you can't join us in person, here are the elements I suggest to create your own:

1. **Acknowledgment and Witness:** Let yourself be seen—not just for what you've done, but for who you're becoming.

2. **Release and Renewal:** Let go of what no longer serves. Set intentions for the next chapter.

3. **Wisdom Gathering:** Own what you've learned. Share it not as advice, but as a possibility.

4. **Community Connection:** Create spaces of support. Build bridges across generations.

This is how we restore meaning to a phase culture tried to erase.

Celebration is not a luxury. It's a declaration: *I matter. This transition matters. And I will not walk it unseen.*

But the ripple doesn't end with women.

As we speak more openly about menopause—what it really feels like, what it's asking of us—it inevitably reaches into our relationships, especially with the men in our lives: partners, sons, fathers, friends.

For them, this transition can feel disorienting. While we're going through rapid transformation—physically, emotionally, hormonally, spiritually—they're not. Their hormones decline more slowly, and their changes are less socially disruptive. They don't wake up one day feeling like an entirely different person.

We do.

So when we start changing—how we feel, what we need, how we relate—it can catch them off guard. They may not understand why what once felt "fine" now feels intolerable. Why the woman they've known is suddenly craving more depth, more space, more fire, more stillness.

I've seen too many relationships strain under this disconnect. Women navigate this transition alone while partners interpret the changes as rejection or moodiness. "He looked at me and said, 'You've changed,'" more than one woman tells me as if that were a problem. Of course, we've changed. That's what this transition is about—*the* change.

With increased awareness and language around the change of menopause, we can educate and support friends and the men in our world to meet us in this metamorphosis so that we can offer each other presence, not perfection. We don't need men to walk the same path—we need them to walk beside us with curiosity and respect. When that happens, the ripple becomes a shared current. And something real becomes possible: a new language, a new legacy.

The Spiral Continues

It's 3:00 a.m. again, but this time I'm awake by choice. The kitchen is quiet, but not empty—it's filled with the energy of creation. I'm not scrolling through my phone to escape insomnia. I'm here putting the finishing touches on this book—a love letter to women everywhere navigating their own transformation.

The same space that once held my mother's solitary vigil and my desperate prayers to find sleep again now holds my purposeful work.

Think about the journey we've taken together. We began with Connection. Through it, you've reclaimed your relationship with your body's wisdom and your heart's deepest desires. You've learned to trust the whispers of your soul and honor the rhythms that nourish you.

Through Clarity, you've cut through the layers of conditioning that once clouded your vision. You've distinguished between what was handed to you and what is truly yours to carry forward. You've discovered your authentic values and aligned your life with what matters most.

Through Creativity, you've opened pathways to express your essence in ways that feel alive and true. You've learned that creativity doesn't require perfection, only authentic expression and the courage to let your unique gifts be seen.

Through Congruence, you've aligned your inner truth with your outer life. You've learned to live in integrity, making choices that respect both your wisdom and your values.

And through Contribution, you've discovered how to share your gifts from a place of alignment rather than fear or scarcity. You've learned to choose where you invest your energy and how to create a legacy that energizes rather than exhausts you.

As I shared at the beginning of this book, this journey was never just about surviving perimenopause or even thriving through it. *It's about who you have become in the process.* The woman reading these words is not the same woman who began this journey. She has been transformed in the most beautiful way.

Here. This is where we've been heading all along.

Where the Queen fully arrives. Not to prove or perform. Not in her striving, but in her stillness. Not in sacrifice, but in sovereignty.

And then there comes a moment when you realize you're no longer in the middle of the storm. Life may not be perfect, and the answers may not have fully landed—yet something inside you has shifted.

This is the return—not to who you were before. But to a life you're designing and choosing with perspective, power, and a vision of who you are *now*. That's the *elixir* you've gathered through the wildness and wisdom of your journey.

My deepest wish is that you feel this. That you know deep within: you don't have to hustle for your worth. You don't have to be perfect to lead.

This book is just the beginning. If you're ready to go deeper, to have support as you navigate this transformation, I'd be honored to walk alongside you.

You know where to find me.

The call to adventure never ends for the heroine, and the next one already awaits. Evolution is cyclical—a spiral that moves upwards. Each time we move through growth and transformation, we do so from a higher level of awareness. Evolution is not a destination; it's a way of life.

There's always a deeper truth to uncover, another layer of self to meet, another way to share your gifts with the world.

And if you feel called to walk this path more fully—to be witnessed, supported, and celebrated as you integrate this new self—know that the journey doesn't end here.

Whether the *Larger Life Lab* spoke to you, or you feel drawn to a *Wise Woman Weekend* here in Mallorca, or you simply long for a deeper conversation, there are many ways we can walk together.

The world needs your wisdom.

Your story.

Your voice.

You've chosen to meet this transition with consciousness and courage. To turn what could have been merely endured into something meaningful, creative, and shared.

The best truly is yet to come.

And I can't wait for it to find you.

With love,
Daniella
Mallorca, October 2025

About the Author

Daniella Schoch guides women through menopause's transformative passage with the wisdom of someone who has walked the path herself—and emerged crowned.

Born in Switzerland and shaped by a life of exploration, from childhood years in the United States to formative chapters in New York and Spain, Daniella eventually found home in a small village in the heart of Mallorca. There, surrounded by ancient olive trees, sea breezes, and her beloved rescue cats, she continues her own unfolding journey of reconnection and renewal.

Her path to this work was anything but linear. With a Master of Law degree and years in corporate leadership within financial services, Daniella once believed success meant climbing higher, performing harder, and suppressing the parts of herself that didn't fit the boardroom mold. Three life-altering accidents in her late thirties shattered that illusion, awakening a deep spiritual and creative calling to reimagine what it truly means to thrive.

Today, Daniella brings together an extraordinary tapestry of training and lived experience as a coach, therapist, and healer. She is a certified Art Therapist, Strategic Intervention Coach (trained by Tony Robbins and Cloé Madanes), Feminine Power Coach & Facilitator, and Integrative Health Coach. For over two decades, she has also practiced Pranic Healing and Arhatic Yoga, drawing inspiration from the esoteric teachings of Alice Bailey and Master

Choa Kok Sui. This daily devotion to meditation and energy work infuses all that she creates.

Known for her grounded yet soulful approach, Daniella bridges the worlds of science and spirit—combining the practical tools of neuroscience and positive psychology with the depth of esoteric psychology and spiritual wisdom. Her unique ability to translate profound concepts into accessible, embodied practice helps women not only understand transformation, but live it.

Through her masterminds, one-on-one coaching, and transformational retreats—powered by Positive Intelligence®—Daniella helps women view every crisis, challenge, and transition as an initiation: a call to evolve, awaken, and embody their Queen energy.

Wiser. Hotter. Stronger. is her love letter to women standing at the threshold of menopause—a map from disconnection to sovereignty, from confusion to clarity, from depletion to radiant contribution.

Connect with Daniella and continue your journey at daniellaschoch.com.

Printed in Dunstable, United Kingdom

73178506R00102

GROW YOUR BUSINESS WITH VIDEO

Position your business as the obvious choice in your industry using the most powerful form of marketing

Alex Wardle

Published by WriterMotive
www.writermotive.com

Contents

ABOUT THE AUTHOR

Since 2014, Alex Wardle has helped businesses design, create and deliver effective video content. He's worked with big brands such as the largest musical instrument retailer in the UK, plus one of the biggest entertainment agencies, as well as smaller businesses like coaches, personal trainers and musicians. He and his cameras frequently travel up and down the country and also overseas – some of his favourite film-making projects to date have taken him to Warsaw, New York City and Rome.

As is the case with many entrepreneurs, it's all been a bit of a blur for Alex. Once an aspiring music producer with a passion for all things audio, his focus (pardon the pun) shifted to the moving image after he graduated with first-class honours in Music Technology and Production. During his time at the University of Derby, and then on his return home to the north east of England, he obtained what camera equipment he could afford and sought a film-making education from a select few friends … as well as YouTube. Applying the attention to detail his tutors had continually praised him for to the world of video, Alex approached film-making from both artistic and scientific viewpoints, aiming to create wonderful videos that told compelling stories, but also attained the highest quality possible and capitalised on his advantageous background in audio.

Now armed with more than a handful of professional film-making tools, the knowledge to create successful films and the experience to show for it, Alex seeks to help more people get the most out of video. To only create films that are *effective* is his mantra.

He hopes you enjoy this book, and he'd like to stop speaking in the third person now.

INTRODUCTION

Is this book for you?

Congratulations! By buying this book you've taken the first step towards better marketing, a better business, maybe even a better life …

Don't worry – you won't find much woo-woo marketing guru theory here. This book contains nothing but useful, valuable, tried-and-tested information and guidance on how to grow your business using the powerhouse that is video marketing. If you put into practice what you learn across the following 11 chapters, your business will look a whole lot different before long.

In order for this book to prove most effective and useful to you, there are a few prerequisites. This book and its teachings, plus my values and opinions on all manner of topics, are certainly not for everyone. Most importantly, this book is designed for a certain kind of individual who is both in a particular situation right now, and has a specific target they want to reach. Let's see if you fit the bill:

- You're a business owner, a marketer, part of an advertising agency, or perhaps a blend of all the above. You own or form part of a business – be it online or offline, offering products, services or both – and you want it to grow. You want more fans and followers, more qualified leads, more clients and customers, and more sales.
- You're already pretty good at "the thing" – that is, the delivery of whatever it is you offer (e.g. marketing manager, personal trainer, online coach, store owner).

You're an expert in that field and want to convey such status to your audience … but there's something missing. Ultimately, your marketing doesn't reflect the level of authority you know you and your business are capable of. You're not sure how best to show the world how good you are, but you know you need to.

- Being a smart cookie, you want to position you and your business as top-tier, premium and high grade. You want your business and brand to be associated with luxury, with reassuringly expensive prices backed up by nothing short of the utmost quality. You want to become the obvious choice in the eyes of your ideal customers – the ones who are willing to pay for the very best. You want to come across as professional, but still fun. Yes, you're part of a business, but you're still a real person with a real personality, with real values and a genuine desire to help others. As such, you're not afraid to place yourself (or at least a willing ambassador or two) front and centre in your marketing.
- You're open to new things, advancements in technology and tectonic shifts in social interaction. You embrace the rapid pace of change we're all experiencing every day; you see it as an opportunity, not a threat. You're willing to learn new concepts, develop new skills and engage in new practices in the pursuit of building a remarkable business.

Did you tick all the boxes? If so, good news – video was meant for people like you. High-quality films that are built on the foundations of solid strategy will make you so much more attractive to your prospective (and indeed existing) clients and customers. Shared on a consistent basis, these videos can help gain the all-important trust of your target market, so that people have no qualms in paying for your supreme service again and again. Your competition will look amateur in comparison, and you will become the go-to, the obvious choice, in your industry.

Of course, anyone can jump in front of a camera and wax lyrical about how brilliant they are, how great their business is, and why you – the viewer – should cough up your cash and buy their stuff. But few can grasp the attention of those on the other side of the screen for more than a few seconds. Very few people are actually a true representation of themselves on camera. Not many people do a good job of the actual filming. And even fewer can use video in a tasteful, genuinely helpful way to *compel* their audience to take action.

The ones that can are dominating – they're seen as leaders in their industries, with their top-level positioning unwavering and highly resistant to challenge. By the time you reach the end of this book, you'll have the knowledge at your disposal to join the club.

Grow Your Business With Video is highly pragmatic and deals with observable, measurable, real-world issues. Think practicalities, not soul-searching. Technicalities, not tears on command. We will be looking at the artistic, emotional side of film-making, but the primary aim of this book is to equip you with the practical knowledge to create and utilise more effective video for your business. Not only will you learn how to create videos that look and sound excellent, but you'll also discover the many different types of videos that your business can utilise along with how, why and when to use them. You'll discover the ingredient list for remarkable videos, and the not-so-tasty recipe for poor content, so that you can create more of the former. You'll learn how to incorporate video into your marketing system as a whole, how to avoid spending excessive time and money in the pursuit, how to systemise and strategise your content based on your objectives, and how to measure the performance of your videos so that you can learn and improve. The foundations of the advice you'll find in this book are built on years of experience both in front of and behind the camera, in a multitude of industries and with all manner of stories to tell along the way. It's all there for you to learn from, with an abundance of tips, techniques and real-life exercises to help you put it all into action.

As a freelance videographer since 2014, I have less experience behind a camera than many others out there who are playing similar roles to me. In fact, I bet there are some fellow film-industry folk who will turn their noses up at this book. They'll be thinking things like:

"Who does this guy think he is? How can he write a book on video when he's barely been in the industry five minutes?"

But this book isn't for them; it's for you – a business owner and/or marketer who wants to get ahead of the curve. It's not written for someone who operates a camera on a film set every day; it's designed for business owners who would consider themselves "hyper-implementers" – clever folk who recognise that video is a format whose popularity and thus importance is sharply on the rise. They know that the application of this medium has become a *minimum requirement* for any business to market themselves effectively, and as such they want to know how to make the most of it.

Furthermore, this book has been written by someone who's helped many businesses – small and large – get brilliant results from video: more sales, more leads, better staff knowledge, more event attendees, more membership subscriptions … all manner of positive outcomes. I love making good films any day of the week, but what you don't find in every videographer is the appreciation that for most businesses, video is simply *a tool* used to get a certain job done.

You see, there are droves of camera folk out there who make gorgeous films that are technically and artistically excellent. Ask them to make you a pretty little promo, and they'll see it done. The problem is, most of them don't have the faintest knowledge about marketing. They're brilliant with a camera in their hands, but ask them about the purpose or intention behind the expensive video they've just made, or how they might optimise its delivery to ensure the best results, and you'll get a vague response – if any at all.

Here's the cold, hard truth (expect a lot of it to follow): unless you're a giant brand like Red Bull or Coca-Cola, throwing your valuable time and money into a single, gorgeous video that exists just for the sake of being pretty is *not* a good idea. Sure, its high-end look will help associate your brand with a high level of quality in general … but for the viewer, it likely won't serve any specific purpose. It doesn't help them solve a particular problem, or answer a pertinent question. Ultimately, it isn't *valuable* to them, and so they probably won't see your business that way, either. So while a film like this might do okay for your "brand awareness", don't you think there's a better way to truly win over the hearts and minds of your audience? Surely there must be a way to use video in such a way that it nurtures the most highly qualified prospects over time, provides them with valuable, useful, entertaining and engaging material to help strengthen your business's positioning, and thus in turn promotes long-term, repeat customers and clients who are true evangelists of your brand?

Early in my career, I saw all too often the negative effects of non-strategised video content that was heavily lacking in purpose. I would go along with any and every video job that came my way, even if I had the niggling worry deep down that it would probably amount to nothing for the client in the end. I can recall far too many times when, as the presenter's dull, boring, monotonous words came through my headphones, and the camera screen showed an emotionless face against a dull, boring, lifeless white background, my mind repeated the words over and over again … "*This is terrible.*" The video might have been planned out with all the best intentions, it might have been approved by the brand's marketing manager and it might have promised to be effective on paper, but I knew that it would fall completely flat through being irrelevant, uninspiring, unentertaining or just plain worthless to its target audience. The business in question was wasting its time, money and effort, but it simply wasn't my place to say, so I kept my mouth shut and the camera rolling.

But thankfully, on many more occasions since those grim ol' days, I've had the pleasure of helping create and implement some really effective films that are engaging, entertaining and useful to the viewer, as well as serving a purpose to the creator. I've met and worked with some very gifted people who run awesome businesses built on the foundations of *effective* marketing. I've learnt invaluable marketing lessons from those considered true experts in their industries, who have put solid principles into action and are enjoying the endless benefits of having done so. Today, I only make videos that tick all the boxes, and that I *know* will be worthwhile investments of a client's time, money and energy. It's my job to work *with* my clients to create videos that are going to serve their interests, perform a particular function and prove valuable to their audience. In this book, I've taken what I've learnt and distilled it down to the actionable fundamentals for people like you – business owners who deserve to make the most of video.

So, you know you need effective video. But it's tough, isn't it? Whether you're doing the filming yourself or you've hired a pro, video is inherently complex; it's technical by its very nature, and there's absolutely no hiding in front of the lens. It can be difficult to portray you and your business in the intended fashion. You might be a super-approachable, lovely, outgoing person in the real world – a truly knowledgeable expert in your field – but come across on camera as unconfident, unconvincing and dull, like a fresh-faced kid on his first day of school.

What's more, with technology's ever-quickening pace, it might be easier and cheaper than ever to make and share a video, but it's just as easy to get it wrong. There are videos that look and sound remarkable, and there are those that appear outdated and have clearly just been slapped together. Furthermore, the fact that more people are creating video means there's so much *garbage* out there to compete with. How do you cut through it and push aside all the inferior content that's distracting your viewers? Or worse, the videos your competitors are posting?

The answers lie within this book. Or, at least, my thoughts on the above. Another truth: there is no single correct way to use video marketing in your business, because your business is unique. By that I don't mean "pretty little snowflake" unique – I simply mean that you have, to some degree, a distinctive product or service that is obtained or experienced by an exclusive set of people. What works for one business may completely bomb for another. But by the end of this book – providing you pay attention, make notes and follow the action steps at the end of each chapter – you'll have the knowledge to make videos that look better, sound better, engage your audience, leave them wanting more and encourage them to take action. You'll be churning out regular content for a loyal tribe of followers, with many of them becoming long-term clients and customers as a result. With your awesome videos, you'll be seen as premium and professional, likeable and relatable – the unshakeable foundations for a successful business.

It's relatively *simple*, although not *easy*, to get good at this whole video thing, and so you will probably hit some quit points along the way – especially when it feels like making snow angels on gravel would be more comfortable than what I encourage you to do. But persevere and navigate through them, remembering that the spoils are found in the long game – my friend and client Dom Hodgson first told me that a long time ago. I didn't think much of it at the time; now my entire business is built around serving me and my clients in the long term.

Oh, and one more thing – we'll touch on this again soon, but if you can't already talk passionately about why you're in the business you're in, and you don't get a genuine kick out of helping people fix their problems, you're in trouble. I'm not saying you should aim for Oscar-winning performances on camera, but if deep down you don't enjoy whatever it is that you do, and you can't express how good it feels to help whoever it is that you help, you won't get much out of this book. Your videos might look a little better, but ultimately you'll be spouting the same tripe as 90% of other businesses – "I'm great, buy my stuff."

And *no one* wants to hear that.

How to use this book

As you make your way through *Grow Your Business With Video*, you'll be encouraged to view examples of certain concepts we discuss – it wouldn't be a very valuable teaching resource on video without showing some videos! You'll be prompted to visit **artifactmedia.co.uk/resources** at various points – this section of my website contains a range of videos, images and screenshots, as well as links to other learning materials I've created, that are all referenced throughout this book. In order to reinforce your learning and extract maximum value from this book, I'd highly recommend visiting this resources section whenever prompted.

Speaking of other learning materials, you'll also hear about several video courses I've put together that are available to download from artifactmedia.co.uk. While I highly recommend that you do obtain these courses, I'd advise reading *Grow Your Business With Video* in its entirety first, not least of all because as a reader you can take advantage of a special offer relating to these courses, which is detailed in the very last "Bonuses" section.

I've learnt from experience that multitasking is, counter-intuitively, a less-than-ideal way of working – while it can feel like you're achieving more, often the quality of the end products of your efforts suffers as a result of stretching yourself too thin after trying to achieve many things at once. As such, I'd urge you to give this book your full attention and focus until you reach the end, *then* solidify your newly found knowledge and skills by taking advantage of the aforementioned offer and downloading the separate video courses.

Chapter One
Why is everyone raving about video?

The rates of video creation and consumption have grown exponentially over the past few years. Changes and advancements in technology, as well as more cultural shifts, have defined the many ways we view the moving image. It wasn't long ago that primitive television sets incapable of displaying even basic colour information were among the most exclusive, expensive and envied consumer products. Now, over two billion people have a high-definition display in their pockets with unprecedented, immediate access to quite literally endless video content, and they're consuming more of that content every day.

Why is it that the popularity of the moving image has advanced at such a pace, to the point where one third of all people on the internet are users of YouTube? Why are shoppers who watch video almost twice as likely to make a purchase as those who don't? Why does 100 million hours of video get watched on Facebook every single day? Before we start creating good video ourselves, we need to understand what makes it so powerful, and thus why it has rapidly become an essential part of any business's marketing.

Here are the 11 big reasons why everyone is raving about video.

1) It's the most human form of digital communication

Video creates, extends, solidifies, breaks and challenges relationships. It allows people all over the world to communicate in a way that's both artificial, and yet intrinsically human.

If you and I met for coffee for the very first time, according to the Harvard Study of Communications it would take a mere seven seconds for us both to make a judgement on the other. Then, based on our interaction and communication around our respective interests, experiences, values and beliefs, our initial judgements would be either compounded or contested. At the end of our meeting, we'd both walk away and, to some extent, like or dislike the other. We all do this every time we encounter someone new.

But what if, instead of the face-to-face meeting, we just had a phone call instead? If our first "meeting" was a faceless conversation where we only heard a low-quality version of the other's voice, or perhaps we simply wrote to each other and thus couldn't read the other's facial expression, would we be as well informed to make judgements as we would in person? Would either of us feel like we really "knew" the other? No – you can't *really* get to know a person that way. Meeting in person, or at least being able to digitally communicate as though you were, is much more powerful because it's much more human.

Apply the same principle to your tweets, your Facebook status updates, your adverts and even your Instagram uploads. Is a paragraph of text, a still image or a generic plea for someone to buy your product really giving your audience the ability to get to know you? Are you offering any kind of real insight into the kind of person you are, the sort of business you run and the things you stand for? Are you allowing them to get to know you as another person over a coffee, or are you simply showing up at the café with a sales pitch?

Video can absolutely be used to sell products, services and solutions, but as you'll learn throughout this book, its primary function is to serve as a communication tool. Video allows you to strike up a conversation and start a meaningful interaction with anyone anywhere, and most of us find the experience very natural and true to life.

Consider the difference between an eloquent, grammatically perfect text-based advert that has been edited to perfection, and a simple video of someone speaking to the camera casually and instinctively, as though it were another person. Both of these forms of communication have their places in marketing, but I know which would be most likely to seize (and retain) my attention. I know which format, if used consistently over time, would make me feel like I knew the other person and thus place great value on that relationship.

2) It bonds well with other marketing methods

Video isn't the Holy Grail of marketing, and it shouldn't be used exclusively – well-written copy, high-quality photos and valuable audio content all have their merits and best uses in any marketing system, just as websites, landing pages, podcasts, brochures and webinars are all valuable tools.

But a business with great video at its disposal has an ace up its sleeve. It's like the turbo in a racing car engine – used in harmony with a bigger machine it can propel you past the competition. As you'll discover, video can be put to good use in a variety of ways and integrate seamlessly with many other marketing tools and practices. When incorporated correctly, these tools feed off of and benefit each other, allowing you to extract the maximum value from the system as a whole.

3) It's essential

The internet has become a truly saturated place, and we're drowning in information wherever we turn. Go anywhere – the streets of your city, on the bus or train, in the park, on the couch, even in the countryside – and it won't take you long to find someone staring down at a rectangular device in their hand, swiping their thumb up and down the pane of glass again, and again, and again …

While we could dwell on the current state of human social interaction, let's instead put our business caps on. The fact that so many people are consuming so much content and information every day puts anyone with products and services to offer in a hugely advantageous position. It's never been easier or cheaper (or more effective) to get your name and brand "out there" in the big wide world, and to do so using an incredibly rich and dynamic form of media. Gone are the days of only the largest, most powerful and cash-rich companies dominating the advertising space – now in just a few minutes and for a few quid, you can get your name in front of thousands. Previously you'd need to invest huge sums of money in TV, radio and print ads if you wanted to be heard. But the times have changed dramatically, and now it's the screens of phones, tablets and laptops that have become the most valuable arenas for marketing.

In his Brand Minds 2017 talk, marketing mogul Gary Vaynerchuk rightly said: "We are living through the greatest shift in human communication since the radio to the television." He took his own smartphone out from his pocket, held it high and continued: "This is it. If you do not storytell, communicate, [and] market on this device, and the eight or nine platforms that dominate this device, you are barely existing."

The inherent problem with the democratisation and affordability of digital advertising in the form of video (whether it's paid for or not) is that every day more content is being created, uploaded and shared. It's no longer information that's scarce – it's *attention.* We'll look at this important issue, and how to counteract it, later. For now, here are some statistics you may or may not be aware of that help demonstrate just how prevalent video has become online:

- In March 2018, YouTube had over a billion users – or, in other words, one third of all internet users.
- In 2017, video content represented 74% of all internet traffic.
- As early as 2015, Facebook video views were reaching 8 billion per day.

It's easy to feel overwhelmed at these numbers, particularly if your business is on the smaller side, but they're actually good news for all marketers; more people have their eyes on their devices than ever before, and on the whole people prefer to consume video over other forms of content. Coupled with the excellent (and often undervalued) advertising systems on the likes of Facebook and YouTube, that means you've got better, more affordable, more efficient and more targeted access to potential customers than ever before, too. As a business owner in today's world, you are in a very powerful position that you should be exploiting; this book will show you how.

Every business or brand worth its salt is using video, right now. They're putting it to good use in all sorts of ways, for all manner of purposes, and every single one of them clearly appreciates that to neglect the richest form of content available today is to miss out on a huge opportunity.

Even since you started reading this book, the necessity for video in any and all businesses' marketing strategy has increased. Every day its prominence grows, pushing other forms of content to the side. It certainly wouldn't be outlandish to speculate, as one high ranking representative of Facebook itself has said, that one day all content online might be video … It makes sense seeing as the cost of producing videos has plummeted, whether it's done in-house or with the aid of a production company. Technology is also making the whole process incredibly fast; practices that would take several hours to accomplish even just a few years ago can now be done in minutes.

But businesses aren't flocking to video just because it's easier to create – they know that it captures and retains attention better than any other medium, which leads to more fans and followers, which leads to more customers and clients, which leads to more subscriptions and sales. They're fully invested in the long-term value of quality video content, safe in the knowledge that, if done correctly, it will serve a great many uses for years to come.

Of course, as a videographer who makes a living helping businesses and brands get the most out of video, I have a vested interest in preaching about the wonders of the format. But I'm not alone in my enthusiasm – can you imagine how dire the consequences would be if a company like Apple suddenly stopped using video to promote its products, or if Red Bull canned its extreme sports films and just stuck to making drinks? I shudder at the thought.

Put simply, video is "where it's at" right now. It's the best way of communicating online. Your business deserves it, so use it – it's there for the taking.

4) Video accelerates the Know, Like, Trust process

People buy from other people, as a result of their relationships with other people, and we buy only from those we trust. You might make a one-off purchase from a vendor you've had no previous experience with, like a newsagent on the high street or a random seller on eBay, but there will be a select few suppliers with whom you feel a much stronger sense of connection. These businesses, and the people behind them, invest heavily in establishing, developing and nurturing their relationship with you to the point where you ignore their competitors; you simply have no reason to go elsewhere and so become a loyal, long-term customer.

The reason most businesses are less than extraordinary is because they commoditise their customers – they focus on reaching and selling to as many people as possible, rather than building a strong foundation of the most loyal customers and clients who are far more likely to do business with them for years to come. Attaining your own "tribe" requires more long-term thinking and a potentially radical shift in your marketing strategy, with video being one of the best tools available to help you do it.

It's often said that marketing is like dating, and without wanting to sound clichéd, understanding and applying this one principle dramatically changed my business (and my clients' businesses) for the better.

Let's say you match with someone on a dating app, or a friend hooks you up with someone they think you might like. Besides having an underlying sense of attraction to (or, at the very least, being intrigued by) this person, you don't know much about them. So you go to a café or a bar and spend some time getting to know each other over macchiatos or mojitos. You need to determine whether or not you and your new acquaintance are a good fit, and the only way to do that is to get to Know each other. Over the course of an hour or two you share stories, ask and answer questions, and discuss values and beliefs – all of which helps paint a more detailed mental picture of the other, which you can then compare against yourself. If it goes well, you might agree that you'd both like to meet up again.

On the next date, the conversation is even healthier. You both Know each other a little better, and so you share even more. You start to speak your minds more, instead of reserving some of your opinions through not wanting to cause offence. There are many things you agree on, and others you don't, but the energy is overwhelmingly positive. It could well be that at this stage, you start to feel that you Like this person. What's more, you opened up about a problem you had and it just so happened that your date has some experience in that subject. So they did what any well-meaning person would do and offered you some help.

Jumping forward six months … and perhaps skipping some of the, ahem, details … you and your date have become an item. You Know a lot about each other, which in turn has led you to Like each other, and because throughout the journey you've been helping each other out with problems and issues, you've developed a sense of Trust. What started as a chance encounter has grown and developed over time to become a healthy, lasting and mutually beneficial relationship.

I'm not suggesting you wine and dine your prospects or take them on dates, but in a way that's exactly what you should be doing – treating your customers like the human beings they are, inviting them to take a journey with you and allowing them to get to Know, Like and Trust you over time is undoubtedly the most valuable investment of your time, energy and money when it comes to marketing. Appreciating the *long-term value* of each and every one of your clients is something that very few business owners think about, let alone maintain and develop, so by being extraordinary and treating your customers more like people than commodities, you stand out as one of the special ones.

With video being the most human form of digital communication, and because it's being consumed like no other type of content, it's the obvious method for all types of business communication, from establishing the very first interactions with complete strangers, all the way through to nurturing the relationships with those you've known the longest – your most loyal, long-term clients. In order for a loyal tribe to form, Trust is required, and the only way to build Trust is to open up a window between you and the world where everyone can see what kind of person you are, what sort of business you run and all the ways you can help them, so that they can decide for themselves whether they want to get involved.

5) Video inspires action

I really dislike the terms "ask for the business" and "close the deal". They're a bit "Wall Street" for my liking – the kinds of phrases shiny-suited emotionless corporate robots use, and that makes me feel a bit icky. But I suppose they are valid – at some point, in one way or another, we have to ask our potential clients and customers for "their business". If we didn't, we'd soon go *out* of business.

But how do you do it in a way that isn't overly salesy, tacky, off-putting or so discourteous that it sends people running for the hills? Well, one way is not to ask at all.

In my early twenties, I found myself torn. I'd just about saved up enough cash to treat myself to some new music production hardware – I had my eye on a sampler-come-synthesiser called Push, from a company called Ableton. At the time I was still working a day job and filming on the side, so spending £500 on a "toy" made me feel anxious. For the longest time, my inner sensible self kept the cash safe in the bank because I wasn't 100% sold on the product. I knew it was good, and it was hugely desirable, but I just couldn't justify the hefty investment. The benefits of owning a Push did not outweigh my objections and concerns.

That was until YouTube suggested a video that it thought might be relevant to my interests. It was on the official Ableton channel, but it wasn't the glossy launch promo for the product – I'd seen that months ago (several times). It was titled "JNTHN STEIN making a beat with Ableton Push 2". I didn't know who JNTHN STEIN was, how to pronounce his name, or whether I'd like the beats he was apparently creating, but anything involving Push 2 had my intrigue at the very least.

For the next 10-and-a-half minutes, my eyes did not leave the screen. I'm sure my ears grew 10 times in physical size as I cranked the volume up and took it all in. It was kind of a documentary, partly a story, somewhat a feature, but undoubtedly it was bloody brilliant. JNTHN told his interviewer how he composed, arranged and produced a full song in one day using his Ableton Push. The cinematic interview footage was interspersed with fly-on-the-wall clips captured in JNTHN's apartment-come-studio; a handful of cameras candidly captured his creative process, showing how he used Push from initial idea generation and noodling around with sounds and samples, all the way through to performing the finished (glorious) song.

The next day, Ableton became £500 richer courtesy of Mr A Wardle. The video had debunked all my objections, worries and queries about whether this was the right product to buy. It showed me first-hand how intuitive, powerful, inspiring and fun it would be. It proved that similar musicians to me were using the same product to good effect, and gave me more than a few ideas of how I could use it myself.

The most profound part was that Ableton didn't hard-sell the product once during this video. In fact, it didn't really have a call to action at all; the video merely served as an entertaining and insightful piece of content. In my case, and no doubt many others, Ableton simply didn't need to ask for the business.

This isn't exactly a tear-jerking story of gut-wrenching emotion, but it does demonstrate a point – a good video can take an anxious, cautious, reluctant prospect to a paying customer in just a few minutes. So imagine what kind of passionate brand advocate that buyer might go on to become if subsequent video content continued to delight them in this way over a longer period of time.

6) Video is memorable

In 2017, Hubspot discovered that branded video stuck in the minds of consumers more than photographs and written material – hardly surprising, but worth knowing. Making sure your content (and thus your brand) is memorable and noteworthy has never been more important; it's one thing to create quality content that appeals to a specific type of viewer, but it's another to *remain* distinctive and noteworthy against the multitude of other information that increasingly demands your prospects' attention every day. As you'll soon learn, great video is the culmination of many ingredients blended together, but there are two elements in particular that help make videos unforgettable, even for viewers who've never heard of you before.

Emotion

As a species, we're wired to react emotionally to almost everything. When our primitive ancestors' main concern was merely to stay alive, humans felt the instincts of fight and flight on a daily basis. Life-and-death situations would unavoidably result in feelings of incredibly strong emotions, which helped us remember and learn from both mistakes and successes. Thankfully most of us don't have to face such threats today, and so we rarely engage fight or flight mode, but studies have shown that emotional events still have the same effect of aiding memory retention.

In other words, attaching some level of emotion to a stimulus, be it positive or negative, happy or sad, excites the area of the brain responsible for encoding and recalling memory; the event is more likely to prove memorable for the person experiencing it.

Because video is such a rich and dynamic form of media, it's very effective at conveying powerful stories, and thus instilling strong emotions. Films make us laugh, cry, gasp and feel fear, and the more emotion they cause us to feel, the more profound their long-term effect. Videos that play to particular emotions and feelings are more likely to be remembered for longer, and thus have a lasting, valuable impact and effectiveness.

Most people probably don't find courier companies and parcels very interesting, but UPS challenged this with their *Driver for a Day* film in 2014. Over just a couple of minutes, it tells the story of four-year-old Carson, who looks forward to seeing Mr Ernie – his local UPS driver – doing his round of deliveries, and hopes that he will eventually become a driver himself. When I first came across this video, I was sceptical that it would keep my attention at all, let alone make me feel emotional; how can parcels possibly be that exciting? But after finding myself fully engrossed in the short film from start to finish, smiling with glee watching this little boy getting the chance to live out his dream, I was proven wrong – and here I am telling you about it too. Check it out at **artifactmedia.co.uk/resources**.

Amazement

For the right audience, big, bold films that aim to astonish and astound are among the most memorable. The viewer's unwavering gaze is fuelled by awe, admiration and wonder, leaving them feeling inspired, enthused and eager to spread the message. Amazing videos stick in our memories as a result of being truly unique and unlike anything we've seen before.

As such, they most often demand high production value with beautiful visuals and captivating soundtracks being pushed to the limits of what's technically possible. Rally driver Ken Block stunned petrolheads everywhere with his first Gymkhana film in 2008, in which he burned insane amounts of rubber off the tyres of his Subaru Impreza through an epic display of perfectly choreographed driving skill. The video proved so popular that Ken and his team made several more, each more ambitious than the last (one even required downtown San Francisco to be closed to the public for several days). Now, for many enthusiasts, the word "Gymkhana" no longer refers to an overarching motorsport discipline, but instead conjures up the image of Ken Block and his signature vehicles in a cloud of tyre smoke.

Videos don't have to be complete masterpieces to be memorable; even the simplest, most stripped-back content can stick with a viewer long after they've finished watching, providing it positively affects them in some way. But the combination of emotional impact with a generous helping of amazement will undoubtedly prove memorable to thousands of viewers.

7) Video is worth it

Developing anything for a business requires investment, not just in terms of cash but also the precious resources of time and energy. The most successful business owners calculate and justify all of their actions and efforts by their potential return on investment (ROI); they invest in products, methods and strategies that will give back more than they cost. Effective video content is among the top priorities of the cleverest marketers because they know that, if done correctly, it will deliver results that far outweigh the cost of creation.

Video is inherently technical and time-imperative, and can cost almost any figure imaginable to produce – from a few hundred pounds to purchase a smartphone with a good camera, to several million dollars for a 30-second spot during the Super Bowl. But it's only in these extreme cases where the question of whether it's worth the investment applies; video has the potential to deliver so much value back to the creator that it's almost always worth it.

Later in this book you'll learn how to track and measure the results of your videos so that you know whether or not they're delivering on their objectives (hint: it's not just about getting lots of views). Then, we'll look at the significance of video as an asset of your business – one that does require planning, investment and commitment, but has the potential to be one of the most valuable tools at your disposal as a result.

8) Video can explain anything

While video – like anything – has its limitations, compared to most other forms of digital marketing it's easily the least restricted. Written words can be expressive, emotional and intriguing, but in a way they can't go beyond mere description; they require us to use our imagination. Photographs can be cherished for many years and open up windows to another time, place or experience, but they only capture a single moment of time – a mere illustration of a more elaborate event.

Video is the richest form of digital media, immersing the viewer through the use of vision and sound that both flow over a period of time. It allows for a greater sense of involvement and connection between creator and consumer, and really is the next best thing to being there in person. As such, the practical applications of video are immense – entertainment, information, demonstrations, tutorials, lessons, guides and stories are among its endless uses, all of which a business can benefit from utilising no matter what the end offering is. For example (and unsurprisingly), four times as many customers would rather watch a video about a product than read about it.

Technologies such as virtual reality and 360 video are certainly changing the way we engross ourselves in visual content, and as these exciting innovations become more widespread and democratised, the landscape will shift dramatically. But ultimately video as we know it is a tried-and-tested formula that's proven successful at engrossing audiences for many years, and no matter what specific form it takes, it isn't going anywhere any time soon.

9) Video spreads the word fast

All businesses rely on having a presence in the appropriate marketplace that they use to reach potential customers. People need to know not only that a company exists, but also what it does, how it works and – crucially – how it can help *them* before they make an informed purchase. There are, of course, all manner of ways to achieve this, but wherever you turn and whichever successful business you come across, you can almost guarantee they'll be using video in their pursuit of attaining market authority.

The fast-track way to establish presence in your market is to understand the behaviours and traits of your audience and make sure your marketing conforms accordingly. Basically, you "show up" to them frequently and consistently, in whatever format and on whatever platforms suit them best, and dish out content that they'll enjoy or benefit from. Thus, the reason more businesses are making use of video is simply because it's being consumed like never before; people can't get enough of it.

Furthermore, the world is becoming more connected and more interactions are occurring between people every day. We no longer keep online encounters to ourselves – we frequently and openly share content with our family and friends, making sure they benefit from it just as we have, opening up conversations around what we've discovered. The combination of video's increasing rate of consumption plus the ever-more-openly connected world is a dream come true for marketers. High-quality, effective video that is optimised for its intended use and encouraged to be shared takes full advantage of these two trends; to not use it would be to miss one hell of a trick. The fact that video generates 1,200% more shares than text and images combined tops this point off nicely.

10) Video is easy (sort of)

As you'll learn throughout this book, video content that adheres to a simple formula based on a handful of fundamentals becomes more than a fleeting, short-term marketing tool with an end result that is difficult to measure. Combining the fundamentals of effective video creation with the knowledge and skill to tailor your content to specific viewers, who are each at different points in their individual buyer's journey, will allow video to become an intrinsic, integral part of your business. Such a library of content increases in value over time, to the point where many businesses cite it as their most important marketing asset.

It does take time and practice to hone these fundamentals and set up the delivery system, which is why most businesses are sporadic in their efforts and in turn don't see major, long-lasting results. But by the end of this book you'll not only have a detailed knowledge of these fundamentals, but you'll know how to use them to maximum effect and in turn create video content that isn't just aligned with the needs, wants and pain points of your audience, but is delivered optimally and works in tandem with your other marketing efforts.

11) Video works with your existing marketing strategies

There are countless ways to market your business, but many methods benefit from the inclusion of at least an element of video to bolster its overall effectiveness. Perhaps you already use email, for example, and have a valuable list of subscribers who frequently consume and engage with your content. You probably have a Facebook page for your business, which has the potential to target and reach very specific groups of people. Maybe you're taking advantage of LinkedIn's unique set of tools and would like to capitalise on your influence there. Whatever you're currently doing to market your business, it can almost certainly be improved with video, both on a systematic level (with most platforms offering some level of support for direct video integration) and in the way people actually consume content. For example, as much as video consumption is on the rise, people still read emails, search for stuff on Google, stumble across articles and blogs, and listen to podcasts. To extract the maximum value from video, it should be utilised alongside these other forms of marketing so that you have a high number of touchpoints with your audience members, giving them as many options for content consumption as possible.

Another result of video's rise in popularity is that many advertising platforms such as Facebook now offer incredibly detailed and advanced tools designed to make the most out of paid-for video ads. Mark Zuckerberg and his team of experts know that the popularity of video is sharply on the rise, and so have given creators a great many ways to utilise their immensely powerful platform. Video ads come in a variety of forms depending on where and how you're interacting with the social network; the more of these you can take advantage of, the greater your market influence will be.

Finally, there are now video-centric features and sharing capabilities on most social networks. Snapchat and Instagram were both designed with quick and easy photo-sharing as the original priority, but have since evolved to focus heavily on video. While there are many occasions where your videos will benefit from detailed planning, preparation and high production value, you can still use spontaneous and less-than-perfect content on these platforms to increase your market influence, promote your offerings and develop your relationships with customers.

Chapter summary

These 11 reasons, while extensive, are still just a drop in the ocean – as the format evolves, trends change and consumption patterns shift, there'll be even more reasons for businesses to use effective video.

Action steps

1. Identify a video, or a series of videos, that has resonated with you deeply.

Think back to the most recent or most profound example of some kind of video content that struck a chord, instigated strong emotions or left you feeling compelled to take action. What factors contributed towards this highly memorable, powerful experience?

2. Brainstorm some initial ideas on how your business could use (and benefit from) effective video.

This book provides a roadmap to designing, creating and utilising highly valuable video content, but no doubt you already have some ideas worth documenting and later expanding upon. Write these down, ideally in a dedicated notebook, be it physical or digital. I personally love using the app Evernote to make sure spontaneous thoughts and ideas are captured quickly and neatly, are easy to find in the future, and don't go missing … unlike sticky notes!

Chapter Two

Who is using effective video?

The ratio of effective to ineffective content online today is weighed heavily towards the latter – most people (and businesses) simply aren't creating or utilising truly effective video. However, there is a growing base of brands and individuals alike who are consistently sharing great content that is consistently well-received by their audience and thus drives their business forward. These people are getting savvy with the process of video creation, and most niches now have their own figureheads – a select few who communicate with their respective audiences in remarkable ways, using video as one of the key driving forces in their marketing machines. This influx of influencers is a wave – one that you can ride alongside the best, or one that, if you decide not to take action, will sweep you out to sea. The fact is that video has become massive, so your choice is simple – either get good at it, or get left behind. Climb the ranks, or be forgotten.

The fact that you're reading this book already puts you several steps ahead of most, because by the end of it you'll know how to create and utilise *effective* video content. But what does that mean, exactly? Well, my definition of *effective* video is simply video that is designed to fulfil a specific purpose and succeeds in attaining desired outcomes for both the creator and the viewer. It's tailored to a defined audience and carries value, which is hugely important given the aforementioned fact that there's so much content now available for consumption. We're all exposed to an increasing amount of *stuff* online, with more of it becoming high quality and thus worthy of our attention. Therefore, your content needs to warrant being watched. Yes – you need to advertise your business, your products and services, but you also need to win over the hearts and minds of your ideal customers. You need *them* to come to *you* after gaining their trust and demonstrating that whatever you offer is genuinely remarkable. You can do that through using effective video.

Learn from the best

So how do we create effective video content ourselves? Well, whenever there's a goal we wish to achieve or an outcome we want to work towards – whether in our personal or business lives – there are usually a few prime examples of people who've done so (or done similar, at least) before us. So before we look at the process itself, it's worth taking a look at those who are already doing what we want to do. Even if the finer details differ from what we specifically want to do, there is always inspiration to be drawn from the actions taken by others and the *way* they've done those things. For example, a band who play a particular genre of music might give a budding guitarist some ideas on how he might create his own music that sounds similar to his muse. In the process of doing so, however, he can't *not* put his own unique, personal spin on his creations, and thus produce something completely new.

The process of marketing is no different. In fact, it's brilliant because there's so much inspiration to be found out there, even from those who aren't in the same industry as you or who are doing completely different things; if you're going to create effective videos, it only seems natural that one would do well to identify and study some examples of films that come under the same definition. I've personally been inspired by films from vloggers, racing drivers, chefs and even delivery companies, to name just a few. Here are some that promise to teach you many things about video marketing, no matter what you do or who you serve; these are some of the special few who are providing value to their audiences while simultaneously achieving their marketing goals.

Gary Vaynerchuk
Web: garyvaynerchuk.com
Facebook: /gary
Instagram: garyvee
YouTube: GaryVaynerchuk

Perhaps the most prolific advocate of the moving image in the online world, Gary Vee can be seen on film pretty much everywhere. In fact, that's one of his self-defined signature characteristics – he's always pioneering new platforms, new mediums, new technology … and often correctly predicts the future of such things. Once a wine critic and now a digital agency owner, he's a true giant of the internet with a handful of books and countless speaking gigs under his belt. That agency – VaynerMedia – is just one of his larger-scale business ventures. He's become a household name among entrepreneurs and small business owners in particular, thanks not only to his unique backstory, but also to his truly unique marketing. Together with a handful of other lucky film-makers, in 2016 I had the pleasure of filming Gary Vee at a speaking event held in a boxing arena in London. His performance did not disappoint.

Gary Vee's life – his business life, at least – is something of a TV show. Across various platforms and in different formats, he uses video to share lessons, musings and insights on all things digital, social media and entrepreneurship. He speaks directly to you – the viewer – through the camera, but his real-world conversations with peers, colleagues and fans are also captured. He pretty much wears a microphone and has a guy with a camera following him around all day. Most notably, his interactions and ponderings are shared at such a rapid, ever-changing pace that in the time between me writing this book and you reading it, he'll be doing so in a completely different way.

Gary Vee uses video to communicate with his audience on a daily basis, most significantly via the "DailyVee" series, which is posted to both his YouTube and Facebook pages. Usually these are filmed by his dedicated in-house video crew (ain't he lucky?), but he'll often upload self-shot clips straight from his smartphone too – everything from meetings and live Q & A sessions to simple "here's what I think of X" videos.

Perhaps most surprising, at least from a film-maker's perspective, is the fact that despite him having a personal videographer committed to capturing much of his working day on film, Gary Vee's content *isn't* prim, polished and perfect – far from it. It's high quality in the sense that it's most often filmed on a "proper" camera, but the content is captured in a scratchy, rough-and-ready way, which actually (counter-intuitively) adds to the sense of realism. Rather than a more produced film with a deliberate sense of flow and structure, there's a sense of inherent urgency in Gary Vee's videos – most likely a natural by-product of his bustling, hectic lifestyle, and if nothing else a reflection of his advocacy of "hustle".

Gary Vee does, however, also use more refined and better-produced content such as the #AskGaryVee Show (which doubles up as an audio podcast). Here, several cameras are firmly planted on tripods for more of a "studio" look as Gary interviews his many and varied guests. Even then, though, as a videographer I can't help but respond to an innate yearning deep inside my perfectionist, oh-so-critical brain and point out the less-than-ideal filming location of Gary's corner office in New York City, where faces are usually silhouetted by the contrasting bright light coming through the windows – it doesn't make for the best-looking videos. But even I can admit that this simply isn't *that* important – it's the content itself that matters, not how the video looks, which is a concept we'll be revisiting throughout this book.

Finally, he makes sure his video content is optimised for the platform on which it resides – his Instagram posts are super-short and his Snapchat updates succinct, while his YouTube and Facebook videos are tailored to those who have more time to watch.

Gary Vee *could* have been just another mogul – yet another faceless name behind a big company with a fancy office in a big city. Instead, though, he's a celebrity with a huge, loyal and enthusiastic fan base. Sure, much of the general public might not have heard of him, but most people who've researched marketing and/or entrepreneurship know exactly who he is. There are plenty of folks who dislike him, but regardless of opinion it's difficult not to respect him. When I co-filmed the man himself at the aforementioned event, he rocked up to the venue a mere three minutes before his talk, sneaking through a back entrance so as not to be seen by the audience and cause a ruckus. This ultra high-level positioning and status is, in part at least, a result of his sustained, consistent marketing activities; quite simply, he's put in the work. After all, it's hard *not* to be considered a celebrity when you have a podcast, several books, hundreds of speaking engagements and millions of YouTube subscribers.

With celebrity status, or high-level positioning of any kind, comes immense opportunities and possibilities – you can charge higher prices, for one thing. More than that, though, you command influence, leverage and true impact within your industry (and indeed others). Gary Vee remains top of mind for thousands of entrepreneurs who want to achieve even just a fraction of what he's done. His aura of confidence and expertise influences his fans' decisions to invest further into his world – everything from £7.99 books to event tickets costing thousands. While I have no doubt that Gary Vee would have found a way to do all this if video didn't exist, it's undeniable that his abundant efforts to capitalise on this format in particular have paid off … big time.

MasterClass
Web: masterclass.com
Facebook: masterclassofficial
YouTube: Search "masterclass"

I first learnt of MasterClass.com through a pre-roll YouTube ad – those short clips that play for a few seconds before the video you actually want to watch begins. Much like yourself, I imagine, most of the time I reach straight for the "Skip" button when these pop up. But this time, it was different.

Legendary music producer deadmau5 (real name Joel Zimmerman) appeared on the screen, then muttered a line or two before some bold text proudly proclaimed "Meet Your New Instructor". Well, that had me intrigued. Over the next couple of minutes, I gladly soaked up this sales pitch for an online video course, not just because it appealed to my interests, but primarily because I hadn't seen anything like this before. The level of production quality meant I didn't doubt the course's promised value for a second. This was clearly "the real deal" – leaps and bounds ahead of any low-budget YouTube tutorial I'd struggled through before.

Their own description of the site reads: "MasterClass is an immersive experience that offers access to genius by allowing anyone to take online classes with the world's best." Sure enough, they host classes by the likes of Christina Aguilera, Gordon Ramsay, Serena Williams and even former astronaut Chris Hadfield. The celebrity factor is certainly the most significant string in MasterClass's bow, but it's paired accordingly with the absolute highest levels of visuals and audio. You don't need to watch their ads for long to appreciate that they're offering the very best.

There are PDF workbooks and other supplementary materials provided for every course, but obviously it's video that's at the core of MasterClass – movie-grade video, at that. It's all about you, the viewer, granting your utmost attention to the person appearing on screen, to their wisdom, anecdotes and unique insights, no matter what the course is about. The trailers for MasterClass make you feel like you're missing out by not signing up – the content simply looks that good, that valuable, even when the subject matter itself might be concerning a skill or practice you've never even considered before (like investigative journalism or basketball, in my case).

There's a lot to be learnt from MasterClass, and I don't just mean via their courses. The way they convey an immense sense of quality and promise nothing less than excellence in their product is hugely instructive for anyone involved in marketing. You may not have the luxury of A-list celebrities affixing their names and statures to your business, but there's plenty you can do to convey a sense of quality and superiority around your brand. If you want to be considered premium, and thus enjoy the benefits of such positioning, like high prices and an association with luxury, you'd do well to take a close look at how MasterClass have accomplished this for themselves.

Philip Bloom
Web: philipbloom.net
Facebook, Instagram, YouTube: philipbloom

For the best part of 20 years, Philip Bloom was, for all intents and purposes, a cameraman. His 20-year-plus career in broadcast film-making saw him work for the likes of Sky, the BBC and CNN. But things have changed a bit since then; he's become much more than a camera operator, a mere gun for hire, in what I can assure you is a heavily commoditised industry.

Philip still creates beautiful films, including documentaries and fiction pieces, but while his prowess behind a camera is what he's primarily known for, he's become a highly influential key person of influence for a great many other things too. He has a substantial list of subscribers on YouTube, with his video reviews of cameras amassing hefty view counts in particular. He posts frequently to his Facebook page and consistently sees high engagement when doing so. Perhaps most notably, he's invited to speak at high-profile industry conferences like NAB, for many reputable brands in the video business want his expert, influential name and seal of approval attached to their products, which is also why he's partnered up with a select few film-making brands to endorse their products; if Philip says it's good, it must be so. Thus, Philip has become one of the most well-known faces in his field – a true expert with a great deal of influence and an enviable level of positioning. His actions have ultimately set him well and truly apart from the 99% of film-makers who simply go through the same motions day in, day out.

So how did he do it? Well, as you'd expect, he uses a lot of video – his reviews are second to none in their quality and depth. His classes – both online and offline – are brilliantly put together. But once again, it's not *just* the quality of his videos that has contributed towards his success. Philip, like all good marketers, puts his personality front and centre too. He's a likeable guy, but he doesn't hold back when it comes to expressing his opinions, particularly on gear and technique. He's actually somewhat polarising; despite his esteemed career in broadcasting, he's an advocate of using minimal filming equipment to get the job done. He admits that he prefers smaller cameras and less elaborate set-ups; he's kind of "been there, done that" with regard to the complex, expensive and cumbersome stuff. Undoubtedly there will be many who frown at Philip's approach to film-making, but clearly there are many more who are fully behind it – present company included.

What's also noteworthy is that Philip uses less-than-perfect video alongside his polished, high-value content. Despite being someone with an obvious eye for beauty and quality, he doesn't think twice about uploading rough-and-ready clips onto his Instagram Story, because this is "throwaway" content anyway. But he does clearly put in the effort to make his evergreen content as high value as possible. He doesn't take himself, or indeed video as a whole, too seriously. He uses it fully to his advantage, and has done a better job than most in transforming himself from "just another camera guy" to a prominent industry leader.

Dominic Hodgson
Web: mydogssuperhero.com & growyourpetbusinessfast.com
Facebook: /PackLeaderUK & /GrowYourPetBusinessFast
Dom "The Dog Guy" Hodgson and I first crossed paths way back in 2014. He was pretty much my first client, has remained as such, and quickly became a very good friend. He's one of those hundred-miles-an-hour guys, which is reflected in his various and ever changing business ventures … so here's the short version.

Dom has used video in just about every way imaginable. When we first started working together, we mainly created generic promotional material for his dog adventure business (Pack Leader Dog Adventures), as well as product reviews for his online store. But in hindsight, we didn't *really* know what we were doing. The videos themselves were okay, but it's plain as day to us both now that they certainly missed the mark in a few areas. I wish my future self could have handed this book to me all those years ago! Ultimately the store was canned, and Dom put his efforts into creating The Superhero Dog Owner's Inner Circle – an online community where members received exclusive training designed to improve the relationship with their dogs. He did this after learning a shedload about marketing from some of the world's best, and writing his first (excellent) book *How To Be Your Dog's Superhero.*

As we both studied marketing and sought inspiration from people not unlike those described in this chapter, our video content became more focused, refined, purposeful and valuable. I also got better at the actual filming, which helped quite a bit. Hence, a video podcast was born, which helped grow Dom's audience by providing them with regular, high-value content. We also directed our efforts towards creating video courses and guides for the same purpose, and also to cement Dom's status as a true expert in his field. In sync with all of his other marketing mediums, he made his personality one of the defining characteristics of this content, embracing the polarisation of his audience. We also created content optimised for Facebook, such as Twenty Second Dog Training Tips and short "teaser" sections lifted from the podcast. In the case of the latter, we were able to do this easily and quickly because all of our footage was designed to be evergreen and repurposable. We created a structured archive, an ever-growing library of video material that could only ever grow in value over time; the more we filmed, the more quality video Dom had at his disposal. The combination of high-quality, valuable video content, plus Dom's signature daily emails and direct mail campaigns, also allowed him to perform a sell-out UK tour, speaking to eager audiences up and down the country.

Clearly recognising his growing influential status, Dom then wrote his second book – *Walk Yourself Wealthy* – aimed at owners of pet businesses, not just pets. Around the same time, he launched another membership programme that has since become his most successful venture to date. The Poodle to Pitbull Pet Business Bootcamp first ran in 2016, and saw pet business owners trek hundreds of miles to not-so-sunny

Sunderland just to be in the same room as our Dom. He's been on the radio, has been featured in print media, has interviewed and formed connections with people literally all over the world, and has scaled his business more than anyone I know.

Was it all because of video? No way – while Dom has undoubtedly used video to a greater extent than the majority of marketers, he's also an avid advocate of email, plus direct mail and other offline practices. The cold, hard truth (that most videographers know deep down, but seldom speak the words) is that it takes a great deal more than good video content to position you and your business as top-tier. You need more than high-quality films to win over the hearts and minds of your target audience – Dom is proof of that. He serves as one of the best examples of someone who *utilises* video as the tool that it is alongside other tried-and-tested marketing techniques, all of which come together to form a solid, strategised system that works in synergy to bring about his business goals.

Hireaband
Web: hireaband.co.uk
Facebook: /hireaband

Hireaband are another long-standing client of Artifact Media. The clue is in the name – Hireaband are an entertainment agency serving up some of the best wedding, function and tribute acts in the country. And they really do serve the whole country, with offices spanning Glasgow to London. They represent a lot of acts, and therein lies the problem – how do musicians set themselves apart from the competition? How does one band differentiate itself from another in what is yet another saturated marketplace?

MD of Hireaband, Del Cotton, had this to say in a guest blog he kindly wrote for my website: "Estimates vary, but it's thought that there are more than 10,000 UK covers bands looking for bookings at any one time. That's a lot of competition for a finite number of gigs.

At a time when many bands are wondering where all the gigs have gone, some switched-on players are cleaning up. What are they doing differently? Are they just better musicians?"

(You can read the full blog post at **artifactmedia.co.uk/resources**.)

The short answer is no – just like any industry, it's not always the most talented who get all the gigs (literally, in this case). The few who attain superior status and high-level positioning are the ones who get the marketing right. Of course, being good at "the thing" you do is a basic prerequisite – you need to actually be able to follow through on your lofty claims and promises. But the opportunity to do so needs to be earned. You need to *prove* to your potential customers that you're the right choice. In Hireaband's case, their acts need to communicate that they each offer something unique, something different from the rest, *while* demonstrating that they're expert musicians.

When it comes to booking a musician or a band for any kind of occasion, much of a customer's choice will come down to personal preference and individual taste – you'd be quick to disregard heavy metal bands if you wanted a traditional wedding complete with classical music from a string quartet, for example. However, where a lot of people would assume that a band's defining of their category, genre or classification is pretty much the most they can do to market themselves, i.e. that their musical style is the primary thing that defines them, Del and I would argue otherwise. An act can and should differentiate itself from others, even those who reside in the same categories or come up in the same search engine results, in a host of ways – starting with effective video content.

People who need music for an event obviously want to listen to potential acts beforehand so that they can make a prior judgement on whether they'll be appropriate for the big do. But by the same token, I'd be amazed if a potential customer didn't consider a band's visual aspect as well. Furthermore, the personalities of the individual members should also come into question. After all, a band doesn't really *just* play music at a gig – they become part of the event itself. They set the tone and shape the mood, because ultimately they're attendees just like everyone else. They might play great music, but their mannerisms and characteristics, in the eyes of some, might leave something to be desired (looking at you, Gallagher brothers). The act needs to be right in more ways than just sounding good – they need to be appropriate for the gig as people, too. Thus, the best way to showcase what an act is *really* like – and to give a potential customer a detailed insight – is through video.

The videos I've produced for Hireaband acts have been varied. Some have simply captured on-stage performances of a handful of tracks from the band's roster, but others have been more documentary-like and taken a closer, more personal look at the act in question, such as that of The Chosen Few, which featured footage of their studio recording and an interview with the band members. In both cases, the personality and temperament of the band as a whole was a hugely important factor to try to communicate to the viewer, second only to the band's musical abilities. Interviews with band members open up a completely new line of dialogue, allowing the viewer to get to know them a little better *before* they have a phone call or arrange a meeting. It's not even that complicated – I just asked the band what they do, how they do it and what they love about it. Rather than the prospect wondering whether they'll actually get along with the members of the band, by the end of a video like this they already feel like they know them. Even if it's just a little, it's a whole lot more than the 99% of bands who don't open themselves up in this way, simply blending in with the rest. Del told me that within just one week of posting the video, the band received 15 new bookings. I hope you can see how this fast-tracks the sales process, and how you might apply something similar to your own business. You can see some of Hireaband's films at **artifactmedia.co.uk/resources**.

Chapter summary

This list of some of my favourite video marketers is varied, but certainly not extensive. There are countless examples of people using video for a great many purposes in a host of businesses in a plethora of industries. I'm sure you have your own examples, too …

Action steps

1. Take a look at the videos used by those listed in this chapter.

You might not be a dog trainer or run an agency, but there are lessons to be learnt from these wonderful examples of people using effective video regardless of what it is you actually do.

2. Make your own list of those who create and share inspiring, effective videos.

I'm sure you'll have had a few names or brands in mind as you read this chapter; make the effort to identify some videos that have proved memorable, inspiring, educational or entertaining to you, collating them into a list. Again, even if they're not at all related to your profession, there are always lessons to be learnt and techniques applied to your own marketing. I personally use YouTube's playlist feature to keep track of any standout videos, and also take notes on the very best films I come across in Evernote.

Chapter Three

What's your "Why"?

Given the recent popularisation (and commercialisation) of all things mindset and mindfulness, plus the oft-debated subjects of chakras, visualisation, manifestation and fulfilling one's potential, phrases like the title of this chapter may lead you to believe we're teetering on the edge of "woo".

But fear not, dear reader – you're reading this book for its practical, real-world teachings, and that's how it shall remain. But I do firmly believe that, to become more than just "good" at video marketing, you need to know your Why.

Your Why is a succinct summary of the stuff at the core of you and your business – the driving force behind it. You could also call it your mission statement or your elevator pitch … whatever. It doesn't have to be a grand, elegant and eloquent vision, it doesn't have to be perfect, and it certainly doesn't have to be something you write on a mood board at the start of each day.

But it does have to be something of a genuine cause, a task that your business is dedicated to championing, a philosophy that influences everything you do and helps separate you from your competitors. If it isn't, or you don't have one at all, people will see right through it – especially on camera. As mentioned in the introduction, you need to be genuinely passionate about what you do and demonstrate that, like a real person, you're not just in the business of making money and becoming successful; you also want to help others. Aside from anything else, a less-than-all-in attitude to your profession means you're probably in the wrong business in the first place.

Your Why is so important because, as Simon Sinek (author of*Start With Why*) says, " *People don't buy what you do; they buy why you do it.*" Consider the almost-clichéd analogy of the comparison between a top-spec Windows laptop and an Apple MacBook Pro. On paper, the Windows machine has a comparable technical specification to the Apple device, yet the latter is priced much higher and is widely considered to be more valuable and desirable (and yes, I'm writing this book on one now).

Why is that? Well, Apple have always been all about doing things *differently*, offering inventive and idiosyncratic alternatives to the status quo. When they launched the iPod in 2001, they didn't sell a "5GB MP3 player" – they sold "*1,000 songs in your pocket*". Their Why is the driving force behind their actions, opinions and decisions, and it's been communicated and demonstrated consistently over time, which in turn has positioned them and their products as premium, high-end and ultra desirable – three characteristics that I'm sure you'd agree your business would benefit from being associated with.

There are many benefits of defining your Why:

- You present yourself as an enthusiastic advocate of your craft
- You do so with ease and in a natural way, because that advocacy is genuine
- You come up with content ideas more easily
- You polarise your audience because you show that you stand for something, attracting more of your ideal customers and repelling those you don't want to deal with anyway

- You position yourself as an expert in your field – one who shows they're in it for all the right reasons

For example, here's my Why (or at least, one version of it):

To design, create and deliver effective videos.

And here it is broken down:

'design'

I plan and strategise video content; I don't just create it.

Most videographers are "guns for hire", taking on whatever job is available so long as it involves using a camera. That's fine – it's their decision to make.

But personally, I resent being involved in projects just for the sake of it, or if I know that very few people are going to enjoy or get some use out of the end product. No matter what figure is on the invoice, it's unfulfilling, ungratifying and just feels wrong, so I stopped taking on such projects a long time ago.

Thus, clients of Artifact Media get me not only as a camera operator and video editor, but also as a key influencer in the pre-production stage. I've developed a systemised process that helps business owners and marketers create video content which serves a purpose and is effective, based on consultations and strategy sessions that take place long before the cameras start rolling. I don't call all the shots – the most successful projects are the result of collaboration and consolidation of different ideas, perspectives and opinions – but I simply decided that I wouldn't go blindly forth to create videos that I knew weren't going to be worth it for the client. Plus, the videos need to work <u>with</u> the other parts of the marketing machine to deliver maximum return … otherwise, what's the point?

'create'

I wear two consecutive caps – camera operator and editor.

I use appropriate film-making equipment to capture all video and audio necessary to bring the aforementioned plan to fruition.

Cameras, lenses, filters, microphones, lights, framing … all the physical stuff.

Then I stitch all this wonderful content together into edited, polished, sophisticated …

'effective video'

Linking back to the Design stage – it has to be effective and built for purpose or I don't get involved.

Quite often, when someone asks what I do or what makes me different to others in my field, my response is something along the lines of: "I help businesses make the most of video content." As such, my Why isn't necessarily just one phrase, and yours doesn't need to be either. The purpose of defining your core message like this is simply to give you a solid foundation upon which all of your marketing is based. Consistency, as you'll learn throughout this book, is crucial, and so it's important to give yourself something to be defined by, something to be so closely associated with that people immediately think of you whenever they encounter the subject. Only by doing this will you successfully stand out from the vanilla marketers who don't stand for much, and so don't stand *out* much at all.

At **artifactmedia.co.uk/resources**, you can download a PDF guide that runs through my entire, systemised video production process, from initial consultation to filming, editing and (importantly) beyond. I send this to new clients before we discuss the details of the project itself, and as you'll see, my Why is at the core of it. It won't surprise you to learn that this core message also underpins my emails, blog posts, copy on my website, even Instagram captions.

Since I nailed down my core message, after tweaking it over time, scrutinising it and justifying each component word, I've approached (and gained) new clients with increased confidence, maintained existing relationships for years and positioned myself appropriately in the marketplace.

Having something clear and defined to underpin your business means it's easy to come up with ideas for content and you're always thinking of new ways you can help your ideal customers. When discussions and debates arise, you unwaveringly take a stand on one side or the other; you don't sit on the fence all bland and beige, and in doing so you attract the people you want, repelling those you don't – it's great. And obviously, all of this plays into the hands of video *perfectly* – in its simplest form, all you need to do is show up and speak.

Obviously, the first Why you write probably isn't going to be the one you stick with. A good tip if you're stuck is to precede it with "My job is …", and go from there. Write down one idea, think on it, then write another. Don't delete the first one. Keep going until you've got half a page or so, where you can pick and choose the best bits. And anyway, it never has to be perfect. A phrase I'd like you to keep in mind both as you work through this book and even when you're creating videos is: "done is better than perfect".

Chapter summary

Your audience is out there and many of them *already* want what you're offering. It's your job to show them why *you* are the best option, how you're different and why you're worth choosing over the offerings of your competitors. Having a robust and sincere Why to underpin all the communication between you and your ideal customers will bolster your marketing like a bulletproof vest.

Action steps

1. Research the mission statements of companies and brands that inspire you.

Look at those of TED, Uber and Google. How do they succinctly communicate their Why?

2. Define your Why.

As per the advice in this chapter, write down a brief summary of what you do, how you do it and why you do it. Repeat the process until your Why becomes more accurate and eloquent – but remember it doesn't have to be perfect, and you don't have to stick to a specific wording for evermore. However, the underlying principles and driving force of your Why should remain true and congruent always.

Chapter Four

The all-too-familiar recipe for an ineffective video

I'm not much of a "Negative Nigel", so let's keep this chapter brief …

As much as it might make you wince and cringe with discomfort, it's important to recognise not only what makes a *great* video, but also what kinds of ingredients spoil the dish. Being able to identify these elements will deter you from making similar mistakes yourself, and seeing as your goal is for your business to become premium-positioned, you wouldn't want anything less than great marketing material out there for the world to see, would you?

So before we learn how to craft truly effective videos, here are a few ingredients that should be left out of the recipe.

Poor quality

Contrary to the belief of many marketers (and to the disdain of most other videographers), the technical quality of your videos is *not* the most important factor. Some viewers simply won't be able to tell the difference between one film that was shot on an outdated smartphone and another that had £30,000 of camera and a crew behind it. As a videographer it pains me to say it, but there are some who either won't care or will be oblivious to how good your films look and sound. But most viewers can and do recognise any work of high quality, and given the high standards of modern TV shows, films and indeed the content put out by certain brands online, the majority of us are well versed in acknowledging a "proper" production.

As such, to skimp and save on quality is to shoot yourself in the foot before you've started shooting! Your audience relates every facet of your content and communication with them to your brand as a whole. How you and your business are portrayed on film directly reflects you, your products, your services, your values and ultimately your worth in the eyes of your viewers. Having low-quality video content harms your business by literally damaging its image.

Imagine what your viewer's internal monologue might sound like as they watch your material. Will they be completely immersed in the experience with their full attention on what's unfolding before them? Will they feel involved and connected? Will they feel a sense of awe and inspiration at the beauty of your film? Or will they be thinking that your video doesn't really stand out from whatever they watched previously, that it doesn't look particularly special and thus doesn't warrant their time or attention? If your videos *look* like they were cobbled together, created using average or inferior equipment and poor techniques, then they probably were – and your audience will be able to tell. Premium-positioned businesses only associate themselves with high-quality, effective video content.

If you were looking to sell your business or acquire some kind of investment, you'd want to steer clear of anything that threatened to devalue your brand. You'd want your name to be trademarked, your unique products and services to be copyrighted, and your intellectual property to be protected in order to attain the maximum valuation. All business owners – no matter what stage they're at in their entrepreneurial journey – would benefit from applying this kind of thinking to their marketing. A high-quality, premium-priced brand should *only* associate itself with high-quality, premium content if it is to be perceived in this way by its viewers, as per the owner's intentions.

You might think that technical quality is largely out of your hands – you've only got access to the gear you own or can afford, you need to have some level of technical knowledge in order to make the most of it, or if you've hired a videographer, it's up to *them* to handle quality. True on all counts, but as a business owner it's your responsibility to attain and maintain a certain level of quality in your marketing, regardless of your level of involvement in the creation. It's the same as if a supplier fails to deliver on their promises, or you find yourself battling a legal dispute – it's not necessarily your fault, but it is your obligation to sort it out.

It's up to you to take your marketing (and by extension your whole business) by the horns and strive for the best quality you can get. There are many ways to do this, ranging from solutions that are super-cheap and fast to implement, to those that require more substantial investments of time, energy and cash. You could upgrade your camera, your microphone, your lighting and even your filming environment with relative ease and very little investment. In fact, you're already taking a bigger step than most by reading this book. But even if you've invested more substantially by hiring a videographer, you can make sure you're getting your money's worth by setting a few things straight upfront. Ask them about the equipment they use, why they use it and in what format you'll receive your videos. Ask them how your video(s) will look and sound, for examples of similar projects they've produced in the past, and what they'll specifically do to achieve the level of quality you desire. Make sure they're delivering the highest quality possible, and make sure they know that you'll only accept the best.

As mentioned, I systemised this process by creating a downloadable guide to Artifact Media video production, which specifically details to my clients how we strategise, create, deliver and measure the results of the content we create. You can download this yourself at **artifactmedia.co.uk /resources**. I also write blog posts and case studies as well as making explainer videos that offer behind-the-scenes insights into projects, all of which come together to form an information-rich system that delves deep into the production process so that my prospects (and indeed existing clients) know exactly what to expect and what their investments are worth. Put simply, the supplier of any product or service should be able to sufficiently demonstrate the value of their offering long before you decide to commit to the investment.

When discussing potential video production projects, I've been asked a few times: "Can't I just do this myself? Isn't my smartphone good enough?" Ultimately, it's not up to me, or indeed any supplier, to decide if it's a good idea for you to bypass their service. I've had business owners operating in the exact same industry, and indeed offering near-identical services, react to my video production proposals in completely opposite ways; one would clearly see the value on offer and move through each stage of the process with no questions asked, while the other immediately voiced their objections to the price and time investments required. Of course, no two businesses are identical in terms of where they're at on their journeys or what levels of investment they're able to make; to some, professional video production or even an upgraded camera would put pressure on their financials. But in my experience, whether or not someone chooses to invest in any aspect of their business, not just video marketing, primarily comes down to their "inner game" or mindset (for want of a less clichéd term).

Where one business owner sees a great opportunity and a chance to back up their premium-level offerings with impressive marketing material, the other sees a large cost and the potential for many things to go wrong along the way. There are few things in life that are clear-cut, black and white, one or the other, but most business owners do fall into one of the two camps of thinking: abundance, or scarcity (Daniel Priestley, author of several excellent books on entrepreneurship, calls it "balance sheet versus profit-and-loss thinking"). There's nothing wrong with cutting costs by using basic film-making equipment yourself or going for a cheaper, less experienced videographer, and, by doing that, saving your money for other things; as much as I do love video, I'd much rather spend several thousand pounds on two weeks' snowboarding in Canada than a new camera. But the fact that you're reading this book suggests that you're prepared to spend a little to gain a lot, and you probably don't need me to tell you that cutting corners means risking the quality of the end product. In the pursuit of attaining high-quality video, you'll undoubtedly feel some resistance in parting ways with your precious resources of cash, time and energy. But if you're in "Camp Abundance", you'll know that so long as it's an informed decision, it will be worthwhile.

As is the case with most things in life, you get what you pay for, so if you're browsing for a new camera and see an unbranded or second-hand model that looks like a bit of a bargain, or if that production company down the road has surprised you with a low price estimate for your project, you should probably reconsider your investment. Good stuff rarely comes cheap, and the best videographers will have no problem in demonstrating the value of the service they offer in relation to their prices. And just while we're on that point, remember that video (done properly) really is an *investment.* The return of high-quality, strategised video always justifies the cost.

> If you're due for a phone upgrade, consider the latest model with the best camera – the one sporting high resolution and frame rates. Even then, you'd do well to go one step further and invest in a compact camera or DSLR. They might seem unnecessary at first given how capable smartphone cameras are these days, but if you go for a mid- to high-range model you'll definitely see the difference. Combine that with a good microphone from a reputable brand, and watch with glee as your content shines like a beacon against the "normal" stuff from your competitors.

"Me, me, me!" (Old-fashioned marketing)

Most businesses and brands market their products and services like it's still 1950. In the post-WWII era, according to an article published by Bournemouth University:

"*Marketing was … focussed on distribution, communication and persuading customers that one manufacturer's goods were better than another's.* "

As though they were merely digging through the archives of old tobacco companies and regurgitating their archaic material, most of today's businesses go through exactly the same motions and recite the same not-so-inferred message:

"*We're great – buy our stuff.*"

But while the tactic of merely presenting the *features* of your product or service brings about some positive results on a small scale, the vast majority of your viewers will react in the same way:

"*Who cares?*"

And who can blame them? This shoved-in-your-face approach does nothing for most of us, and in fact it often results in an aura of negativity hanging over the brand in question. It's like when you get stopped in the street by one of those life insurance salesmen. Life insurance is certainly important, and perhaps wrongly at the bottom of absolutely everyone's list of things they must sort out, but surely there must be another, gentler way to inform people of the merits and benefits of such a service other than strong-arming them into a conversation with a stranger on the street in the cold while they're in the middle of shopping?

And yet, even today, businesses perform the digital equivalent in the online world. Their videos serve no purpose other than to unappealingly reel off a list of features and facts. The creators apparently don't even get as far as considering the needs, wants or troubles of the viewer; they simply want to sell a product or service that they consider superior, and want the viewer to make the purchase now – right now.

I hope you can see how flawed and antiquated this approach is. It may have worked in the '50s, but you'll be hard-pressed to gain anyone's attention these days if you metaphorically jump in their path and demand they give you their time of day. It'll be like that scene in *Airplane!* in which a gentleman walking through an airport lobby politely declines the first aggressive salesman who stands in his way, but by the time another dozen of these annoying fellows have demanded his attention, he's dished out a few right hooks and knocked them all clean out. In today's saturated online world, people will actively dislike and disregard you if your only strategy is to bombard them with "me, me, me".

Lack of substance, personality and/or value

The phrase "all fur coat and no knickers" rings true for this point. A video with no substance, story or intrinsic value to the viewer – no matter how good it looks or how well it's been put together – is not going to stand your marketing in as good stead as a film with real purpose, value and significance.

Ron Howard, director of *Apollo 13* and *The Da Vinci Code*, sums it up perfectly in the trailer for his MasterClass video series on directing:

> *Ultimately, you are the storyteller. At the end of the day, it doesn't matter how big your crew is, it doesn't matter how much money you have to spend; it's what you're capturing inside the framelines that's going to have this impact on the audience … or not.*

For every poor film out there that's lacking in pretty much every department – technical quality, story, substance, value to the viewer, etc. – there is another that looks and sounds fantastic, but *still* isn't worth much. You simply can't make an epic-looking film with all the production value in the world, neglect to couple it with substance and value to the viewer, and expect great results (hence my point that if there are any fellow videographers reading this book, most of them will be sitting there frowning with discomfort, because most of them take on any and every job that lands in their inbox). It *might* be successful – if your business is inherently visual, then a gorgeous film bursting with pretty shots might do well for getting people on board. But most of the time, it's simply not enough.

Think of some ads you've seen for cars, perfume, sofas, kitchens, home improvements or chocolate. Chances are, if they were from a big, reputable brand, they looked fantastic (and cost thousands to produce). But as impressive as these films are, it's very rare that, as marketing material, they are used in isolation. You don't just see perfume ads on TV before Christmas – you see banners in shopping centres, posters at bus stops and billboards on the sides of buildings. You're made very much aware of the brand and the product long before you head down to the department store, but then – crucially – you get a sample to decide whether or not it's right for you. The fact that an A-list celebrity whom you like has endorsed the product might make you feel more aligned with the brand and thus more interested in the product, but if you don't think it smells nice, you won't buy it. You might be impressed at how great a new car looks on TV, but it's highly unlikely that you'll buy one before learning more about its features and benefits, seeing it in person, and taking a test drive.

In these examples and countless others, it's more than just one video that seals the deal. Even if your business operates on a much smaller scale than Chanel or Audi, it's unlikely that anyone will buy from you if all they've seen is a single film. As you'll learn more about in Chapter Nine, every video you make should be tailored to a specific type of viewer who is at a particular point in their relationship with you and your business. They need to be taken on a journey that addresses their needs, wants, problems, objections and questions at various stages – not all at once.

Consider the difference between a film that, through high-grade visuals, simply screams "look how great we are", and one that looks great *and* makes the viewer stop, think, contemplate, wonder, feel inspired, question, or otherwise absorb some kind of value. Which one is going to prove more effective? Again there's no real right or wrong answer, and it's different for every business. But in an era where businesses are fighting to be given a moment's notice as they battle with the infinite distractions facing their viewers online, I would argue that putting all your eggs in the "production value" basket is a very risky move, and like any decision is certainly not without consequence.

But this is where things actually get really exciting for you, and the reason why I'm bringing these points to your attention: by combining a high level of technical quality with great stories and subject matter, you'll be leagues ahead of your competition, who are stuck in the Stone Age with their dreary sales ads.

You *could* do the opposite and cut corners, like many business owners do, by opting for ease, simplicity and time-saving tactics. You could film and upload a quick 'n' dirty, one-take attempt at a video because it's easy, doesn't take much effort and will "get the job done". But believe me when I say your audience – your potential clients and customers – will see through this like X-ray vision. It's painstakingly obvious when a so-called marketer has done something in a rush or not given it their all. I'm not saying you should dedicate four days a week to making awesome videos, but I am saying that you need to look at what your competitors are doing and aim higher – *much* higher – if you want to stand out. That takes time, effort and investment, and it's certainly painful at first, but it's so worth it when your business becomes truly first-rate in the eyes of your viewers.

Ignore what your mum says

I'm going to end up in some bad books for this one, but I promised you the truth … so here goes! (Also, I don't have anything against mums – I love mine dearly. This concept applies to any and all of your close relations and acquaintances, including your dad, spouse, partner, best mate, whoever.)

When you do something big like start a business, most of your family and friends will react with the following:

"Wow, that's amazing! Go for it – I know you'll work hard and do brilliantly."

While this is lovely and can provide some much-needed reassurance and generally make you feel really good about yourself, it's important to remember that your closest relations aren't giving you the full picture. For example, when I quit my job in 2016 in order to grow my business, I had a lot of support. I'd already moved to a part-time role after producing videos on the side for a while, so the decision to go fully "lone wolf" wasn't unexpected by my peers. According to my family and friends, I was making wonderful videos that would be huge successes. But in hindsight I've realised that while they certainly had their merits, for the most part they were crap.

Of course, to this day I'm immensely grateful for all the kind words of encouragement; I don't recall ever receiving any negative feedback. If I had, it's likely I wouldn't have jumped the employment ship so eagerly, as I would have been afraid of not being good enough or not being ready (especially considering I'd never studied video production and was learning very much on the fly). But I do wonder if I would have become a better film-maker, sooner, if people had been a bit more honest and given some constructive criticism on my less-than-brilliant work so that I could make steps to improve.

In the same vein, here's the truth when it comes to your videos, and by extension your marketing and your entire business – your mum, your spouse and your friends are going to tell you that what you're doing is great. They're going to sing your praises, spur you on and give you the drive to carry on. "*I saw your video,*" they'll say. " *Great job! Check you out, appearing on camera.*" This is a good thing that I'm sure you'll benefit from and be grateful for.

But your audience is another matter entirely. The people you're actually targeting your videos towards – your ideal customers and clients who are complete strangers at present –

will not necessarily be so kind, or forgiving. If your videos are crap, they'll say they're crap. If they don't agree with your views and values, prepare for a heated debate. For many people, sitting behind a screen with a keyboard at their fingertips is very much like when you get road rage in your car – you feel safe and cocooned and are perfectly comfortable throwing all manner of insults and damning gestures at the guy who just cut you off. That feeling of supremacy, invulnerability and having the opportunity to speak your mind in an uncensored way and without harmful consequence is shared by motorists and internet trolls alike. Thus, just like lunatics on the road, you're bound to come across a few nasties in your video marketing travels. They might be offensive, and you may get genuinely upset, but they're just being honest, so you'll need to grow a thick skin in preparation for the odd colourful comment.

If you don't believe me, go to the comments section on almost any YouTube video. Lying within will be the full gamut of reactions, ranging from positivity and admiration all the way to the most derogatory, pejorative and scornful remarks you'll find anywhere on the internet. It's foul, it's disheartening, but for the most part it's just their honest opinions.

I don't mean to take the wind out of your sails; I merely want to prepare you for what it's like out there in the big, bad online world, if you didn't already know. How much of this "constructive" criticism you'll have to deal with will depend largely on where you post your videos – as mentioned, YouTube, for all its excellence and value to us marketers, has become the clichéd hub of harsh audience feedback. Facebook seems to be a more hospitable place, although is not without its share of keyboard warriors.

You can actually use being on the receiving end of offence to your advantage. The "Celebrities Read Mean Tweets" segment from US talk show *Jimmy Kimmel Live!* is the perfect example of turning a would-be frown upside down by pulling some positivity out of contemptuous audience feedback. The simple idea of having stars like Gary Oldman, Gal Gadot and Katy Perry read out some of the harshest verbal attacks on themselves is pure genius, for three reasons:

1. It's hugely entertaining (thus provides valuable content for the viewer).

2. It demonstrates that the creators are listening to the audience.

3. It shows that you, as the creator, don't take yourself too seriously.

For Professional Music Technology's final video of 2017, drawing inspiration from *Mean Tweets*, Dagan and I sat in front of a tinsel-donned fireplace and read out some of the worst YouTube comments we could find (most of which attacked Dagan's twin-like resemblance to Russell Brand). At the same time, we also went through some of our favourite bits of gear we'd filmed throughout the year. In 24 minutes we ticked all the boxes – entertaining, engaging, consistent, useful and high quality. Embrace the haters!

You'll find links to both these videos at **artifactmedia.co.uk/resources**

Chapter summary

For every factor that contributes to a great video, there's another that will reduce its value and in turn threaten your business's image and positioning. It's important to see and understand both sides of the coin, so that you are not only equipped to create videos to the very best of your ability, but are also in possession of the rarer skill of self-evaluation; keeping up a high standard of quality with all aspects of your videos will help position your business as nothing short of premium and high-quality.

Action steps

1. Compare how often you talk about your prospects and customers to how often you talk about yourself, across all of your marketing material.

Look at your website, your social media pages, your emails and – of course – your videos. Do you speak about yourself more than the needs, wants and problems of your viewers? Or are you attracting attention and gaining loyal followers by putting them first?

2. Compare the quality of your video content to that of your competitors, or the businesses you look to for inspiration.

What are the discernible differences between your videos and those that are competing for the attention of your target audience? Which brand appears more premium, professional and high quality? As a consumer, which one would gain your trust?

Chapter Five

The secret recipe for a great video

We know that there are droves of crap videos out there failing to achieve anything of merit for all kinds of businesses, but we also know that there are some epic films that are working wonders for the most successful businesses and brands.

Before we look at *how* to create the stuff of legend, we need to understand what makes these videos so damn good in the first place. What separates an average video from a brilliant one? What are the secret ingredients for a great video recipe?

I say "secret" very deliberately, because even though there are bazillions of videos out there, hardly anyone seems to know how to make a good one. It may be easier and cheaper than ever to physically produce a video, but whether it's any good or not is an entirely different matter. Think about it – how many videos have resonated so strongly with you that you felt *compelled* to take some kind of action, had to share it with all your friends or were reduced to tears? I'm guessing, compared to the total amount of videos you've seen, not many at all.

Crucially, though, it's not just about making great videos on their own – those films need to be incorporated into a marketing system, a strategy, a framework designed with a specific type of viewer in mind and one that takes them on a particular journey. By the end of this book, you'll not only know how to create excellent videos in the first place, but you'll also know how to actually use them – something very few business owners take the time to master, and even fewer videographers know much about.

There are a few technical concepts in this chapter – you need to know about these in order to understand the ingredients for high-quality videos, which will in turn allow you to make informed purchasing decisions on filming equipment you might be considering. But I've distilled each of them down to simplified forms so that you can spend less time worrying about numbers and facts, and more time on making better videos.

Alex's "works like a charm" video excellence layer cake

Enticing, moreish and oh-so-satisfying

Ingredients:
Quality – a generous lump
Consistency – enough to keep them wanting more
Engaging content to keep things interesting
A purposeful message to win their hearts
A clear call to action for when they've finished consuming

For this recipe to really work, you'll need all of the above. Don't try to cut corners – it's amazing how well they gel together when they're combined in just the right amounts.

Let's take a closer look at how you work with each ingredient.

Quality

When it comes to a format like video, there is very little room for hiding. What your customer sees is what they think they're going to get. That's worth repeating …

What your customer sees is what they think they're going to get.

Thus, the importance of visual and auditory quality in your videos cannot be overstated. The more premium you look and sound, the more premium you are perceived to be in "reality", i.e. when they purchase and thus experience your product or service. High-quality, premium content reflects a high-quality, premium business, and vice versa. As alluded to in the introduction, if you don't want to be premium and are happy to serve people who buy solely on price, you're reading the wrong book. And if you don't offer a high-grade, remarkable product or service in the first place, you're *definitely* reading the wrong book.

At **artifactmedia.co.uk/resources**, you'll find two screen grabs (still frames taken from videos, but the videos themselves are there too). Both were taken in the same environment and feature similar subjects – the dashing, bearded chops of Dagan Wilkin, Product Demonstrator at Professional Music Technology and the poster boy of the brand's YouTube channel; and … me. One video was captured with an iPhone 8 front-facing ("selfie") camera with a less-than-ideal lighting situation in front of the lens. The other was recorded on £2,000 worth of Sony camera with another £2,000 worth of lens attached, under lovely studio-grade lighting. They're worlds apart in terms of visual quality. Can you tell which is which?

I do hope so …

The second image, taken with the pro video camera under a proper lighting set-up, is clearly superior. Various elements, such as colour, dynamic range and depth of field, combine to create a produced, professional look that screams "premium". The visual quality of this image is the kind you'd see on TV, and is akin to a contemporary documentary you'd find on

Netflix or Amazon. Clearly this video has *not* been rushed, and it *has* had time, money and effort put behind it, which reflects the values of the brand for which this video was produced – they obviously favour high quality and want to present themselves in the best light (pun intended).

The other image is perfectly fine in many respects, but it doesn't go much further than that; the visual quality pales in comparison, and there's nothing separating it from the kind of video a teenager would post nonchalantly to their Instagram Story. Indeed, this video *was* part of a spontaneous, rough-and-ready Instagram Story that would disappear from existence after 24 hours, and so didn't warrant a huge amount of time or effort being spent on it … a point we will revisit later.

Professional Music Technology have been a long-standing client of mine because they want their YouTube channel to be bursting with high-quality, valuable video content. They want to combine all the elements that make up their brand – expert staff, remarkable service, a huge range of products and a "rock 'n' roll" personality – and communicate these defining characteristics through their marketing. PMT don't really do anything in half measures. Their super-cool Crew Members greet you when you step into any of their stores across the UK, and their musical instrument displays are beautifully organised and maintained whether you're in the guitar room or the keyboards section. Quality is at the core of the business – it's certainly part of their Why – and so their marketing needs to reflect that.

Every viewer is different, of course, and as much as it pains me to say, some people won't care (or will be totally oblivious to) how good your videos look and sound. But they're certainly in the minority, and for the most part you should be striving for nothing short of excellence. Most of us recognise a remarkable video as soon as we see it, even if we're not sure what went into creating it, and, once again, if you want to appear premium and professional, why wouldn't you want the best?

Don't worry – you don't have to shell out thousands on a pro-level videography set-up, nor do you necessarily need to invest in someone like me to do it for you. You just need to develop and nurture a keen eye (and ear) for quality, which will allow you to attain the quality content your premium business deserves.

Here's a crash course in some of the elements that make high-quality videos like PMT's, and what sets them apart from the average stuff. Armed with just this basic knowledge will put you ahead of most business owners and open the door to creating supremely higher-value content.

Detail and clarity

When you look at the level of detail overall, one image in our example looks like a standard "shot on a smartphone" video, and the other looks much more produced, high-end and superior. Yet it might surprise you to learn that both of these videos have the same resolution of 1080p high definition – the standard of most TVs. But how can the image from the pro video camera look better than the iPhone if they're both HD?

Well, as much as camera manufacturers would have you believe otherwise, the "resolution" of a camera simply means the physical size of image it produces – how many pixels long by how many pixels tall, the digital equivalent of a canvas. Thus, a higher resolution doesn't necessarily mean a better image – after all, you could paint an amazingly detailed watercolour picture on one canvas, and a pencil-drawn stick figure on another; they're both the same size, but the difference in quality is another matter entirely.

While it's generally true that higher resolution means more detail, there are many other factors that go into making a great-looking image, and resolution is just one of them. You could order a 4K camcorder off Amazon right now that will give you a higher-resolution image than what you see in these examples, but you may not necessarily see an actual increase in quality. This situation is one I see (and get asked about) very often – business owners flocking to buy the kit with the most impressive specs, with little knowledge as to what results these arbitrary figures actually bring.

So in the case of our screen grabs, resolution itself doesn't really play as big a part as you might think when it comes to visual quality. Instead, the "pro" shot has higher detail and clarity mainly because the sensor of the Sony camera (the bit behind the lens upon which the light is focused) is what most of the £2,000 price tag is attributed to. Basically, it's much more advanced than the iPhone camera's sensor and is physically huge in comparison, so it absorbs tons more light and renders details much more clearly. This is one of the reasons why it's worth considering getting your hands on a compact camera or DSLR, rather than just using your smartphone to create videos, as you'll learn more about in chapter seven.

So with resolution, it really all comes down to – yes, I'm going to say it – not how big it is, but how you use it.

Lighting

Cameras are just tools for capturing light. They're not as sophisticated as the human eye, and certainly not as forgiving. If you're in a dark room looking at someone standing in front of a bright window, you can still make out their features while being able to clearly see the outside world behind them. Most cameras don't have the ability to do this, and as a video creator filming in this situation, you'd have to pick one or the other to "expose" the camera to – either the bright exterior, or the dark interior.

> In my video course *Effective Video Fundamentals*, I demonstrate this exact situation in the module *How to Film Indoors*, and then show you how to avoid the kinds of lighting situations that look weird and threaten to distract your viewers. I also show you how to create great-looking videos indoors without buying any lighting equipment, and how to do the same when filming outside. You can get access to the course by heading to **artifactmedia.co.uk/guides**, but there's a special offer at the end of this book that you'd be silly not to take advantage of.

Anything that you're filming – be it a person, a product or a landscape – needs to be well-lit. It needs to stand out, be distinguishable and be super-clear. You still see incredibly complex and elaborate lighting set-ups surrounding the most expensive cameras in the world on film sets, which should tell you something.

How you light and what equipment you need could be (and is) a book on its own. But fear not, because even if you don't have any professional gear, lighting is never *completely* out of your control. There's always something you can do to get a more flattering image, even if it's simply facing in another direction. Just being aware of the light around you and how your camera sees it will put you leagues ahead of most other business owners and marketers, who simply point their camera any which way and expect a half-decent result.

Colour

It's no longer 1970 – all videos are just "in colour" now, right? Not exactly.

Each camera responds differently to colour, in the same way that they respond differently to light. Here's a "blow your socks off" fact: most consumer-level cameras capture around 16.78 million colours, which sounds great until you compare it to the 1.07 billion colours captured by those at the pro level. What's more, because of the way they store that colour information, those higher-end cameras grant editors the ability to tweak and refine the colour of their videos to a huge degree. That's why movies and TV dramas just look so damn good – because the creators have been able to shift, alter and fine-tune the colour to a very high standard.

Your business's videos don't need to be of Hollywood standard, of course, but as with lighting, it pays to at least be aware of the impact of colour on their quality. You might notice that the second screen grab in our example has a certain "look" to it – the shadows aren't actually fully black, they have a purple tint to them, and in general the colours are more vibrant than the image from the iPhone. I was able to subtly dial this in while editing in order to give the video a more "produced" feel, rather than have the colours 100% lifelike. Purple is also the primary colour of PMT's branding, so it's a little nod to the other visual elements of the company as a whole and allows the video to look great when embedded on their website.

The most extreme example of this that I've seen is in my favourite movie of all time: *The Matrix*. Every scene that takes place within the computer-simulated world of the Matrix has a green cast to it, while the shots in the "real world" are more cool and blue. Even if you don't consciously acknowledge this the first time you watch the film, it cleverly plays a big part in its storytelling.

If you're on Instagram, you've probably come across a very basic form of colour grading just before posting, where you get the option to add a filter to your clip (or photo). It's worth having a look at these and seeing how they affect your videos (for better or worse), but just remember that less is usually more. Sure, it's all down to personal taste, but to me there's nothing tackier than an overly filtered photo or video. It looks unnatural, kind of "broken", and suggests that the uploader didn't really know what they were doing.

There are other apps out there that give you even more options and room for experimentation, such as Chromic and the excellent VSCO, which can easily make both your stills and your videos "pop" in a variety of ways.

The "arty" or "filmic" look (gorgeous blurry backgrounds and focal points)

Aside from the lighting, the biggest visual difference between the two example screen grabs is how the foreground is separated from the background (known as "depth of field" or DoF). Look at how everything beyond Dagan's face just drops off into a blur in the second image, almost like a smudged painting. This image has a shallow depth of field, and Dagan is the focal point of the image. At other points during the video this is even more obvious, especially during the close-up shots of the music products Dagan is reviewing.

Compare this dreamy, polished look to that of the iPhone camera, which just can't match the lovely portrait-style cinematic look of the video camera and its attached lens. Instead, all areas of the image look sharp and in focus. This image has a deep depth of field.

The arty look of the first screen grab is a result of a camera-and-lens combination, with both assigned to very specific settings to achieve the shallow DoF; you simply can't get this look on a smartphone in video mode. Any emulations of this kind of image are just that – digital recreations that do a decent job of faking the look of a shallow DoF, but don't come close to the real thing.

The biggest benefit of having a shallow depth of field (where there's only a small part of the image that's in focus), aside from the fact that it's just so damn pretty, is that it commands the viewer's eye. Your eyes are immediately drawn to the area of the image that is sharp – the focal point – and mostly ignore the rest. The applications for this type of look are endless – it suits portraits beautifully, it's perfect for product close-ups … and it makes animals look *really* cute. It proudly shouts "this is a film of quality", even if your viewer doesn't consciously acknowledge it.

Epic slow motion

Slo-mo isn't just reserved for extreme sports and *The Matrix*'s infamous fight scenes. It can actually bring something of a new dimension to shots that would otherwise be mundane, and like many technicalities of film-making, it's become widely available.

For example, during the Success Engineers 2018 Business Experience Weekend in Rome, we filmed a lot of slow motion to use in the "highlights" film, despite the event not involving any action or particularly fast-moving objects. Instead we captured people giving presentations, talking, exploring a beautiful city and generally having a wonderful time. The slow motion actually provided a totally different end result to run-of-the-mill real-time shots. It increased the production value of the film massively; each and every use of slow motion helped pull the audience a little closer, focus their attention a little more, and ultimately feel more involved in the experience.

You can check it out (and see similar examples) at **artifactmedia.co.uk/resources**.

Across this shoot and most others, I've used slow motion liberally because it is such a cool effect and allows you to see even everyday actions in a totally different way. It is very filmic, can be dramatic and is always associated with a premium image; aside from it simply looking brilliant at face value, it requires specialist equipment in order to be captured well.

The opposite of slo-mo is a <u>time lapse</u>. These have become very popular, and for good reason; they condense a long space of time down into a much shorter clip, so they're ideal for sunrises and sunsets, travel and landscapes – you could leave your camera filming for an hour, then condense the recording down to just 10 seconds and see some epic results.

If you watched the Success Engineers film mentioned above, you'll have seen a few time lapses – when you're in rural Italy at the height of summer, you can't *not* get a sunset time lapse or two!

<u>To move, or not to move (the camera)?</u>

For some reason, many people think that they *need* to move their camera while they're filming, emulating a dad in the '80s or '90s who, having just bought his first video camera, straps it to his wrist and flings it around the house, filming anything and everything he can see (with lots of zoom, too).

Most of us have been guilty of recreating the Dad cam at some point. What we probably weren't aware of at the time is that static shots actually make for much more visually appealing and even professional-looking videos than shaky ones with unnecessary movement. The "5 Basics" video at **artifactmedia.co.uk/resources** shows this in full effect. I filmed my other half Naomi speaking to camera – once while walking backwards as she walked towards me, and then again with us both standing still. The first pass unsurprisingly gave poor results, with the camera shaking about all over the place, but this isn't dissimilar to the kinds of videos I see many businesses uploading (and then wondering why view counts are low). The second take *felt* more lifeless and boring at the time of filming – she simply stood talking, and I stood filming – but the end result was leagues ahead. By keeping Naomi in the same place in the frame, she looks proud and purposeful. All the attention is on her and what she has to say. She doesn't *need* to walk towards the camera, and the camera doesn't need to move around her … so why do it?

Movie director David Fincher (*Se7en, The Social Network, Gone Girl*) is often praised for the lack of camera movement in his films, or rather for his occasional use of *deliberate* camera movement; for the majority of shots, the camera is firmly planted on a tripod and does not track, pan or do anything other than capture what's happening in front of it. The viewer is forced to focus all of their attention simply on what's occurring on the screen, rather than the way it's being captured. Contrast this with almost any action movie, especially something like Michael Bay's *Transformers*, where camera movement and shake is actually sought-after in order to add energy and excitement.

Each to their own, of course, but while I love using expensive stabilisation equipment to capture super-smooth, gliding footage even when running around like a madman, there's a lot to be said for Fincher's minimalist approach to camera movement, and it's something you should consider for your videos, too. Ultimately, you'll get more views and better engagement if your video is *easy to watch.* If you make it a difficult affair by adding unnecessary, nauseating movement, your audience are more likely to switch off. In the case of our example video – the product review from PMT – there was no reason to include excessive camera movement because the intention was for the viewer to focus on what Dagan's saying, what he's playing on the guitar and thus how the product we're reviewing sounds. As such, we used two cameras to film the review: one wide shot, completely static and unmanned; and another camera that was used for close-ups, still mounted on a tripod but with some simple, deliberate and complementary pans here and there. It depends on the type of video you're filming, of course – if you're giving a tour around your business premises, the camera should probably move around! But we'll discuss shooting styles and techniques appropriate for different types of videos later; as always, your first priority is to keep your viewer in mind.

<u>Sound's good</u> (as in: sound IS good!)

As a graduate of Music Technology and Production, it really does break my heart to know that the most left-out and forgotten element of most videos is sound.

When it comes to videos from small businesses in particular, most of the time I either see great visuals paired with substandard audio (clearly forgotten about or neglected through obliviousness), or bad visuals and even worse audio. The former is more common, because most of us have at least something of an eye for beauty, so we jump at the chance to improve our visuals; but we often just forget all about what our viewer will be listening to. Yet, as George Lucas famously said, *sound is half of the picture.*

Granted, the goalposts have been shifted with platforms like Facebook introducing the "autoplay without sound" feature back in 2016, which created a way for viewers to consume video content without any sound at all. But most videos still have a soundtrack of some description, and the most premium, high-quality videos have excellent sound.

In general, sound is more straightforward than visuals, less subject to personal taste and pretty much speaks for itself (pun intended) – speech should be loud and clear, music should be non-intrusive and complementary to the subject matter, and the video as a whole should have minimal distracting noises from the environment. Basically, use high-quality microphones and don't film near roadworks – easy!

There's a lot more to it than that, of course; we'll look at (or listen to?) sound in more detail soon. But rest assured you can improve the quality of sound in your videos with ease and very little expense.

These are just some of the elements that go into a quality video. And just in case I haven't said already … you should always aim for high quality. A premium video reflects a premium brand, and a premium brand is no less than what you should want to be.

Do all of your videos need to be highly produced films with expensive costs and heaps of your valuable time attached? Not at all. In fact, as you'll come to learn in more detail, I'd actually advise against having a "perfect" suite of beautiful, glossy videos. But your most valuable content, which offers the greatest longevity, deserves only the best. You'll get the most out of it, it will prove valuable for years to come, and your audience will thank you for it.

Consistency

Ask anyone in good physical shape how they got to look so great, and they'll tell you it didn't happen overnight. Being strong and having a healthy physique is the result of hard work, determination, genuine effort, and defining and striving towards a realistic target. If you join the gym after a period of sedentary activity (a situation most of us are familiar with), you'll see limited results at first. It seems like you're putting in a whole lot of effort for not much return. But you know deep down that, given time, your efforts will be paid back and deliver a bigger return.

The exact same is true when it comes to video marketing, and indeed all forms of marketing. It's no good making one beautiful video and leaving it there, regardless of the fact that you might've invested hefty amounts of time, effort and/or money in its creation. Even if you manage to strike a powerful emotional chord with your viewers or have shared something incredibly entertaining, there's only a slim possibility that your video will go viral. Ploughing all your resources into a single film is a short-sighted and thus poor business strategy, and will most likely leave you frustrated, unsatisfied and with a considerably lighter wallet.

A far more sensible and grown-up tactic is to play the long game. Think of the value of your video content in the long term, and think about how a *collection* of valuable, engaging, entertaining videos could easily (and probably will) become the most valuable asset in your marketing machine – as we'll discuss later.

> The folks at SimplyMeasured.com frequently praise the importance of using video consistently. In their downloadable guide *Social Video Marketing 101*, they rightly say that "video marketing is never one and done … by frequently publishing video content, you're not only giving your brand more exposure, but also increasing your opportunities to attract new followers with every video you post". They also claim that with regularity comes improvement. In your early days of creation it can be challenging and intimidating to appear on camera, but the more videos you make, the better they'll become; it's as simple as that. You can get the full guide for free, plus many more high-value marketing resources, at SimplyMeasured.com.

The value of video content grows exponentially – the more videos you make, the more content you have to repurpose again and again, and the greater the perceived value of your brand as a whole. Dominic Hodgson and I know this better than most, after creating video and audio content for his two businesses – Pack Leader Dog Adventures and Grow Your Pet Business Fast – since 2014. We set the bar high right from the start, filming high-quality content underpinned by a solid marketing strategy. Thanks to our ever-growing archive of media, we've proudly revisited and repurposed footage originally filmed years before, finding new and improved uses for it, and continue to do so. Perhaps one of the most valuable long-standing series of content we've made (so far) is Dom's podcast, "The Superhero Dog Owner's Show", which had a total of 55 episodes regularly uploaded over an entire year. Fans of the show had new episodes to look forward to on a weekly basis, just like their favourite TV shows or YouTube channels. That video podcast has since ended and we've moved on to new things, but crucially the content is still there, available for both new and existing prospects and clients to consume, and all the video clips that helped create it are just a few clicks away from being reused in future projects. You can check out "The Superhero Dog Owner's Show" at **artifactmedia.co.uk/resources**.

Giving yourself a regular upload schedule to stick to can help keep your video marketing efforts consistent. How often you upload will depend on the type of videos you're creating – for example, many businesses happily and easily post quick updates on simple topics daily, often through the use of live broadcasts on Facebook or short-and-sweet updates on Instagram or Snapchat. If you're making a more in-depth series on one of your services, however, or you're addressing a larger issue requiring a longer, more detailed video, it will probably be more sensible to upload less frequently, perhaps once per week. This is entirely your decision to make, and varies between marketers depending on their technical proficiency and other commitments in their schedules. You'll have a better idea of the various types of video content you should be utilising after Chapter Nine, and can then plan accordingly.

Maintaining a good level of consistency applies not only to the quantity of videos you share, but the quality too. Quick-and-dirty, spontaneously shot videos offer the most convenience and so they're usually the easiest types of films to film and share. But no matter whether you're filming a highly valuable training series with the help of a videographer, or you're simply throwing a quick clip onto Instagram, you should maintain a consistent level of quality throughout your content. Once again, it's about managing your audience's expectations of you and your business – the last thing you want to do is send mixed messages about the quality of your products and services by having them be associated with poor content.

Consistency matters a great deal to your audience, whether they're consciously aware of it or not, and it extends beyond how your videos look and sound – it applies just as much to your message. Once again, Simon Sinek emphasises the importance of a consistent message in his book *Start With Why*. People are drawn to certain companies and individuals not purely because of the merits of their products or services; consumers consistently buy from particular brands because they share the same values and beliefs and feel a deeper sense of connection with them. The companies speak about these principles in all of their marketing, proudly displaying them front and centre, loud and proud. They stand for *something*, which is a whole lot better than blending in with the vast majority of businesses, who are trying to be "professional", but stand for very little. All of the successful brands' communications are on-message, singing from the same hymn sheet, keeping a consistent theme so that viewers know exactly what they're all about.

In his book *24 Assets*, Daniel Priestley speaks about the importance of brands communicating their philosophy consistently. Companies with strong values gain more loyal customers, he claims, which makes sense given what we already know about the Know, Like, Trust process. He cites Virgin as the perfect example of a brand with a clearly defined philosophy that is communicated consistently, even with their endeavours ranging from banking to space exploration. Most of us also clearly remember Microsoft's enduring mission statement of aiming to put a PC on the desks of every office and every home in America. Both of these businesses were clear and consistent with their message, communicating it at every opportunity. What's your philosophy, and have you communicated it clearly with the world?

Identify the three or four things you feel strongest about in your industry or niche. The things you really believe in – your "gut feelings". Talk about them all the time in your videos, keeping the message consistent.

Look at Phillip Alexander as an excellent example – a Savile Row-registered tailor based in Wilmslow, that I first filmed with in 2016. Owner John Homoky believes: "We don't make wonderful suits. We make suits to make people feel wonderful, which is quite different." This beautifully eloquent message is at the very core of his values, and it's one that he's rightly proud of. His son Alex also shares this view, and so the message is clear and consistent in both of their respective interviews. For a real lesson in how to put your message at the forefront of your marketing, watch the short film we made at **artifactmedia.co.uk/resources**.

Engaging and valuable content

I was never a fan of maths at school, but I invented this formula to demonstrate the relationship between different elements of your videos:

Difficulty of retaining attention = duration of video x complexity of content

It's hardly a perfect, elegant equation … but it makes sense when you think about it, doesn't it? Essentially, your audience will be more likely to switch off if your video is too much, too soon.

For example, if your one and only video is a 30-minute in-depth explainer on the intricate workings of your service, you'll probably be disappointed at its view count, no matter how brilliant it is. The harsh truth is no one cares enough to give you half an hour of their time … not yet, anyway. Never mind the fact that we're all super-busy these days – remember that thousands of other businesses are fighting for the attention of your prospective customer, too.

As such, you need to start smaller and provide your audience with engaging, valuable content that's *easy to consume*. It needs to be stuff that they can digest quickly and easily, but that still addresses whatever problem they're experiencing that you can help them solve, even if only to a minor degree right now. There is definitely a place for longer, more detailed films – after all, the people who *really* get behind your brand will want as much content as they can feast their eyes on. But you simply can't expect a fresh-faced prospect – a complete stranger – to spare a significant amount of their time or attention the minute they happen upon your business. In Chapter Nine, you'll learn how to create videos for all your prospects, no matter where they are in their individual buyer's journey or how familiar they are with you and your brand.

A great example of this unsurprisingly features our friend Dom again. In 2016 we launched a series of super-short videos designed specifically for Facebook and targeted primarily at new prospects, called "20 Second Dog Training". Everything you need to know is in the name, really. Check out the example at **artifactmedia.co.uk/resources** – the view and share counts (the two metrics we were looking to get nice and high) were ace considering Dom didn't put a penny behind this series (which was on his personal profile, not his business page). This series of super-short, high-value videos proved to be a great tool for:

- raising the profile of Dom and his personality
- providing legitimacy to his dog-walking business
- proving that his knowledge and expertise works (he's clearly got the full and undivided attention of no fewer than six energetic dogs, after all!)
- showing that he has genuine, good intentions to help others by providing them with useful information and guidance.

The other interesting thing to note is the subtitle of this one particular video: "Why You DON'T Need to Be a Dog Whisperer". What Dom's done here is very clever – he's polarising his audience from the get-go. He's doing anything but sitting on the fence by making his position and opinion on the subject matter very clear. Having filmed a few folks in the pet industry, I can tell you that "dog whisperers" like the infamous Cesar Millan remain popular among a percentage of the general public, but are largely viewed with contempt by those in the professional dog world (I've been told they're "full of shit"). Thus, Dom's challenge of the status quo is bound to catch a few people off-guard, force them to question his claims and statements, and ultimately spark their intrigue.

Polarisation is another big subject best saved for another book, but the key take-away is that, as Dom says: if you don't stand for something, you don't stand for nothing. If you sit on the fence and remain all goodie-two-shoes, you're at risk of blending in with everyone else, and filtering away into the abyss of boring blandness. But if you share what you really think and give your viewers something to remember you by, you'll push some people away for sure, but you'll simultaneously attract more of the people who feel the same way. So don't be afraid to tell it how you think it is.

A purposeful message

One of my favourite quotes when it comes to business and marketing is from Theodore Levitt: " *People don't want quarter-inch drill bits; they want quarter-inch holes.* "

He means that when you go to a DIY store, you don't *really* want to buy a quarter-inch drill bit. You want the end result that it gives – a quarter-inch hole in your wall. But as copywriter and small business growth guru extraordinaire, Vicky Fraser, says: it goes even further than that, as you don't *really* want a quarter-inch hole in your wall, do you? You want to be able to hang up that nice picture frame of you and your kids, or of a holiday you and your partner went on. You don't even really want to do that either – you want to cherish a memory, to make your house a home. It's a very simple concept, but when I first heard it I realised I hadn't been looking at business this way at all; it was (cliché alert!) a game-changer.

Presumably, your business operates in the same way. Dom doesn't *just* walk his clients' dogs, for example. He relieves his clients of the stress, headaches and guilt that come as a result of their pooch being locked in the house all day by providing it with an outlet for its energy and curiosity, while keeping it safe, stimulated and happy. Your videos need to show *how* your product or service helps fix a particular problem, frustration or pain point. You might think that you do this already, but if you're reading this book, the harsh truth is that you probably talk about *your* business, *your* services and why *you* are so great, rather than thinking of it from the customer's perspective. Vicky Fraser calls this "we'ing all over your marketing", and she's one of the only legitimate experts on the specific subject of making your business stand out. Her book *Business for Superheroes* is a must-read, particularly if you're fairly new to entrepreneurship, and her daily emails are excellent – head to vickyfraser.com to get both.

The worst examples of marketing that just shouts "me, me, me" usually come, for some reason, from the bigger corporates. I once saw two video ads on Facebook in the space of an hour that couldn't have demonstrated this more clearly. One was from a massive UK bank, and had a lady speaking directly to camera in front of a coloured background. Technically speaking the video was fine – she was clearly well-lit, the video itself was high quality and the sound was spot on. But all she did for 40 seconds was reel off a list of things she'd done, how well her business was going and how with the help of the bank she would "continue to find success". There was neither an inferred nor an explicit incentive for me to take any action whatsoever. In fact, the video gave me no reason why I should care at all about this girl or her brand. It did not have a clear or purposeful message – not one deserving of any viewer's attention, at least. The icing on the cake was the fluffy, clichéd and uninspiring caption of the video: "Don't follow your dreams, chase them."

The other, better ad was from car manufacturer Land Rover. Rather than being your typical highly produced TV ad for their latest model, this short video demonstrated some of the features of one of their 4x4 vehicles that many of their customers probably wouldn't know about or have much experience with, such as the ability for the vehicle to detect how deep it's immersed in water and display the information on the dashboard – handy when there's a lake (or maybe just a big puddle) to cross. An expert ambassador of the brand gave two customers a real-time demonstration of and guide to these features while several cameras captured the whole thing. We also heard from the customers directly, who praised the brand for giving them the ability to use their vehicle in a whole new way that they weren't aware was even possible. The *Dragon Challenge* series took this even further by challenging a Range Rover Sport to ascend the 999 steps of Heaven's Gate on Tianmen Mountain, China. Like our quarter-inch drill bits analogy, though, the purpose of both of these videos isn't just to make viewers more aware of the vehicles' functions – they're designed to instil the utmost confidence and a sense of awe in the product. Whether you own a car made by this manufacturer or not, you're left thinking that there must be very few driving situations that it would have difficulty dealing with. Range Rover offer a premium product with a price tag to match, and drivers of their vehicles do so with pride. Films like these keep them safe in the knowledge that they're driving some of the most capable vehicles on the road. See it for yourself at **artifactmedia.co.uk/resources.**

The lesson is this: talking solely about you, your business, your achievements or (god forbid) your problems will do nothing other than alienate your audience, or, worse, rile them up. So, instead, think about how you could entertain, engage, inspire or otherwise provide value to your viewers.

A clear call to action

Unless you love spending time and money on making videos just for the sake of it, there's no reason why you shouldn't ask your customers to do something else once they've finished watching. This extends from the fact that your videos need to have a specific function or purpose in mind; you need to define clearly what your customers can and should do next. This could be as explicit as asking them to make a purchase, or it could be more inferred and subtle – perhaps "click here to learn more" or "if you liked this, you'll also like this …"

As we discussed in Chapter One, a lot of people feel some degree of resistance to this because it can feel quite awkward to ask someone to take action. But if you don't, you run the risk of your viewer simply walking away and forgetting you even existed in the first place.

Naturally, your call to action is a precursor to the type of result you're aiming to get from your video. We'll talk about this a little later, but usually there'll be one or two primary objectives for each of your videos, such as view count, shares, comments or more specific viewer actions, like clicking through to a page on your website, referring a friend or making a purchase. I'll say it again – don't feel bad about asking your audience to do something! Many of them will simply be unaware of your other offerings. When I first shared a post on Facebook about writing this very book, I had several comments from people expressing their interest, surprise and delight that it was on the way; I completely forgot that the only people I'd told up to that point were either in my immediate family or subscribed to my emails!

It's your obligation as a business owner to provide for your customers so that you can provide for yourself. Try not to come across as desperate – just spell it out for them as plainly and simply as you can.

Chapter summary

So … those are your ingredients to cook up some tasty videos. It's easy to feel overwhelmed at this stage and wonder how you can possibly tick all those boxes for each and every video you create from now on. But don't get hung-up on striving for perfection – done is better than perfect, and, like anything, it will get much easier with practice.

Once again, for some inspiration and examples of businesses, brands and individuals who are making the most of effective, strategised video content that fits this recipe, head to **artifactmedia.co.uk/resources**.

Action steps

1. Go to artifactmedia.co.uk/join and download the five-step cheap sheet.

As well as enhancing your video marketing even further, this short but highly valuable document will help you in the areas of consistency and calls to action.

2. Find an example of a video that has all the ingredients of the video excellence recipe.

On occasion you've undoubtedly found yourself struck with awe after watching a truly remarkable video. Maybe you've also been green with envy because it came from one of your competitors. Take note of how the creators ticked all the boxes in our recipe to make their film effective, and think about how you might do the same.

Chapter Six

How to be awesome on camera

I'm going to share with you some techniques and tips that will help you appear more confident, purposeful and assertive in your videos, even if you'd rather be scrubbing dishes than staring down the big scary lens. You should still read this chapter if you're perfectly confident in sticking your face in front of a camera, because putting these tips into action will make you even better.

And if you've been wondering, "Do I even need to be in my own videos?", well … in my honest, humble and correct opinion – yes, you do. If you employ staff, you could get them to be the stars instead. Or you could hire in some professional actors to take your place. But to do so is to hide away in the cupboard under the stairs like a frightened Harry Potter. Why shy away from being front and centre of your business's marketing when you played a part in building the damn thing? Why not be completely transparent with your audience instead of using replaceable avatars?

> I made a video course with the same title as this chapter which you can get my going to **artifactmediaco.uk/guides**. But don't forget – there's a special offer reserved for readers of this book, which you'll find out about after chapter eleven.

Take it from a guy who's always nervous

I know that for some, speaking on camera is about as daunting as it comes. I've met dozens of people who are happy enough to speak about the subject in which they're an expert to a packed lecture hall; but ask them to do the same thing on camera, and they'll crumble into a sweaty mess. It's a curious thing, but it's definitely something that I can empathise with.

Despite playing to big crowds of people as a guitarist in a rock band as a teenager, I've always had issues with self-confidence. In many ways, I genuinely don't mind what people think of me and I don't pay much attention to how I look, but I definitely ponder and worry about things like making a bad first impression, upsetting or offending someone, or doing/saying anything that might result in conflict or disagreement.

I was very shy and reserved until I made the decision to go to a university several hundred miles from home, where I knew I'd have to push myself to speak up and make new friends, or I would face a very lonely and depressing three years. Looking back, it's clear that my current level of confidence is worlds apart from what it was at university. While these social worries aren't as much of a concern these days (purely the result of two factors that you'll learn in a second), as I write this book I've not long since accepted having a form of clinical anxiety that I'll probably never completely get rid of, to the point where at its worst, it reveals itself in physical symptoms. Those heart palpitations and clammy hands I felt when meeting new people in Derby make a lot of sense in hindsight.

This might be surprising if you've met me in person, seen me in videos, or perhaps even been at a presentation I've delivered; I don't show many outward signs of being nervous or uneasy or of lacking in confidence. Because I'm not, really. Sure, there are points when I realise I've rambled on a bit, or perhaps haven't put a point across as eloquently as I'd like, and I think, *Damn. What now? Argh. I'm on camera / in front of people! Panic!* But they're usually nothing more than fleeting moments, and I'll happily appear on camera just about any time, anywhere, with little to no preparation beforehand.

So how did I go from *Scared Little Alex – the Shy Boy Far from Home* to *Big 'n' Proud Alex – the Video Guy*? Easy:

1. By accepting that even if I royally screw up on camera (or indeed any social situation), it won't mean the end of the world. Nothing truly terrible will happen, really.
2. Practice.

Comedian Ross Noble (of whom I'm a big fan, being a fellow Geordie) famously improvises just about every part of his stand-up show. When I saw him live at Newcastle City Hall, he made the fact that he'd seen the same group of lads attending three of his gigs in a row an integral part of his performance. He must have pulled 50 jokes out of this one occurrence, and certainly couldn't have delivered the same hilarious one-liners at any other performance on his nationwide tour. While I'm sure he prepares his material to some extent, the crux of his act (and what makes it so unique) is that he's the king of keeping cool and making it up as he goes along. He's completely at ease with the possibility of things going wrong because – somewhat ironically – the more confident he is, the less likely it is that something bad will happen.

While I'm not saying that you should necessarily throw all caution to the wind by hitting record and just hoping it'll all be fine, there's a lot to be learnt from Noble's technique. Really – what IS the worst that can happen? With video, if something does go wrong you can usually just do it again – have another go. Learn from what happened, and try again. And even if you're broadcasting live, how important is it to be 100% flawless? I'll tell you one thing – to be perfect isn't to be very "human".

Of course, you still need to be careful and not be completely reckless or ill-prepared. We've all seen videos where the presenter is clearly being a little too spontaneous and fails to create something with real meaning or value due to their stumbling around and apparent lack of direction or focus. But by far and away my biggest pet peeve when it comes to "talking head" videos is seeing someone blatantly reading from a script. I think autocues are horrendous things and should only be used by newsreaders, who might as well be robots anyway. Striving for "perfection" in your performance will only lead to two things:

1. Frustration, because nothing is or ever will be perfect
2. At best, a boring, robotic, uncreative video that very few people will be interested in or take value from

So keep it cool, sunshine. Go with the flow and don't give yourself the unnecessary pressure of reading your scripts verbatim.

I would argue that this applies to videos made for big corporates, despite the fact that in my experience, the marketing managers of these companies usually insist that videos are 100% scripted. In fact, if anything, being more human and less scripted is more important in Corporateland than anywhere else, because 99% of films made for these companies are exactly the same – emotionless, dull, uninteresting. I was once asked to hold up a dog-eared sheet of A4 covered in scribbles and strikethroughs for a lady who insisted that she needed to read her script word for word because she wouldn't be able to think on the spot.

I find this hard to accept. This lady suggested that she couldn't talk confidently about her industry to a camera, yet presumably as the CEO of a firm she would have had countless conversations with other human beings about topics similar to that of the video we were trying to film, relating to her business. I can only presume that at every juncture, she must have used scripts then, too.

I understand that staring down the lens while the red light flashes can be daunting and unnerving. But the sooner you treat speaking to the camera like speaking to another person, the quicker you'll be creating videos that people actually pay attention to and engage with.

By keeping the filming process unfixed and open to certain degrees of variation, you grant yourself the opportunity to deliver your best performance possible. On countless occasions, the person I'm filming on a production will start with a very good idea of what they need to say and how they're going to say it. Others will have an actual written script close by, or memorised in their heads. But during the course of filming a few takes, they identify expressions to rephrase and words to swap out based on how the whole thing flows; your script might read great on paper, but you'll likely find that a direct conversion to the spoken word results in some unnatural-sounding sections, or certain parts may cause you to trip up on your words. If, on the spot, you come up with something that flows a bit better, you'll deliver a more real and human performance, as opposed to producing something wooden and super-scripted that could have been delivered by absolutely anyone. A more human performance allows your viewers to get to know the real you and, as a result, to find out whether they're aligned with your specific personality and values.

Kick the habit

Not long after graduating, I was offered the chance to head back to Derby twice a week to be an associate lecturer on the course I'd studied – Music Technology and Production. I ran tutorial groups and recording-studio sessions, and at the end of the semester each student was required to deliver a 10-minute presentation on their coursework, receiving immediate feedback from me. Both the presentation and my feedback were audio-recorded … and let me tell you, listening back to it was a real ear-opener.

It seemed like every other word from me was "errm", "uhhm" or "like" (the hallmark of any northerner). I remembered my English Language teacher in sixth form calling these *filler words* – meaningless utterances "interjected when the speaker is groping for words or at a loss for the next thought", as eloquently defined by ThoughtCo.com (https://www.thoughtco.com/what-is-a-filler-word-1690859). Clearly my discomfort and unease at being responsible for both praising and criticising the efforts of all these students had made itself verbally apparent – my anxiety was obvious. Did anyone else notice these not-so-subtle hints that the ginger bloke with the northern accent wasn't feeling 100% comfortable in his situation? Probably not as much as myself. But it was definitely "a thing", so from that day on I vowed to put an end to bad speaking habits.

The next week, during the subsequent group's presentations, I concentrated much harder. I was still mindful of the task at hand, but tried to assign a decent proportion of my brainpower to speaking with more fluidity and eloquence. In between sentences, my mouth opened to give a big long "errrrrrrm" to fill the gap, but I resisted the urge, replacing it with prolonged, lingering, haunting, persistent, godawful … *silence.*

After what seemed like an eternity, the next few words came, and this cycle was repeated until all the feedback was given. As soon as the final student left the room to head off for their next lecture, I hastily shoved my earphones in and listened back to what had just been recorded. Just how many seconds did that tense, awkward silence last? How cringeworthy was it?

Not at all, actually.

There was silence, but it didn't go on forever. In fact, the whole thing sounded smoother and less rushed, and certainly suggested greater confidence and authority on my behalf. At the core I was still far from fully relaxed, but the effort to eliminate silly little filler words had a profound effect on the outside. Not only did I immediately appear more self-assured with this more purposeful and deliberate use of language, but the students benefited from more accurate feedback that was delivered much more fluently. Win, win.

This is just one example of how you can improve your speaking to camera relatively easily. Take your time, slow things down and listen not only to what you're saying but *how* you're saying it. I've filmed people who haven't done much video stuff before and nail it straight away, and others who need much more guidance to deliver their best performance. You're probably somewhere in between, but even the most seasoned vloggers and TED Talk speakers make the effort to stop, watch, listen and evaluate themselves, always striving to improve.

By the same token, though, as we've said already, never strive for 100% perfection. Aiming for flawlessness will take you two steps back, as it costs you more time and effort (and thus probably money too). If you make a few mistakes, by all means have another go. But if you've spent all afternoon failing to deliver a perfect one-minute explainer video, it's probably time to lower your criteria. And anyway, what kind of viewer only wants to see perfect videos delivered by perfect people? The fluffy ol' cliché says *your imperfections make you perfect*, and despite feeling a bit nauseous saying that, I have to agree – showing your audience that you *do* have flaws, you *do* get things wrong sometimes and you *are* willing to carry on regardless only strengthens your image by letting them see that you're a real person. I'd much rather watch Jeremy Clarkson mess something up on live TV and make a joke out of it than endure the usual robotic dreariness of a perfectly rehearsed autocue-reading news anchor.

Done is better than perfect.

Be confident from the start

Kiwi pop star Lorde, whose beyond-just-a-bit-catchy single "Royals" exploded onto the music scene in 2013, is someone who radiates confidence and presence. Despite being one of the youngest musicians out there and a self-professed "weird little screwball" (she's even got her own South Park caricature), on stage she completely lets go and delivers a super-cool, captivating performance full of frenetic, wild dance moves. Thing is, though, it's all a façade … to an extent.

She apparently suffers "crippling" fear before her shows – little wonder when you've only been in the music business five minutes yet are sharing stages with the likes of Green Day and blink-182. But is this anxiety at all obvious? No way. Maybe deep down she *is* worried about delivering a substandard show, but she gives her viewers and fans no outward reason to believe she's anything less than 100% confident.

Unsurprisingly, this is a brilliant lesson for you to take notes from. Appearing in any kind of video – whether it's a 30-second selfie clip or a full-blown documentary on your business – means putting on a performance. Performing means putting on at least something of a show – an example of what you can do, an insight into what you're all about, a demonstration of your abilities and skills. To do yourself and your business justice, you need to execute this performance as best you can, and you'll only do that if you carry with you an aura of confidence and self-assurance.

Once again, if we bear in mind the principle of " *what your audience sees is what they think they'll get*", it's safe to say that a video featuring a less-than-confident presenter who doesn't show much conviction in the words coming out of their mouth isn't going to inspire many viewers. After all, if you're not confident in the very thing you're talking about, how can you expect cold leads to become raving fans and customers?

An assertive nature isn't something that can be created overnight – it takes time and practice to build up your confidence. But what you can do immediately is try to *appear* a little more authoritative, from the very start of the next video you shoot. Keep your viewer in mind while you're filming and imagine what they might be thinking as you enact your performance. Do you look and sound like someone who truly knows their industry and empathises with the viewers' wants, needs and problems like a genuine expert? Because the harsh truth is that anything less than that isn't going to convince many people that they should give you their time of day.

Your "script" – as structured or spur-of-the-moment as it is – is very important. The words and phrases you choose combined with *how* you say them has a massive impact on how you're perceived by the viewer. But to state the obvious, paying attention to the way you look is imperative in making effective videos, too. This one shouldn't need much explaining – if you look neat and tidy and are dressed well, you'll convey a different level of gravitas than you will if you look like you haven't made much effort. How much you should consider your appearance will depend on your industry. In Corporateland, the standard is suits and ties all day long (although there's nothing to stop you being a bit different). But in the world of fitness, a personal trainer who wears a tailored suit in his videos would be swiftly tagged as a bit strange.

I learnt a lot about the art of looking good when filming for Phillip Alexander, a Savile Row tailor based in Cheshire. The sharply dressed experts there told me (and the camera) about the importance of looking beautiful, and how a gentleman in a handmade suit designed for him and him alone will almost certainly command more gravitas than a bloke who's picked up a cheap selection off the peg. One of my favourite quotes from that shoot was: "We don't make wonderful suits for people. We make suits to make people feel wonderful."

Check out the quite frankly gorgeous videos we made at **artifactmedia.co.uk/resources**.

Regardless of whether you feel the need to fix up and look sharp or tone it down and keep it casual, just remember that with video, it's the combination of many elements that determine whether a viewer sees you as "the real deal" or an amateur, and just like in the "real world", you only get one chance at a first impression.

Amplify your persona

We've said already that you should be yourself in your videos and put your defining qualities, imperfections and values front and centre. But there's a lot to be said for amplifying your current persona, or adopting an entirely new one.

Ella Yelich-O'Connor *becomes* Lorde when she goes on stage. She pulls weird faces, stares out audience members and pulls some quirky dance moves. Jeremy Clarkson *becomes* the politically incorrect, controversial exaggerated version of himself when he's presenting *The Grand Tour*. Vincent Furnier dons thick eyeliner and a look of evil intent to become rock star Alice Cooper. Are these entertainers anything like their on-stage personas in "real life"? Probably to an extent, but not as much as their performances might suggest. Celebrities and influencers amplify the quirks and oddities of their personas in order to stand out from the crowd and provide truly unique content for viewers to either love or loathe.

You could do something similar, and take it to any extreme you like. You could literally invent a character for yourself, in the way that Leigh Francis created Keith Lemon, who started as just one small part of the sketch show *Bo' Selecta!* before going on to have several of his own TV shows and make many guest appearances elsewhere. If you're unfamiliar, Keith is a fictional ex-businessman with lavish fake tan and eye-catching combo of blonde hair and ginger moustache. Other than his loud visual appearance, his defining traits include an unrestrained Yorkshire accent and the ability to turn pretty much anything into an innuendo. He's perfect for prime-time comedy TV … maybe not a great ambassador for your business, though.

Of course, this is taking it to the extreme for the purposes of entertainment, and only a few marketers take the plunge to do something similar. *Adopting* a persona, while fun and almost certain to intrigue many viewers, requires a lot of effort and prior planning. You'll need to don your Hollywood Actor cap and immerse yourself in the mindset of your invented character whenever the camera is switched on. You'll need to create mannerisms, quirks and one-liners that are congruent not only with each other, but also with the industry to which you're trying to appeal. You'll need to be entertaining yet informative and appropriate; it's a delicate process.

So if, when it comes to marketing you and your business, you think a Keith Lemon-esque personality might be a bit too much or downright inappropriate, you could consider *amplifying* your persona instead. This is where you identify some of your own defining characteristics and simply turn them up a few notches when you're in front of the camera. I've filmed two people in particular who are excellent examples of this.

The first is Dagan, who you know well by now – Product Demonstrator and Guitar Expert for Professional Music Technology. As many of his YouTube comments suggest, he and Russell Brand were seemingly separated at birth; aside from their similar appearances, Dagan's flamboyant and somewhat theatrical performance in his gear review videos can definitely be compared to the British comedian's unapologetically flashy personality. Some of the keyboard warriors of the internet have suggested that his energetic nature must be the result of copious amounts of caffeine (or even harder substances) being consumed before filming, or that while filming is taking place he may desperately need to use the lavatory. "Haters gonna hate" … But while Dagan does receive criticism for his antics, praise and admiration come in equal measure.

This amplification of personality not only makes for a more interesting, engaging and spirited performance, but also serves as a polarisation tool – some people love Dagan's immense enthusiasm and animated guitar playing, others just don't. As we've said already, in the pursuit of creating remarkable content, some people will declare that they're not fans; however, this is to be expected and should actually be welcomed, as it means you're standing out from the vanilla crowd at the very least. In any case, the people who voice their negative opinions are also unlikely to be a good fit for your business as customers or clients.

Being in a PMT store and chatting with the Crew Members is a very casual and informal experience, yet still with an air of professionalism. Most of the guys and girls who work there sport jeans, tattoos and piercings. They'll happily bring down any guitar off the wall and let you give it a try, even if it's a £4,000 Gibson Les Paul, then draw upon their expert knowledge to run you through the features of the product and suggest any appropriate alternatives. There's a down-to-earth, rock 'n' roll vibe no matter which store you visit. Despite them catering for the vast majority of musicians, there will be some people who simply don't enjoy this kind of atmosphere and would rather shop elsewhere. This "real world" concept bleeds into the online arena too – some will prefer to watch a non-talking video of someone robotically demonstrating each and every function of a music product, rather than see someone like Dagan clearly enjoying himself and throwing some humour and personality into his product review – that's fine. For those who are aligned with the values and nature of the self-professed House of Rock, stepping into a PMT store or watching a PMT video means they're in the right place, and watching the right videos.

The other example of persona amplification comes from business growth expert Jon McCulloch (proudly touted as the most expensive copywriter in Europe). Jon *is* the Evil Bald Genius. It's on his website, his emails and his (highly recommended) book *Grow Your Business Fast.* But he takes it one step further by being the EBG in person at his events. At both of the events I filmed for him in Ireland in 2017, Jon carried a certain aura and communicated with his attendees in a very particular way. He sported a tailor-made waistcoat decorated with comic-book-style drawings of female superheroes and action heroes, later telling a story about how he came to own it (and relating that story back to the subject of his presentation). At first it might seem that Jon's choice of attire for his events is fairly insignificant, but this waistcoat in particular served two purposes:

1. There's a story behind it that hooks in your mind.
2. It's polarisation in full effect, in person, literally, in physical form. It matches Jon's "no filter" personality, which is carried through in the presentation itself.

Adopting or amplifying your persona is another area where you'll have to consider the trends and conventions of your industry. The creation of a rude and lewd character like Keith Lemon probably won't go down very well in Corporateland, but it might work wonders if your business aims to appeal to the younger generations, who have little to no concern for being formal. On the other hand, look at it this way – you could become the person who becomes *known* for being ultra different in your industry, thanks to your divisive way of "showing up" to the world. One thing's for sure: it beats blending in.

Either option is definitely worth considering, particularly if you're not feeling too enthusiastic about appearing on camera. It sounds counter-intuitive at first, but pushing yourself to consciously be a bit livelier and more animated can really help break through the confidence barrier. Just remember that whether you amplify or adopt, your values still need to come first. There'd be no point inventing an elaborate character to appear in your videos, or putting heaps of effort into becoming an excellent on-camera presenter, if your authenticity was mitigated in the process. If Leigh Francis hated vulgar jokes and swear words, he wouldn't have invented Keith Lemon. If Jon McCulloch wasn't truly comfortable with the occasional politically incorrect remark, he wouldn't risk offending potentially high numbers of his viewers and event attendees. If Vincent Furnier was scared of vampires and horror movies, he wouldn't have created Alice Cooper. See what I mean?

Who are you talking to?

One of the most common mistakes I see in businesses' videos (and indeed all of their marketing material) is the way they address the audience. Most of them will deliberately and explicitly speak to a *collective* group of viewers with phrases like "you guys", "some of you" and "those of you who …". This isn't a huge blunder, but it's certainly a minor snag that ought to be corrected.

Why bother with a seemingly trivial alteration? Because acknowledging that there are several people watching undermines the individual viewer and makes them feel less special (and we all like to feel special). By affirming that you're trying to speak to as much of your target audience as possible, you're implicitly acknowledging to each person watching that to you, they're something of a commodity. They're just one piece of the puzzle, one slice of the pie, and in reality it's not specifically *them* that you want to convert into a follower, customer or client – it's lots of them, ideally.

Of course, we all *know* that companies, brands and marketers usually aren't picky about the individual components of their target markets. They're not necessarily bothered about *who* engages or buys; they just want *someone* to do it, providing they fit the target market criteria. But it's one thing to know this fact deep down, and another to market your business in a way that actually makes it painfully obvious and runs the risk of putting off potential buyers, sending them running for the hills.

Use powerful storytelling

We all love stories, whether they're written, spoken, or depicted on the screen. Providing they're compelling, intriguing and thought-provoking, we latch onto and become fully immersed in them. The best stories appeal directly to our intrinsic human endowment of imagination; they capture our curiosity, and we find ourselves craving to know the resolution, to answer the question "what happened next?" Many of us are so victim to our own curiosities that we succumb to spoiling the plots of films and TV shows for ourselves by looking up the synopsis online, long before we actually reach the end itself!

Stories are powerful, and so you can and should put them to work in your business's video content. They don't have to be akin to Hollywood levels of grandeur, scale or production value (unless you *really* want to create something special and have the appropriate amounts of time and money to invest in such a thing). The stories you tell can be as simple as recalling an event, sharing an anecdote, or drawing a comparison between the topic you're discussing and an experience you've had that was in some way similar. Incorporating an aspect of storytelling in your videos provides your viewer with something much more influential, noteworthy and memorable than an average business film. Even if that film is beautifully shot and provides genuine value to the watcher, it almost undoubtedly would have greater impact if it also told a captivating story.

More than anything, though, just like any of your videos (and indeed any of your marketing material), the stories you tell should appeal to your audience in some way. At the very least they should be entertaining and interesting, but ideally you should teach them something, offer some advice or help them fix a problem. After all, a factory owner who wants to tell the story of an average day at their premises would certainly find themselves with the opportunity to capture some wonderful footage and go into great depth as to the ins and outs of their facility, but the number of people to which it would prove valuable would likely be negligible.

Conversely, if the same factory owner told the story of how they came to run such a successful business through years of struggles and setbacks, mentioned the influential people who helped shape the company, spoke about their constant desire to fix problems their customers faced, and – all the while – capitalised on the power of video by using stellar footage tastefully edited together, then that business would soon find itself positioned in a completely different league to its competitors.

Nicola Wood's personal story was one of great difficulty. In 2017 she told it on camera at the end of our day's filming at her beauty salon, Kitui, in Sunderland. She'd battled cancer and wanted to help others who were going through similar situations themselves. Her salon underwent a transformation into specialising in treatments based around hair loss, with Nicola's own story being the foundation of the message she wished to spread; her empathy and compassion towards the people she aimed to reach was irrefutable. Posted on the Kitui Facebook page, it was shared by over 400 people completely organically. You can see it yourself at **artifactmedia.co.uk/resources**.

Lights, camera, practice

Now that you're armed with a few techniques that will instantly improve your performance on camera, it's time to get filming … right? Well, before you go all-in and start shooting your next quick "proper" video, I'd encourage you to spend some time concentrating on giving the best-possible performance by means of practice and review.

You don't have to give up hours of your valuable time, but if you want to be at your best in front of the lens, I'd recommend that you shoot a few trial runs on your camera or smartphone, and then watch them back. If the deathly silence that comes just after you hit record is a bit off-putting, put some music on to bring up the ambient sound level. You won't actually be using this practice video in your marketing, so background noise doesn't matter; if it helps you to speak louder, clearer and with more confidence, do it.

What should you say for this trial run? Well, you could talk to the imaginary viewer (singular, remember) about a problem they might be dealing with that's related to your industry, or you could start by simply explaining what you and your business do. The subject matter isn't too important at this stage; it's your on-camera performance that you're trying to hone.

When you've finished, play back the video. It's likely that, if you're new to this, you'll think it's rubbish and worthy of deletion, but don't be so hasty – you're trying to identify areas of strength and improvement respectively, so have a proper watch and ask yourself some critical questions.

- Do you appear confident?
- Is it clear that you're an expert who knows what they're talking about?
- Do you have any bad habits, like using filler words or not giving the camera eye contact?
- Is your speech engaging, or is it a bit monotonous?

Make some notes – written or mental – then have another go. Don't delete the first video. Just try exactly the same thing again after learning what you've learnt. Having paid close attention to the way you appear and articulate yourself on camera, you'll definitely do a better job the second time. Unsurprisingly, this "rinse and repeat" process is a good one to follow when it comes to shooting your *actual* videos.

More often than not, particularly with those who aren't well versed in being on camera, I find that recording a practice run first followed by the "real" take means the best performance possible is captured. The very process of saying out loud whatever it is you've got to say sets you up appropriately, like an athlete warming up before the main event. You've already done it (or at least part of it) once, so it'll be very easy to do it again, better. And anyway, if you record your practice run instead of just pretending that the camera is on, you've got two versions to choose from – another top tip.

Chapter summary

Being the centre of attention with all eyes (and lenses) on you can be a daunting affair if you haven't had much prior experience. But if an anxious ginger lad with glasses will gladly appear on camera, comfortably speaking about his business, his values and his beliefs with a good dash of polarisation thrown in, you can too. Practice never makes perfect, but in your case it will make you feel more confident and in turn a more trusted, authoritative expert in the eyes of your audience.

Action steps

1. Make a conscious effort to amplify some of your defining traits in order to make your videos more interesting.

If your performance and on-screen personality are incomparable to those of your competitors, you're on the right track.

2. Improve your on-camera performance by filming and reviewing practice videos.

Watch them back and take note of how you're delivering your material. What could you change or improve to come across as more confident and authoritative?

3. Become a captivating sharer of powerful stories.

Write down some of your own life experiences – as simple or as complex as you like – that could relate or draw a comparison to the needs, wants and problems facing your prospects.

Chapter Seven

Your roadmap to better videos – part 1: equipment

You know the ingredients for excellent videos, and you know what to avoid. You know that you need genuine passion for what you do, and you know how to appear as an expert on camera. You're well on your way to creating highly effective videos and thus positioning your business in a class of its own.

In Chapters Seven and Eight, we'll drill down into the practicalities and technicalities of creating videos that fall into the requirements of our secret recipe – films that reflect your business's **quality**, are**engaging** and **purposeful** to the viewer, and give them a clear **call to action**. Then, in Chapter Nine, you'll learn how to put it all together, building your own video content framework to give your business a properly sustainable, **consistent** marketing strategy.

Let's start with the hands-on stuff – looking at what equipment and techniques contribute to creating the most effective videos – so that you can ascertain what you and your business would benefit from having access to. No two videos are created the same, and technology's rapid evolvement means there are now countless filming equipment choices available. This chapter looks at the practical side of video creation, whether you'll be filming yourself ("in-house") or bringing in an external producer.

Naturally, much of what we'll discuss is dependent on your available budget, your time, and your skills and knowledge with regard to said technologies. I appreciate that you may or may not have the capacity to use expensive, high-grade equipment, or similarly rated production companies, or both. As such, we'll cover the full spectrum – quick, cheap and easy solutions, plus those that require more substantial investment (with results that reflect accordingly).

Video creation is as much a scientific endeavour as a creative one. Thus, tech-savvy geeks like myself will find it easier to grasp the fundamentals of filming than those who aren't as knowledgeable or interested in technology. At the same time, it's no good buying an expensive, feature-packed camera if the complex workflow that inevitably comes with it won't fit snugly into your already-busy schedule. This chapter aims to paint the most accurate picture of the many options that are available to the business owner who wants to make the most of video, delving much deeper than just tech specs and product features.

Before we dive in, let's very quickly define the video creation process from a purely practical perspective. By knowing the entire process and what's required at each stage, we can make more sense of the options available to us and thus make more informed decisions. In its simplest form, it goes like this:

Filming -> editing -> sharing

The filming stage is self-explanatory – appropriate equipment is used to capture moving images and sound. A camera creates a digital representation of an image by focusing light through a lens onto an image sensor. As this happens, a microphone captures sound.

Editing is more open to interpretation. In its most basic form, editing could just mean trimming the start and end of a recorded video clip to appropriate points, e.g. just before the presenter starts speaking, and just after they finish. Video clips can be cut – sections can be removed entirely, placed elsewhere or played back in a different order. Various video clips can be used alongside or after each other. New assets can be incorporated, such as music, sound effects, text, titles, motion graphics, still images, logos and subtitles. Or perhaps no editing is required at all.

When it's ready, the final video is shared for others to watch.

Each stage is as important as the last, and this book covers each one. With that in mind, let's look at what film-making options are available, and at the same time talk about some of the most important concepts in video creation.

Cameras

Before we start, there's an important distinction you should be aware of, if you don't know it already: a camera and a lens are two separate entities. Both may be housed within the same physical body, but they are very much independent components. One doesn't do much without the other – the camera (more specifically its image sensor) takes in light, which is then converted into a digital image that we can make sense of, but it can't do that without a lens, which focuses the light in a certain way. As you'll learn as you progress through this chapter, despite the plethora of camera models, types and classifications on the market today, it's often the lens that has the greatest influence on the final image that is produced. Thus, the ability to pick and choose from different lenses that are each best-suited to certain scenarios can prove very powerful; ultimately, choosing the right lens for the job creates a more effective video.

Smartphones

Smartphones are the easiest route into video creation, not only because you almost certainly have one already, but because it's nearly always within arm's reach. The cameras in our mobile devices have come along hugely since their introduction, and the gap between them and professional-level cameras, while still vast, is definitely shrinking; in the time between me writing this book and you reading it, some kind of visual technology will have become somewhat antiquated as a newer, more advanced one casts a threatening shadow.

The generally accepted fact of smartphone video creation is that you can indeed get great results in both the filming and editing stages, with the caveat of a few limitations along the way. The idea is that *everything* is quick and easy – all stages of the process are designed and optimised for convenience above everything else. For this to be so, some options and features need to be removed.

This is great if you just want to hit record and get a decent result in most situations. For example, at the time of writing, my iPhone produces a great image from either one of its two "main" cameras, but while I can shoot awesome 4K and even super-slow-motion footage, I don't have access to many features available on dedicated video cameras, such as shutter speed and white balance – they're locked away and automatically dialled in by the phone's software. There's also no option to change the "look" of the image; the colour and contrast are set in stone. Even with the ability to tweak these parameters in an editing app afterwards, the degree to which you can do so is limited (a point more obviously demonstrated when comparing smartphones to larger cameras, as we'll discuss shortly). These settings affect the image to a huge degree, so if I was adamant that a very specific look had to be achieved, then the stripped-back smartphone wouldn't be the most appropriate equipment to use. However, if I just wanted to shoot a quick and easy video for my Instagram Story (which by default will expire in 24 hours and be gone forever anyway), then it'll do the job just fine.

One way to get around this (to an extent) is by using a third-party camera app like FiLMiC Pro, which opens up many of the features that are hidden by your phone's standard camera app. The advantages granted by apps like this are plentiful, and are well worth checking out if you want an advanced set of filming tools coupled with the convenience and speed of a smartphone.

To get the most out of a smartphone camera, many third-party accessories can be used to increase your videos' production value. Lenses like those from Moment or olloclip can be attached to your device to completely change the look of your films. Wide-angle lenses capture a broader field of view; telephoto lenses bring distant objects closer; and macro lenses let you get physically closer to your subject while keeping a sharp, focused image. Stabilisers like the DJI Osmo Mobile do a good job of eliminating shaky, unstable footage; you can walk or even run with your phone and still get beautifully smooth, gliding shots. Microphones can increase sound quality tremendously, and can be attached just as easily as lenses. The RØDE smartLav+ allows speech to be captured much more accurately and produces close, rich, detailed and professional audio, while being super-affordable. Out of the thousands of pounds worth of video equipment I've invested in, it's one of my favourites – so much so that it has its own module in my video course *Effective Video Fundamentals*, which you can get by going to **artifactmedia.co.uk/guides**.

The convenience of smartphones doesn't end when you stop recording – they also serve as worthy video editors. There's no need to copy or move the footage you've recorded onto a computer – just edit on the phone itself, straight away. Once again, though, it doesn't take long to come across limitations, and while for many the editing features and capabilities of smartphones will suffice for the most part, the end results pale in comparison to what's possible with a computer and a more sophisticated editing program.

The cherry on top is the fact that using a smartphone is undoubtedly the quickest way to get your videos online. Once again, there's no need to move your films to another piece of technology – just hit Share and watch your video upload directly to your platform of choice.

Smartphone pros:

+ Quick, easy and convenient to use
+ Can increase production value easily with additional equipment
+ Immediate editing
+ Instant access to video-sharing platforms – get your videos online fast

Smartphone cons:

- Only basic filming functions available
- Limited visual competency (it's easy to tell the difference between smartphone-filmed video and that of a higher-grade camera)
- Battery life and memory can quickly run short

Compact cameras

With smartphone cameras now being so capable, you might question the need for a "point and shoot" camera. Indeed, with both devices you'll get a very similar feature set, especially if you opt for one of the aforementioned third-party camera apps. But a modern, mid-priced compact will boast several big advantages, the most notable being its superior and larger image sensor – the business end of the camera. This is the digital equivalent of film, upon which light falls after it is focused through a lens.

As you'd expect, the sensor of a smartphone's camera needs to be tiny for it to fit inside such a sleek shell – somewhere around 18mm^2 on average. The sizes of sensors in compacts average at about *18 times larger* than that. Okay, so it's bigger … so what? Well, in the same way that a bigger sponge absorbs more water, a larger sensor absorbs more light. Light is food for cameras and, generally speaking, the more you can give it, the better.

It all gets very technical very quickly, but you only need to know of a few key benefits that come with using a camera with a larger sensor, and thus why you might consider opting for a mid-range compact to film with instead of your smartphone:

1) Overall quality

The larger the sensor, the better the image … usually. And before you say, *"But my iPhone shoots 4K – won't that look the same as a compact that shoots 4K?"* , remember back to what we discussed earlier – resolution is just the *physical measurement* of an image. 4K is just a size; it doesn't denote quality, necessarily. Whereas a smartphone is designed to be a Swiss army knife capable of performing many different tasks, from filming videos to booking an Uber, a compact camera from a reputable brand is designed to do just one. As such, the technology and sophistication of its image sensor will almost certainly eclipse the device in your pocket. The images from the two cameras might contain the same amount of pixels, but that doesn't mean the images will be identical; you'll probably find that that of the compact will "just look better".

2) Depth of field

As we discussed earlier, a shallow depth of field means beautiful, blurry backgrounds – perfect for portraits and product close-ups, and a sure-fire way of making any footage of people "pop" with a premium shine. Just like effective videos themselves, there's a recipe for this arty look, which goes like this:

Larger camera sensor + *longer* lens + *closer* subject + *further* background

It's nigh on impossible to attain this look using a smartphone camera, because the sensor is so small and the focal length of the lens is too short (it's not "zoomed in" enough). Granted, there are digital emulations available on many smartphone cameras, which do a wonderful job of *simulating* a shallow depth of field, but as they're only emulations, they don't quite have the same beautiful characteristics as the real thing.

Take a compact camera, use the lens to zoom in on a subject, get as close as you can to the subject while retaining focus on it, and have your background as far away as possible, and you'll see a huge difference to the standard image coming from a smartphone camera. The subject will stay sharp while the background spills off into an attractive blur. This could be one of your physical products on a table, which you pull closer to the camera and away from the background of the shelves in your store. Or it could be your lovely face filling the frame, against the picturesque background of your local park.

Whatever the combination, you'll immediately see this effect in action by following the formula above, but *only* if you use a camera with a larger sensor – a compact pretty much being the minimum requirement.

And, aside from it "just looking good", why would you want to achieve this look? Having a shallow depth of field and as few focal points as possible (one is ideal) draws the viewer's eye to the part of the image that you really want them to focus on. It's rare that you'll want them to pay attention to each and every element making up your frame – even when capturing complex landscapes, there are usually one or two significant components that photographers and videographers want the viewer to focus on. Isolating the most important part of your image in this way is almost like physically pulling the viewer closer to what they're looking at, ignoring everything else and being as immersed in the experience as possible.

3) Low-light performance

Do you know why telescopes are so ridiculously huge? Because the night sky is so dark, and distant stars are so incredibly dim, that our naked eyes can't make them out even if there's no light pollution fogging up the atmosphere. Telescopes, with surface areas many times larger than our eyes, collect and focus the light down through the eyepiece so that we mere humans can see the unseeable.

Cameras work under the same principles. As mentioned above, a smartphone camera's miniscule sensor will only be able to absorb a relatively small amount of light, thus it won't be able to film a decent image in dim or dark conditions (if you've ever tried to show the world what you're about to have for dinner at a restaurant, you'll know exactly what I mean). But use a compact or other larger-sensor camera in the same scenario and you'll be able to record a much cleaner, less noisy image because the sensor is physically collecting much more light. This won't be a huge benefit unless you find yourself filming in dim conditions often, but the benefits of a compact's ability to take in more light usually extend to a cleaner image than that of a smartphone, regardless of lighting conditions.

Most compacts will also open up many of the settings and features that are locked away from your smartphone's default camera, like shutter speed, aperture and white balance. Of course, to get the best results, you'll need to be familiar with what these mean and how they affect your image, which is a topic for a different book … but if you take the time to learn and master them, you grant yourself the ability to really dial in the look you desire, in any situation, ultimately equating to far superior video.

The same or similar accessories that aim to increase the production value of smartphone videos are also available for compacts (and larger cameras). In fact, there are some that can be used in tandem for maximum benefit – for example, you could use a compact to attain higher-quality visuals, but use the aforementioned RØDE smartLav+ connected to a smartphone to record crystal-clear audio of your presenter speaking.

Compact cameras are absolutely worth considering – they're capable, practical and, all things considered, very inexpensive. But don't just take my word for it – at **artifactmedia.co.uk/resources**, you can see just how proficient a mid-range £500-ish model is. For a while, I actually used a Sony compact as a second camera for many shoots, and was so impressed with its performance that I used it to capture our entire trip to Florida in 2016, opting to leave the "big camera" at home. It managed to be super-practical and non-intrusive to the holiday experience itself, yet still capture excellent-quality video – far beyond what was possible with my smartphone. It was the ideal compromise; I would have achieved a better-looking image if I'd taken the much more expensive and advanced camera, but the drawback of carrying something much larger, heavier and less practical outweighed the benefit. The video from the compact wasn't quite as clean or deep with detail, but it certainly wasn't far off, and thus it also served as a worthy B-cam for many Artifact Media productions. At the time there were also several superior models available in the same range, all of which would have increased my videos' production value even further, so for a slightly larger investment I (and you) could have an amazingly adept camera that still fits in the palm of your hand. I know of many fellow videographers who swear by these small-footprint cameras because they offer so much bang for your buck; if they're good enough for pros, that should tell you enough.

After the filming stage, the biggest difference between smartphones and compacts (and indeed any variant of any camera) is that the footage you record is on a separate device to that upon which you will edit and share. You'll need to transfer your video files onto a computer in order to work with them. This is hardly a painful or time-intensive task, but it does add another section to the process as a whole.

Compact camera pros:

+ Small footprint – almost as practical as smartphones
+ Potentially dramatic increase in visual quality
+ Easy to use – automatic filming modes available
+ Access to more video-centric features and settings, e.g. white balance, shutter speed, aperture

Compact camera cons:

- Requires transfer of footage onto another device
- Shooting modes other than Fully Automatic require knowledge on how to best use settings like white balance etc.
- Many compacts don't have flip-around screens, so "selfie" videos become more difficult!

DSLRs

Once favoured for their competence in the world of photography, DSLRs are now also highly sought-after because of their video capabilities. In case you're wondering, it stands for Digital Single Lens Reflex, which basically means there's a mirror in front of the sensor. This allows you, when taking *still photographs*, to look through a mini-periscope and see exactly what you're shooting. When you press the button to take a picture, the mirror flips up for a split second, but when it's time to shoot video, it's locked up out of the way semi-permanently.

Ask any videographer about the "DSLR boom" and they'll tell you the story of how, around 2008, professional film-making suddenly became democratised after brands like Canon started to include proper video features in their mid- to high-end stills cameras. Functions and capabilities that were previously reserved for video-only cameras costing tens of thousands were passed down to DSLRs retailing for as little as £600, and a whole new wave of film school graduates and enthusiasts found that they could offer professional video services without selling their kidneys to pay for a camera (I was one such enthusiast!).

Unsurprisingly, in the years since the infamous Canon 5D Mark II first shook up the industry in this way, technology has come along even further, with the newest DSLR models boasting highly sophisticated features that create truly stunning results. I've often found myself amazed to learn that some beautiful-looking videos weren't filmed on tens of thousands of pounds worth of camera, but a DSLR costing a few hundred quid.

Here are the main benefits of a DSLR over a compact:

1) Interchangeable lenses

I, and many others, would argue vehemently that a film-maker's choice of lens is more important than the camera upon which it is attached. The difference between a wide-angle lens that takes in a vast, expansive landscape, and a telephoto that can isolate a single subject in a crowded environment, is visually immense. But this potentially dramatic shift in how an image looks translates to the *storytelling* of your films too.

For example, picture an episode of everyone's favourite '90s sitcom – *Friends*. What can you see? I'll join in – I can see all six of the gang in Monica's apartment, half of them on the couches, half hanging out in the kitchen. Not only can I make out all of their faces in the one shot, but I can see all the little details of the set too, like the rain coming down on the balcony outside and the brand of milk that Joey's pouring on his cereal. I can see all this because, for the most part, sitcoms are filmed with wide lenses – pretty much everything on the set is visible. The vast majority of episodes are filmed on exactly the same set, so the cast and crew have their work cut out for them to keep things visually interesting for the viewer. Thus, there's usually a lot of to-and-fro dialogue and actor movement happening in front of the camera. For this type of action, wider lenses, which take in more of the scene, are more practical.

Of course, the director will switch to a close-up of a particular character when it's their time to be the centre of attention – when the *story* calls for it. It could be a pivotal moment in the plot of the episode as a problem or conflict suddenly arises, or it could be Chandler delivering one of his classic sarcastic comebacks. Whatever's happening on screen, and whether it's an episode of *Friends* or your next business video, there's a lens choice perfect for the moment.

I'm not saying that you should necessarily draw film-making inspiration from *Friends*, or that you should try to create your own sitcom. What I am saying is that swapping and changing lenses depending on the scene, mood or story of your videos is just about the most powerful facility at the disposal of a DSLR owner (although some compact cameras have interchangeable lenses, too).

As for what lens you should choose, well … that's going in the same book as shutter speeds and white balance.

2) Even bigger sensors

You already know that bigger is usually better when it comes to camera sensors. So it might surprise you to learn that some of the largest sensors available are found not in expensive video cameras, but in mid-range DSLRs.

For the most part, there are two standard sensor sizes found in DSLRs: APS-C and Full Frame. Why one of them flows quite nicely off the tongue and one does not, I can't tell you … but what is widely considered a fact is that Full Frame, with the right lens attached, looks *bloody beautiful.*

Why? Because it's roughly the same size as good ol'-fashioned 35mm film – a nostalgic imaging format that, similar to vinyl, has made something of a resurgence. If you're anything like me, you'll have a stash of dusty pre-1995 photographs in your attic, captured with film, which never fail to put a grin on your face. Even if they're rife with imperfections and flaws, film photos have a certain "look", a particular quality, that just looks … nice. Shallow depth of field, crisp areas of focus, deep colours and a very "lifelike" overall image.

Being the same physical size as 35mm film, a Full Frame sensor in a DSLR means you can combine the signature style of old with all the benefits of new digital technology, like face recognition and fully automatic shooting modes. And once again, manufacturers just keep cramming more and more features into their cameras, to the point where the end results they're capable of producing are quite frankly incredible.

Even though they're smaller, APS-C sensors can still give you an arty, filmic look, but the best results undoubtedly come from Full Frame cameras. And just in case I couldn't sing their praises any more, you'll find that most of the sample videos available at **artifactmedia.co.uk/resources** were filmed on a Full Frame camera adapted for video applications – a very conscious decision from someone who simply can't get enough of this beautiful, premium-looking image.

3) Ergonomics

Most DSLRs are built with photography functions as the priority, but the majority have video features that are beyond adequate (in many ways, you get two cameras in one). The knock-on effect of this could be seen as both a pro and a con.

Compacts are inherently, erm … compact. They're small and weigh very little, which is great for keeping you light on your feet but can prove to be a bit fiddly when it comes to actually using the damn things. Changing settings and reviewing footage often results in lots of button-pressing and menu-navigating. DSLRs make use of their larger bodies with more dedicated buttons and dials for the most often-used functions, so once you get to grips with how these functions work and your camera's specific button layout, your workflow will undoubtedly speed up.

You'll also find that if you're shooting handheld, you'll film more stable footage with a chunky DSLR in your hands than with a featherweight compact. But the inevitable downside is the fact that a larger camera is a heavier, bulkier one, and you'll struggle to fit a Full Frame (or even an APS-C) DSLR in a laptop bag.

That being said, you can enjoy all the benefits of a DSLR in a sleeker, lighter package by picking up a mirrorless camera. These are pretty much what they say on the tin – APS-C or Full Frame cameras without a big, clunky mirror system taking up precious space inside. The aforementioned Florida holida video available at **artifactmedia.co.uk/resources** was filmed with a Sony a6000, which is small and rectangular enough to be declared a compact but secretly houses an APS-C-sized sensor – the only thing it's missing is a mirror, but ever since I ditched my last DSLR for a mirrorless in 2014, I haven't missed it one bit.

Naturally, you'll find all the standard film-making settings available to tweak to your liking on a DSLR, and while they can be a little trickier to learn and master at first, it's worth the perseverance in order to obtain an image that looks super-premium. As far as makes and models go, it's a bit of a minefield out there, and there are thousands of camera-and-lens combinations you could choose – far too many even to start to make sense of in this book. But if you're keen to obtain the arty film look for your business's videos, set yourself a budget and look for well-reviewed cameras that fall into it.

The subject of what specific video equipment to buy, and indeed how to use it, plagues many business owners. They spend hours trawling through YouTube, trying to make sense of various demos, comparisons and instructional videos. And by the time they've done that, a new model has been released and thrown into the mix, restarting the whole process.

The quickest way to determine what equipment you need, what you don't and how to make the most of what you have is through a Consultation with yours truly. This is an hour's one-on-one video call where you're guaranteed to walk away equipped with the know-how to put your gear to good use. Sam Visnic, a health business owner from sunny California,

The subject of what specific video equipment to buy, and indeed how to use it, plagues many business owners. They spend hours trawling through YouTube, trying to make sense of various demos, comparisons and instructional videos. And by the time they've done that, a new model has been released and thrown into the mix, restarting the whole process.

The quickest way to determine what equipment you need, what you don't and how to make the most of what you have is through a Consultation with yours truly. This is an hour's one-on-one video call where you're guaranteed to walk away equipped with the know-how to put your gear to good use. Sam Visnic, a health business owner from sunny California, had this to say about his Consultation:

"My primary outcome was to find out the best settings for using my DSLR camera for video. I wanted to speak with an expert so I would not waste time, energy or money trying to figure it out for myself.

"I learned the fast-track tips to making my video the best it can be based on the equipment I was using, and how to determine the best settings to make editing a breeze.

"I would absolutely recommend a Consultation. You don't want to waste time and energy creating videos that have non-ideal settings when you find out during the editing process that the quality wasn't good. Then you have to either live with the less-than-ideal video, OR, worse, you have to shoot it all over again!"

To book your own personalised Consultation, go to **artifactmedia.co.uk/consultation**.

As you'd expect, the popularity of DSLRs means there are endless accessories and add-ons that aim to complement the video-creation process. Finally, one big caveat to note, which is present in most compacts and DSLRs, is that they only allow for 30 minutes of recording time before you need to press the red button again. It's to do with tax laws, believe it or not – if it can't record more than half an hour of video in one sitting, it's technically not a "video" camera and is thus classified differently. You can still record as much video as your memory card can store *in total*; just bear in mind that you won't be able to record longer takes.

DSLR pros:

- + Massive leap in visual quality
- + Droves of production-value-enhancing add-ons and upgrades available
- + Access to video-centric features and settings as well as beginner-friendly automatic modes (most models)

DSLR cons (same as compacts, plus):

- Larger, heavier and thus less practical
- Can be intimidating to use at first
- Higher price

Action cameras

If I had a penny for every time someone asked me if they should buy a GoPro, I'd have a decent stack of pennies. Action or sports cameras have become insanely popular thanks to their ever-plummeting price tags yet ever-increasing feature lists. Not to mention the fact that their ridiculously small footprints make them ultra practical, non-intrusive and non-intimidating.

For the record, there are action cams available from brands other than GoPro, but the American manufacturer is hands down the most popular and arguably the best. Although mine only sees a handful of shoots per year, I suspect I'll always own a GoPro of some description.

But why would you use an action cam if you're not involved in the kinds of activities that they were designed for, like surfing, skiing or motorsport? Because on paper, at least, it would appear that for less than £500, you could own a 4K-capable camera that has a smaller footprint than a rich tea biscuit. No-brainer, right? Well, most action cams share a few characteristics that you need to know about before you splash your cash.

GoPro founder Nick Woodman famously pioneered the first Hero camera after a surfing trip to Australia, where he found he couldn't easily capture decent close-up images of the sport without investing in either super-long lenses (and remaining on the beach) or waterproof camera housings, both of which were very expensive. So he invented a camera that could be right there in the heart of the action – small enough to not get in the way, but capable enough to take stunning pictures.

Unavoidably, the GoPro needed to have a wide-angle lens that could take in all of the activity despite being so close to it, which of course most action cams have gone on to emulate. In fact, the lenses on action cams are so wide that they fall into "fisheye" classification, distorting the image to the point where it takes on an almost spherical nature, especially towards the outer edges of the frame. Check out some sample footage from a snowboarding trip we took in 2018, filmed primarily on a GoPro Hero 4 Black, at **artifactmedia.co.uk/resources**, to see just how extreme (but very cool) this effect is.

While the super-wide look gives extreme sports an otherworldly feel and truly opens up previously unseen perspectives of these thrilling pursuits, using an action cam for your next business video might not necessarily give such flattering results. For example, I'd never recommend that you buy a GoPro if you're only ever going to be filming talking-head videos of yourself speaking to camera in your office. It's pretty much impossible to get a flattering portrait-style shot from a camera with almost 180 degrees worth of field of view. That being said, it depends entirely on what you do and what you're filming. Some of the more visually interesting aspects of your business might benefit from a little creative thinking and the unique form factor of an action cam, and the image it produces. They're easily mounted to would-be awkward places like vehicles and windows; they're even more easily attached to tripods, stands and stabilisers; and there are even chest, head and wrist mounts for a truly point-of-view look. They can create some very visually interesting results, the best examples of which are truly stunning; some have even reached the stratosphere. Just don't expect the same "arty" look that you might get from a larger camera.

While the audio quality of compacts and even DSLRs isn't great, action cams score the worst out of any type of camera. Although most do record sound and perform averagely in the most controlled, quiet filming environments, they were never designed to capture brilliant audio, and so they don't. There are additional audio accessories and workarounds available, but most are a little awkward and still won't give you great results. Ultimately, an action cam is a film-making tool built for quite a specific purpose, and as such I'd always recommend owning and using one *alongside* a more traditional and versatile video camera.

Action cam pros:

+ Tiny form factor means a variety of unique uses
+ Very easy to use – most are designed with "just hit record" in mind
+ Excellent-quality images from the higher-end models

Action cam cons:

- Fixed wide angle lens can be unflattering
- Not really an alternative to a "normal" camera
- Poor audio quality

Video cameras

Before the DSLR boom, when most cameras were designed exclusively for capturing stills, you had to buy a dedicated video camera in order to capture the moving image. But now that many compacts and DSLRs feature highly capable filming functions, are cameras that focus solely on video still worth considering?

In my view, this depends on two things: what kind of filming you're intending to do, and the subcategory of video camera that you'll be using. On paper, one of the most significant differences between a camera such as a compact or DSLR – one that is primarily designed to take photographs but has had video features thrown in for good measure – and a "proper" video camera is that the latter will allow you to record for longer periods of time. The aforementioned 30-minute record time limitation doesn't apply, so you can hit the red button and rest assured that you'll be recording for as long as you like (until either the battery dies, or you run out of memory).

After that, it's important to establish whether the device you're looking at is a camcorder or a cinema camera (although these two terms are often interchanged, and different brands use slightly different terminology). In my view, at least, the former is an all-in-one unit aimed at the consumer market that can be operated easily, even when handheld, and has features like a built-in zoom lens, a flip-out screen and an electronic viewfinder. The latter technically does the same job, but is a different beast – it's aimed at professionals who do a lot of filming and want the best quality coupled with the most advanced features. Cinema cameras have interchangeable lenses and are highly upgradable and customisable. Download my *Essential Video Gear for Marketers* document at **artifactmedia.co.uk/essentialgear** to see examples of both types.

As mentioned, the ever-increasing capability of modern compacts and DSLRs means that it's become more difficult to justify using a camcorder to record video. It's easy to find yourself endlessly comparing these different camera types, which, on paper at least, share near-identical specifications, wondering how they can possibly be dissimilar to each other or how their end results might be different. So, in keeping with the theme of this book, here's my simple, no-nonsense advice:

Unless you're adamant that you need to record video clips for longer than 30 minutes at a time, use a compact or a DSLR rather than a camcorder. Not only will you get more bang for your buck (because you're essentially getting two cameras in one – stills and video), but it's likely you'll get a much nicer image. A good mid- or top-range compact/DSLR, combined with a good-quality lens appropriate for its intended use, will almost certainly produce a prettier, more "arty" look than a camcorder with a fixed, "catch-all" lens. Furthermore, most camcorders also have very small sensors, which you now know hinders the ability to create beautifully blurry backgrounds and a shallow depth of field. They also usually carry higher price tags, which is kind of the nail in the coffin. All this being said, camcorders are a good choice if you're not keen on using a smartphone but still want a decent image coupled with longer recording times.

Cinema cameras, on the other hand, combine the best of all worlds, with the ability to change lenses, film for extended periods of time and achieve the absolute best image quality available. As such, they're used by both videographers and Hollywood film directors who won't settle for anything less than top drawer. There are even more subcategories and grades of cinema cameras, but in general – and unsurprisingly – they come with significant financial investment attached, and are inherently complex to use to their full potential.

Video camera pros:

+ The absolute best video quality (cinema cameras)
+ Hugely upgradable with additional gear
+ No 30-minute recording time limit

Video camera cons:

- Expensive
- Complex
- Heavy and bulky (in the case of cinema cameras)

> Head to **artifactmedia.co.uk/essentialgear** to download my guide, *Essential Video Gear for Marketers*, in which you'll see examples of all the camera types we've discussed here and thus be able to make a more informed decision about the best choice of equipment for your business's videos.

Audio

I've said it before and I'll unashamedly quote George Lucas again: *sound is half the picture*. Do not underestimate the power of the Force – wait, I mean, the power of audio. Sound can (and will) make or break your next video.

The average viewer, from any background in any part of the world, will probably not even realise that a film's audio is good; the sound will just exist and "be there", flowing along with whatever's on screen. But even the most untrained ear cannot fail to notice bad audio. It jars with the viewer, distracting, confusing and even discomforting them. A watcher who is preoccupied with the oddities and awkwardness of a video's soundtrack is one who becomes less invested in the actual source material with every passing second; that's why it's so important to get it right.

Here's the good news. It's something of an oversimplification, but in general audio is a lot easier to work with than video. And I should know – I spent three years at university recording, mixing and mastering all manner of instruments, bands, musicians and soundscapes. Video creation combines the two distinct but naturally intertwined senses of sight and sound. Essentially, films that look good need to sound good, too, if they're to be effective. That's why TV and film productions have one team of people who hang around near the camera, and another who are all wearing headphones and holding microphones.

The fact that I've extensively studied and practised these two disciplines for many years (I first picked up a guitar around 2006 and bought a camera in 2010) means that I set and demand very high standards for both. You don't necessarily need to be as passionate as me, but you should certainly aim to maintain excellent standards of audio as well as video because, quite simply, if you don't, then your audience will soon switch off. I'm sure that you'll be able to recall an occasion where you've stumbled across a video online, enticed by its promising subject matter, only to find yourself disappointed and underwhelmed when it sounds like utter garbage. You then swiftly hop off elsewhere, never to return to that video (or even that creator) again. *What your audience sees is what they think they're going to get*, but don't forget that this applies to sound, too.

But what makes audio "bad"? What separates professional, premium-grade sound from unpolished and amateur audio? As a marketer, most of your videos will primarily feature the human voice, plus maybe some music and ambient/environmental sound. If we're to look at sound for video in a basic form like this, then there are two attributes you need to be aware of: **quality** and **noise**.

Quality means what it says on the tin: the standard, the grade, the class. High-quality speech sounds loud, crisp and clear. It also remains consistent over time, and is perfectly intelligible and easy to understand. High-quality music wouldn't sound out of place on the radio or your favourite streaming service. It's a properly produced composition, is appropriate for the content of the video and (crucially) is loud and clear when it's called for, and more suppressed and "background" when it's not. High-quality ambient or environmental audio captures the auditory essence of whatever's on the screen, adding to the viewer's immersion in the scene, without being too loud, distracting or annoying.

And the flip side? Low-quality speech is either too loud, harsh and distorted, or too quiet, unintelligible and lost in the mix. Low-quality music sounds cheap, out of date or low in production value. Any type of sound can feature noise, be it the hiss and hum of cheap and inferior audio equipment, or the unwanted and unpleasant disruptions emanating from any number of sources wherever the sound was recorded. This is particularly prevalent with ambient and environmental audio. What should be "background" sound can ruin a video's soundtrack if it is too loud and distracts from the intended auditory focus.

Avoid waterfalls …

My favourite example of poor-quality audio comes from a lady in the health and fitness industry who had a Video

Marketing Consultation with me in 2017. One of her clients had created a testimonial video for her, but had filmed it in front of a waterfall. Naturally the video, even though it was only filmed on a smartphone, looked great – the location was stunning. But the persistent white noise of the waterfall completely drowned out the voice of the person on screen. You couldn't hear a word she was saying, which unfortunately rendered the testimonial almost useless. Yes, there are tools, techniques and clever software packages that can help fix and optimise this kind of "damaged" audio. But they're only effective up to a certain point, and in any case – as we mentioned earlier – it's much better to *get it right from the start* and know that you're capturing high-quality material, rather than hoping you'll be able to fix something substandard later, as we'll discuss further in a moment. In the case of the waterfall testimonial, the creator of the video could have avoided this problem and instead created a high-quality and highly valuable video either by filming in a different location (perhaps just further away from the waterfall itself), or by using better sound-capture equipment, like a lavalier microphone, to isolate the presenter's voice against background noise.

Audio quality is the natural by-product of the equipment and techniques that helped put together the film in question. It should go without saying, but there's an ocean between cheap-and-nasty gear and premium film-making equipment from reputable brands – you get what you pay for, always. So what goes into making good audio, practically? What equipment do you need, and what don't you need, to create videos that really sing?

More good news: as it turns out, you don't need a lot of equipment, or a hefty financial investment, to attain great-sounding videos. As I learnt at uni (and as is the way with all creations, of any kind), it's all about getting it right the first time and capturing it correctly at the source. Using the right gear in the right way can only ever provide you with the best-possible media, saving you the hassle of having to "polish turds" later (an endeavour that seldom results in success). The business end of sound capture is, of course, the microphone, which comes in many variants for different intended uses. You'll also find that different kinds of microphones work better or worse with certain types of video equipment.

Again, let's start with the human voice, because you'll presumably be recording a lot of that. In most situations, a lavalier microphone (aka "lav" or "lapel") is ideal for capturing speech. As its name suggests, it's a small clip-on device that attaches to your (or your talent's) clothing, usually eight to ten inches below the chin. They do an excellent job of localising and isolating speech, separating it from all the other noise around it.

But what if the environment in which you are planning to film is nice and quiet? Can't you just settle for your smartphone or camera's in-built microphone? In short, no – not if you want the best quality. That lav mic is specifically designed to capture speech, unlike the catch-all (and probably lower-grade) unit in your smartphone or camera. Plus, your video device will almost certainly be much further away from the sound source (your mouth) than the lav mic would be, so it's not going to capture as rich and "close" a sound – not by a long shot.

Lav mics also have a very small footprint and are unobtrusive, easy to set up and cheap. Yes – cheap! Professional wireless microphone systems will set you back a few hundred (or even thousand) quid, but you can grab a lav mic that plugs directly into your smartphone for under 50 Great British pounds, and from a reputable brand, too. Once again, check out

artifactmedia.co.uk/essentialgear for my recommended kit list.

As you just learnt, the in-built microphones found in cameras and smartphones are *almost never* up to the job. Sometimes they're okay, but more often than not they're built to a price and their audio quality pales in comparison to a "proper" mic. Hence, there are many mics available that will bolt on to your camera or smartphone, offering superior audio quality and easy integration with your equipment at – again – a fairly low cost.

Why would you opt for one of these mics over a lav? As you'd expect by now, it comes down to what you're filming. If you want to capture environmental or ambient sounds – for example, the hustle and bustle of your office, the city centre, the local park or your kids playing – you can't exactly do that with a mic designed to clip on to shirts and blouses. But with an on-camera or on-smartphone mic, you can capture the sounds of the world around you safe in the knowledge that it'll be significantly higher quality than what your device captures by default. These mics really do come into their own when filming in the great outdoors, because aside from anything else, in-built mics usually have terrible wind resistance. If you've ever tried to film outside, even on a mildly windy day, or you have even so much as made a phone call outside, you'll know what I mean. The slightest gust results in an awful elongated crackle as the microphone overloads because of the high energy of the wind. But clip-on microphones often come with windshields to reduce this massively. Trust me – if you want to film outside and have only ever used bare microphones with no wind protection, you'll be amazed at what a fluffy windshield can do. Just be careful that your dog doesn't get sight of it … I've learnt that the hard way.

Makes and models are changing all the time, so check out **artifactmedia.co.uk/essentialgear** for my recommended kit list.

A quick fix for better smartphone audio

If you've got a current smartphone, it probably shipped with a hands-free kit – either wired or wireless headphones, with a microphone built in. Did you know that you can use these as a makeshift lav mic for your videos? They're designed to be used for phone calls, of course, but there's nothing stopping you using them with the camera app. Just plug them in as usual and your phone will do the rest. They almost certainly won't be as good as a proper lav mic, and you'll still have to be careful when filming outside, as their wind protection is just as non-existent as that of your phone itself – but you can increase the quality of your audio immediately, without spending a penny.

Lighting

After audio, the next thing hindering the effectiveness and value of the majority of videos is poor lighting. Remember that cameras are just light collectors, and they're not as advanced or as forgiving as your eyes. As such, if you want your videos to stand out, look pro and reflect the premium nature of your business, you need to pay attention to light and use it to your advantage.

Again, though, don't worry. As much as the study and practice of lighting is very much an art and science all of its own – especially in full-scale productions – you don't need to know all the ins and outs, just enough to make your videos "pop", quickly and easily.

There are two types of light: hard and soft. Before you make any jokes, let me just say I'm not even deliberately keeping it basic for you here; this is how any director of photography or camera operator would describe lighting, to anyone. Here's how they differ:

Hard light

- Comes from a small source
- Creates striking shadows with hard edges
- Is easy to shape and control (little "spill")
- Is generally unflattering

Soft light

- Comes from a large source
- Casts shadow-less light, or reduces shadow harshness
- Is difficult to shape and control (lots of "spill")
- Is generally flattering and can make the subject appear more beautiful

Head to **artifactmedia.co.uk/resources** to see a comparison between hard and soft light.

Both types of light can be altered, manipulated, shaped and controlled to give the image a certain desired effect. You can take this to any extreme – look at any behind-the-scenes images from a Hollywood film production and you'll likely see highly complex lighting set-ups created by an entire team of people – or you can simply get to grips with a basic (but very valuable) understanding of how to use light and how it affects your videos, so that you can create more visually appealing films quickly and easily. Here are the fundamentals:

The easiest way to compare these two ends of the spectrum (geeky pun intended) are to think of the difference between the light on an overcast day, and the light on a clear summer's evening as the sun goes down. The clouds on a dreary day act as a huge diffuser for the harsh sunlight falling onto them, making the light source bigger and thus softer. Compare that to the long, dramatic shadows that occur during sunset – definitely a "hard light" situation. Yes, with a diameter of a few million kilometres, the sun is a pretty big light source, but in comparison to the rest of the sky it's fairly small, so it effectively becomes a small, hard light source.

Directors of photography and videographers will spend a great deal of time finessing the light going into the camera's lens, perfecting it depending on the scene in question and tailoring it to fit the story of the film or the mood of the scene. But unless you're opting for a particularly dramatic look, soft light is generally what you should be utilising for your business videos. There's a time and a place for hard light (it's a cliché that videographers love filming during the "golden hours" of sunrise and sunset – the light is harsh, but it's very pretty), but it can easily produce unflattering results. You'll have encountered this if you've ever tried to film under small spotlights like the ones found in kitchens, cafés and hotel meeting rooms; it's not that the light is bad or poor quality, but it's easier for shadows to run across the face or for "hotspots" of light to glow, which can be distracting for the viewer.

On the other hand, if you've filmed on a cloudy day outside, or with a large window behind your camera inside, you probably won't have run into any issues; you'll likely have achieved a more evenly lit scene, which complements the subject's face, making them look all pretty and stuff. In fact, that's one of my most often-used tips – get yourself in front of a large light source like a window and watch your video quality immediately improve. It fills me with sorrow every time I see someone filming with a dominant light source *behind* their subject, because in this situation the camera can't expose for both the bright light and the relatively dark subject in front of it, and so it makes a compromise. It'll either make the scene too dark to see the subject properly, or too bright, which will give it an otherworldly glow. Nine times out of ten it simply looks very unprofessional and makes it clear that the creator either doesn't know what they're doing, or is oblivious to the fact that their video looks completely amateurish. And that's not what you want if you're aiming for a premium brand image. There's an example of this in my course*Effective Video Fundamentals*, which you can get by going to **artifactmedia.co.uk/guides**.

Finally, the only other thing you need to be aware of with regard to light is colour temperature. Light sources range from warm to cool – think of the difference between the lighting in a dental surgery to that of your bedroom. The lights in your home will probably be warm and comforting with their orangey, candle-like glow, compared to the whiter (or maybe even bluer), clinical look of the surgery. Different kinds of bulb produce different colour temperatures in this way, measured in kelvin. Next time you go to buy a replacement bulb, you'll see the kelvin rating on the box (counter-intuitively, warmer light is around 3000K, with whiter light up at 5000K). Which is better? Again, it depends on the scene you're filming. It might not seem immediately apparent, but the colour temperature in a film can have just as much impact on the story as the actual shaping of the light. Do you want a clean, modern look? Or a cosier, homelier feel?

If you head to **artifactmedia.co.uk/resources**, you'll see the perfect example of this (and some kittens): for PMT's "Best Gear of 2017" video, we had presenter Dagan sat in front of a roaring fireplace which was draped with fairy lights. Both of these light sources obviously produced a warm glow, giving a nice cosy look. But seeing as a bit more light was needed to fill the scene, we also used an LED panel, positioned just out of the frame to the left of the camera, making sure it too was set to a *lower* colour temperature to match the orangey glow of the other light sources.

Crucially, though, you need to be aware that in most situations, mixing two light sources with two contrasting colour temperatures is a big no-no. Once again it's a case of us humans being a bit more sophisticated than even the best cameras in the world. The human brain can determine many different colour temperatures at once – for example, you can be sitting inside a café filled with warm tungsten spotlights, but look through into the kitchen and perfectly decipher the cooler white light from the fluorescent bulbs. Cameras struggle in situations like this. They need to be told what colour temperature they're looking at through the *White Balance* setting (or they'll decide for themselves if it's set to Automatic). So, put both of these colour temperatures in front of a lens at the same time, and you're faced with a choice: have the café lights look true to life but the kitchen lights overly blue, or have the kitchen lights white but the café overly orange.

How much you need to pay attention to white balance and colour temperature depends on where you film, the control you have over that environment and how much of a concern it is to you. As a videographer, I check my camera's white balance setting before every single shot to ensure it produces the desired result. As a business owner who's got things to worry about other than whether the colour in their video is 100% accurate, you can probably afford to cut some corners. But now that you know about white balance, you're more clued-up than the vast majority of marketers, and can use this knowledge to your advantage when the time is right.

You might be worried that changing the white balance on your camera is a highly complex task and may result in its self-destruction … but it's really easy. Just look for the white balance (or WB) function in the menu (there may even be a dedicated button for it if you're using a compact, and a DSLR will almost certainly have this button). Then, choose from one of the presets: it's simply a case of picking whatever colour temperature matches your scene in real life. For example, if you're filming outside on a fairly sunny day, choose Daylight. If you're filming indoors with lots of incandescent light, choose Tungsten. If it's cloudy, choose Cloudy or Shade – you get the idea. If you're feeling really savvy, you can even dial in a specific kelvin value, but the presets are there to make your life easier, so use 'em.

If you're filming on a smartphone, chances are the white balance setting is locked away and predetermined by the internal gubbins of your device. Most of the time they do a pretty good job of setting this correctly, but you may run into issues if your scene has contrasting light sources, as described above. In these situations, it's well worth spending a few quid on a third-party camera app like FiLMiC Pro, which will allow you to manually set a white balance (as well as open up all kinds of other neat video functions).

You can absolutely shoot great videos without spending a penny on lighting equipment – all it takes is a more informed approach to what's being captured by your camera. With a few subtle tweaks to your environment and the knowledge to dial in the perfect settings, you might just be able to achieve a more premium look in a matter of seconds. But as you'd expect, there are droves of lighting products out there that can give your videos the "pop" they need to really stand out. They range from pretty damn cheap to awfully expensive, but in keeping with the theme of this book, let's keep it simple.

Soft boxes – semi-portable mains-powered lights that make use of a large, diffused material in front of a bright bulb – can be picked up for very little, and often come in a set of two. The more inexpensive ones aren't usually that bright, but most modern cameras and smartphones will be able to cope so long as the light itself isn't too far away from your subject, and you can always buy better bulbs separately. Most soft boxes use fluorescent bulbs, which kick out *daylight*-esque light (i.e. cool/pure white). If you want to use these in an environment filled with warmer tungsten lights, I'd suggest turning off all other lights to avoid issues. The majority of our product review videos for PMT use one soft box as the primary light source, and they look great (if I do say so myself) – check them out at **artifactmedia.co.uk/resources**. When you're done shooting, the whole thing disassembles and folds away quickly and easily. I would recommend these to anyone and everyone. The visual quality from using a big, soft source like these is well worth the already-low cost. Just be aware that the very cheapest units often give off light that isn't perfectly white; you might notice an overly green or pink cast on your camera.

Alternatively, portable LED panel lights come in all manner of shapes and sizes. Some will attach directly to your camera's hot shoe (the accessory attachment plate on the top), whereas others need to be mounted on a stand in the same way as a soft box. Most are battery-powered, making them ultra convenient, but their smaller size means that they produce a slightly harder light, creating harsher shadows. However, many have the advantage of being bi-colour, meaning you can sweep all the way from warm orange to cool white light. With regard to quality, it's the same story as soft boxes – avoid the very cheapest units, or you'll see too much nasty green or magenta in your footage.

Chapter summary

It can be an overwhelming, time-consuming experience deciding what video equipment you need and what you don't, but now you're armed with substantially more knowledge than most marketers. There are many devices we haven't even mentioned here, but what we have discussed are the essential foundations of basic, yet high-quality, video creation. With physical gear out of the way, let's now look at techniques you can employ to create more effective videos.

Action steps

1. Download the *Essential Video Gear for Marketers* kit list.

Head to **artifactmedia.co.uk/essentialgear** to get my current recommended kit list for anyone using video in their marketing.

2. Evaluate your current equipment and consider upgrades or improvements.

Your current film-making gear may suffice, or you might be keen to increase your production value by investing in some new equipment. Using my recommended kit list, upgrade or improve the areas where you think you're lacking.

Chapter Eight

Your roadmap to better videos – part 2: techniques

You might have all the gear, but with no idea how to best use it, your videos' effectiveness will be limited. In this chapter you'll learn how to create better videos regardless of equipment – once again, these are the fundamentals that will only ever serve to increase the value of your films no matter what gear you're using.

Composition

To make a video is to convert what happens in real, 3D space into a two-dimensional image. Your filming device gives you a frame in which to place your subject – a simple box with edges. Where to position that subject, plus the placement of all the other elements that make up the environment surrounding it, is very important.

But it is quite a subjective thing, and there's no right or wrong way to compose a shot. You might line up whatever it is you're filming in a particular way and think it looks great, but a certain viewer might not agree, or someone else might have done it differently. That being said, when it comes to composition, there are a few "rules" and fundamentals that you shouldn't necessarily *always* stick to, but should definitely be aware of and bear in mind every time you're behind a camera.

The rule of thirds

This is the most oft-referenced and arguably most significant "rule" of film-making. You simply take your frame and split it into three sections, both horizontally and vertically, resulting in a grid of nine boxes. You then use these guiding lines to influence where you place the elements of your composition. In the vast majority of cases, lining up your subject with any of these lines produces a flattering result, as does placing particular areas of interest on any of the intersections.

Most cameras can display a rule-of-thirds grid over the image to serve as a handy reference (obviously the grid doesn't make its way into the video itself, in the same way as the spellchecker in a word processor doesn't come out in a printed document). Using this overlay is also perfect for getting your image nice and flat, which, unless you're going for a quirky "Dutch angle", you should always aim for.

For your next talking-head video, try lining up the presenter's face with either the left or right vertical line rather than having them dead centre. Or when you're filming a physical product, experiment with having it off-centre instead of slap bang in the middle, and try to line up the most significant areas of the product with the crossover points of the grid. To see the rule of thirds in action, check out my course *Effective Video Fundamentals* at **artifactmedia.co.uk/guides**.

Flattering angles

The other main concern when composing an image is the angle at which you're filming, as it needs to produce a flattering result for the subject. Inanimate objects can look good from above or below, from the side, dead centre, or looking straight down on top of them – it all depends on the item itself. But there are a handful of best practices when it comes to filming people and faces.

In general, the camera should be at the eye level of the person appearing in the video, or as close as possible to it. If the camera is too low, you'll get a frame full of chin (and your subject can even look like they've put on a few pounds). Too high, and you'll have a frame full of forehead, which is never really a good look.

As well as influencing how beautiful the subject looks, the angle at which you're filming actually has an effect on the story of your film, influencing how the subject is portrayed. For example, filming upwards subtly hints to the viewer that the subject is important, powerful, even dominant. Filming downwards suggests the opposite – a state of diminutiveness, lesser importance or even weakness. Again, I show examples of this in *Effective Video Fundamentals*, which you can get by going to **artifactmedia.co.uk/guides**. You should therefore pay close attention to the angle of the camera no matter what you're filming – be it people, objects or landscapes – because you want your subject to look as good as it possibly can.

Keep it in, or leave it out?

Finally, how much of the subject should be in the frame? In what situations should you opt for a wide shot, and when is it best to get a close-up? The general rule is that the closer the subject (and thus the more of the frame it occupies), the more emphasis and gravitas it carries. If you want your viewer to look at just one thing in particular, giving their full attention to only one element of the image, then you should frame accordingly and give them little reason for their attention to drift elsewhere. In general, you should only include as much of the subject as is necessary so that the viewer has as few things to focus on as possible.

For a talking head or interview, it's usually safe to forget about trying to fit in the full height of the subject from head to toe. You simply don't need to see this much, and furthermore the attention is taken off the important bit – the person's face! Instead, get that frame filled by going to a head-and-shoulders shot, making sure to avoid cutting off the top of the head or the bottom of the chin. Then use the rule of thirds to guide the subject's position in the frame and you're pretty much guaranteed a flattering result that drives the viewer's attention to the thing that matters most.

Remember the story

When composing shots, bear in mind your video's mood, story and message, even if it changes over time. A common technique is to jump to a closer shot of an interviewee or talking head when they deliver a really important point, because it almost says to the viewer "look closer" or "pay particular attention to this next part".

It might not be immediately apparent, but the same applies to products and inanimate objects. Rather than simply filming a single shot of the item, it's always best to get a range of footage that shows the item in all manner of different ways, such as wider shots showing both the product and the environment in which it's residing, and then close-up images of the finer details. For example, when capturing footage of a new electric guitar for Professional Music Technology, I'll make sure to capture wider shots that show the product in its entirety as it sits proudly on a stand, and then get right up close to focus on each one of the finer details, like the neck, pickups, tuning heads and even the lacquer of the body.

Got the gear?

The ability to compose a shot in a certain way depends heavily on the equipment at your disposal. If your only film-making device is a smartphone, you've essentially only got one or perhaps two fixed lenses and so will need to physically move closer or further from your subject to change the framing. But as you'd expect, a videographer's film-making equipment of choice will include a host of lenses ranging from super-wide to telephoto, each with its own unique qualities and ideal scenarios in which it can be best put to use. For example, during an interview, I might have one camera filming a wide shot, which shows more of the person's environment and frames their head down to their waist. Then, at appropriate points throughout the video, I'll cut to the shot from a second camera, which has a completely different lens attached and is much more zoomed-in, focusing only on the face of the subject.

As a bit of a side note, the lens attached to your camera actually affects much more than just the field of view – it plays a significant role in determining the final image's sharpness, colour, contrast and, perhaps most significantly, depth of field. What would be a very cluttered frame with a subject surrounded by all manner of visual distractions can actually be made much more focused and beautiful if the right lens is used. When filming in my office, I'd struggle to separate the busy background from the subject (me) if I used a smartphone with its fixed lens – pretty much every element of the image created by this camera-and-lens combination is pin-sharp and in focus. That's great for certain shots, but it doesn't complement my intended end result of the viewer focusing primarily on me. So, instead, I always choose a particular lens from my arsenal that produces a very shallow depth of field (as well as it being a flattering focal length for portrait shots), shifting the background into a blur and ensuring there's only one focal point – my face! You can see some examples of this at **artifactmedia.co.uk/resources**.

Which way up?

Finally, there's the somewhat controversial subject of orientation – whether your camera is horizontal or vertical while filming. This was never a "thing" until smartphones showed up and allowed for filming portrait videos as well as landscape. The videographer in me says, "Never film vertically – videos are supposed to be wide, not tall!" After all, we see the world through two eyes that are side by side, not on top of one another. But, truthfully, there is a time and place to hit record when your phone's stood up. In fact, with mobile usage sharply on the rise, the importance of video *other* than traditional widescreen is increasing. Apps like Snapchat and Instagram's Stories feature were primarily designed to be used with vertical video. When filming content that you know will be used on these or similar platforms, stick with what works best; in many cases, Facebook actually recommend using vertical or square video for video ads, because they appear more seamlessly integrated with the News Feed when viewed on mobile devices, thus increasing your ad's effectiveness. Just bear in mind that it's harder to repurpose vertical video. You can film in widescreen and then crop the image down afterwards to make it fit, without losing quality, but you'll have a hard time getting a useable, high-quality landscape image that's been cropped from a vertically shot video.

"But Alex – my smartphone camera can zoom in and out. Can't I use that to switch between wide and tight shots?"

Yes, your smartphone camera has a zoom function, but I would always advise against this, because it's not "real" zoom. Real zoom is optical – the lens itself magnifies a far-off image, like a telescope or a pair of binoculars. The image is already zoomed-in when it hits the camera's sensor. But digital zoom simply magnifies the *end image*, the digital representation that the camera creates, which means it loses quality very quickly. Imagine taking a magnifying glass and looking closely at a magazine or newspaper. You'd soon start to see the gritty details of the ink on the paper, uncovering the imperfections of what looked like perfect, glossy images to the naked eye. This is essentially what happens when you use digital zoom, and it's another reason why upgrading from a smartphone to a camera with an optical zoom lens is such a significant (and worthwhile) investment.

Camera movement and stability

The Dad cam returns … We discussed this a bit earlier – the tendency for many first-time film-makers to fling their cameras around with high levels of enthusiasm, seldom considering how such unwarranted and zealous motion will negatively affect the end result. Like anything else in film-making, camera movement is a technique to implement when the situation calls for it, and conversely to neglect when it's not so appropriate. It's also very subjective, and even the biggest Hollywood directors don't agree on it.

Of course, your business's videos aren't aiming to rival blockbuster movies (even if you've brought in a videographer to take the production value up a few notches) – they just need to look clean, professional and a cut above the average, and in order to do that you need to think about what the camera is doing while it's recording.

To move, or not to move?

You might think differently, but here's my two cents: the camera should only move if it's warranted. There needs to be sufficient justification for movement, otherwise the camera should remain fixed. Any video, whether it's part of your more structured and strategised content or has just been filmed on a whim, relies on your viewer remaining attentive and focused throughout for it to be effective. One of the ingredients for that is ease of viewing: your content must be easy and pleasant to watch. If the viewer's attention becomes drawn to the camera, i.e. if they become consciously aware that there is indeed a camera, rather than them just "looking through" at what's happening on screen, then something's gone wrong in the process. You want your viewer to focus on and pay attention to the video itself and the message it carries, not necessarily the inner workings of how it was created. Throwing in excessive, unstable and irregular camera movement inadvertently steals the attention away, and so in many situations I'd recommend simply placing your camera on a tripod or stand of some description. The *Essential Video Gear for Marketers* kit list contains a few examples of such devices that are perfect for smartphones, compacts, DSLRs and beyond – you can get it at artifactmedia.co.uk/essentialgear

The flip side is that camera movement done properly can add energy and excitement to your videos, as well as a greater sense of immersion and involvement. It can also give scenes a more three-dimensional look. Static shots are like paintings – beautiful in their own right, but very much flat and unmoving. Shots that combine creative composition with smooth, consistent camera movement can be like donning a pair of 3D glasses (see below). Moving the camera is also nigh on essential for certain types of videos, for example premises tours and walk-and-talk interviews. There are all kinds of ways to incorporate the kind of movement that will give pleasing, professional-looking results, rather than your typical "I'm just walking along with my camera and not paying any attention to how it actually looks" look. I cover this in more detail in my course*Effective Video Fundamentals*, which you can access by going to **artifactmedia.co.uk/guides**, but for now, here are a few quick tips.

This is for the geeks – in the event highlights video for Talladium UK, which you can see at **artifactmedia.co.uk/resources**, there are several shots, particularly those of the room as a whole, that look almost 3D and are deeply immersive. This was achieved by moving the camera in a way that mimics how our eyes work. We have two eyes so that we can perceive depth – we see the world in 3D and can determine how far away objects are because our brain subconsciously compares the two images being received by our eyes. When supplied with two images to compare against each other, the brain can determine where objects are in physical space relative to each other. It's somewhat easier to describe our hearing system, which works in exactly the same way – our ears are on opposite sides of our head so that our brain can figure out where sound is coming from. When someone on your left calls your name, the sound hits your left ear first and so the brain determines that's where the source is. Your eyes work in a similar way, measuring the differences between the two images.

So, if we need two images in order to see in 3D, why do shots like those in our example almost pop out of a 2D screen? Because the camera is both tracking and panning at the same time. In our example, it's sliding one way while turning the other. Rather than seeing two images simultaneously, you're *almost* seeing two images at the same time because a single camera is capturing something similar to what both of your eyes see – the difference is you experience it over a few seconds rather than immediately. This is most often called the parallax effect, and it's perfect for adding a sense of realism to your videos. Cool, huh?

Use technology to your advantage

Even just a few years ago, getting beautifully smooth footage was simply out of reach of most people purely because the equipment required to do so was incredibly expensive, reserved only for films, shows and ads with the highest budgets. Now, though, like many other facets of film-making, it's become much more affordable.

One bit of video kit that is worth the investment is a three-axis gimbal stabiliser. These elaborate-looking devices essentially employ witchcraft to do a fantastic job of eliminating camera shake, to the extent that most models will allow you to walk or run and *still* have your footage look like your camera was mounted on rails. You don't need to know the ins and outs of how they work – just that they're really impressive. Better yet, there are different types designed to work with different video kit. I use mid-sized models that support DSLR-type and compact cinema cameras, but some are specifically designed for smartphones or action cameras or even larger cinema cameras. You simply attach your device, get the unit as balanced as possible, and then switch it on. The three motors kick in and silently counteract any nasty shakes or bumps, making typical jarring handheld footage a thing of the past.

If you haven't seen a gimbal in use and the magic it can do, head to **artifactmedia.co.uk/resources** for a behind-the-scenes look at a music video I shot, which puts beautifully smooth camera motion to good use.

Walk like a ninja

Our brains do a wonderful job of deciphering the visual information received from our eyes in everyday life – even if you're sprinting, traversing uneven terrain or driving over cobbles in your car, the image of the world around you is plain as day. Once again, though, cameras are not as forgiving and you've undoubtedly run into problems in the past by trying to walk and film.

Normal footsteps throw cameras off-balance and create jarring up-and-down movements, so quite simply you need to be a bit gentler. The quick fix is to walk more smoothly! Pay attention to your heel making gradual contact with the ground, and transfer your weight evenly onto first your toes, then your other foot.

Combine this with the use of your body as a stabilisation system in itself – if possible, hold your camera with both hands and bring your elbows close to your body. Having several points of contact will help absorb bumps and knocks, as will holding your device firmly but not so tight that it induces more shake.

You might feel silly employing these techniques at first, but you should make the fact that most people are too self-conscious to care about how you look work to your advantage; you might look a bit strange, but your videos will be better than theirs.

Fix it in post

If a gimbal's too expensive or elaborate for you, rest assured that many cameras and smartphones do a decent job of creating smoother footage without you needing to do anything other than press record – either the lens on the camera itself will have a built-in stabilisation system, or the software will attempt to smooth out the footage digitally, or both. The iPhone 6s Plus was the first Apple device to have such a system, and the benefits were immediately apparent. Phones are convenient for being small and light, but their lack of weight means they're difficult to hold steady or move smoothly, increasing the likelihood of bouncy, amateur-looking footage. But with a stabilisation system in play, videos look much smoother even when shooting handheld.

Optical stabilisation is almost always better than digital (it's the same story as zoom, as we discussed earlier), so check your device's specifications to see if it's included. If not, editing software (on either your mobile or desktop) can be used to smooth out footage after it's been recorded ("post-production"), although its effectiveness is quite limited. In fact, if used incorrectly, it can create very weird results; I can see when someone's done a bad job of trying to digitally fix their bumpy footage from a mile away. As you should know by now, you'll always get better results if you get it right from the start.

The aforementioned event highlights film at **artifactmedia.co.uk/resources** includes many examples of warranted and deliberate camera movement, but also many shots that are completely static. Hopefully you can see how the combination of both helps create a video that is involving and engaging, yet pleasing on the eye and very easy to watch.

Does any of this really matter?

All this talk of camera movement (and indeed the other points covered in this chapter) might seem a bit much – after all, many of your viewers might only give your content a fleeting look before moving on to the next thing, and so you could question its importance. But it's fair to say that no matter how or where your viewers see it, the more professional-looking your video is, the better your business and brand will be perceived. That being said, and as is the case with all film-making, it's a matter of compromise. It doesn't make sense to invest heaps of time, money and effort in your more short-lived or temporary content such as Instagram or Snapchat Stories, which expire after 24 hours of posting. You can certainly pay a little less attention to how polished these short-term videos are; some less-than-perfect camera movement or a slightly overexposed shot isn't going to severely damage your business's image. Far rather reserve your best efforts for longer-term, evergreen content that can be reused and repurposed long after you first create it.

But now that you're armed with the knowledge and skills required to film great-looking footage regardless of its intended use, it doesn't matter what video you're creating or how long it will remain effective – you know the ingredients and can choose when to put them to use, putting you in a much more advantageous position than most marketers.

I often get asked: "Won't simple static shots make my video lifeless and boring?" The answer is: maybe … But how engaging a video is, and thus its perceived value, relies on factors other than just the camera's position. In other words, if your video is boring *anyway*, then throwing camera movement in for the sake of it, or even having crystal-clear audio, is unlikely to increase its worth. In fact, in the case of camera movement in particular, it could even have the adverse effect of coming across as a little desperate.

For example, plenty of video ads for business coaches and mentors crop up in my social media feeds, but almost all of them get swiftly disregarded purely due to their presentation, which, to me at least, screams "I've done this in a rush" or "*please* give me your attention". The presenter will be doing something like walking down a street, holding their smartphone up in the air with the selfie camera engaged, and will reel off a few lines about their awesome business and how I, the viewer, *must* click to learn more. There'll be gesticulation galore as they try to capture my visual attention through any means necessary. To me this looks cheap, nasty, unprofessional, unsophisticated, rushed and difficult to watch, and hence videos that employ such techniques rarely get watched. I find it hard to take seriously someone who has clearly bashed together a video in five minutes that's supposed to convince complete strangers that they're a worthwhile investment of their time, money and attention. And the same goes for those who opt for waving their arms around in my face (either metaphorically or literally) just because they don't have a compelling story or message in the first place.

But if an unknown someone pops up with a video that looks and sounds ace, and is relevant to the viewer's interests/problems or provides swift entertainment, you can almost guarantee they're going to pay attention.

Hey … that might be the most important sentence in this entire book.

Chapter summary

I appreciate that if you're fairly new to video creation, there's been a lot to get your head around in the past two chapters. Production is potentially the most complex part of video, even if it's just smartphone videos you're creating. But it doesn't have to be difficult, especially now you know about the various aspects and considerations required throughout the process.

You'll notice that while we've deep-dived into the many aspects of filming, this book doesn't have a section dedicated to the process of editing. Despite all the potential complexities of capturing video in the first place, this stage of video creation is one of the most intricate. This book is designed to instil you with the energy and enthusiasm required to make effective videos and lay down the foundations of knowledge that lead to video marketing success; to go through the finer details and endless variables of editing would detract from that, and in any case you might not actually need or want to do any editing at all. That being said, you can quickly and easily learn how to do basic editing to make your videos more clean-cut and polished, using nothing but your smartphone, in my video course *Effective Video Fundamentals*, available at **artifactmedia.co.uk/guides**.

More than anything, I hope you can see how important it is to start with at least something of a shooting plan for every video you create, before you press the record button – even if it's mega-brief and super-simple. As well as the actual content and the way the video fits into your marketing system and your customers' journey (more on this in the next chapter), make sure you have at least an idea of how your video is going to look, and thus how it will be filmed. By doing this you not only give yourself the greatest chance of achieving a high-quality, polished and premium final result, but you also increase your efficiency because you know the steps that are required in order to produce it; you'll seldom find yourself backtracking and reshooting videos because, with a plan in place, you know exactly how to attain the results you want.

Action steps

1. Experiment with the rule of thirds when filming your next video.

As mentioned, this is the simplest and yet one of the most significant places to start if you wish to achieve more professional-looking videos. At the same time, take note of how subtle variations in your angle of filming complement, or detract from, the beauty of your subject.

2. Film two videos: one with the camera static, and one where some kind of movement is used.

Step into your ideal customer's shoes and watch the videos back – which one is more engaging? Which one is easier to watch? With the proper film-making equipment, could you incorporate movement without the risk of your video looking amateur?

3. Invest in a tripod, a stabiliser, or both.

Anyone using video in their marketing should own a tripod or a similar device designed to hold their camera steady. You know that static shots are the easiest to watch, and easy-to-watch videos are more effective than those with excessive, jarring movement, so make the small investment – you'll find it useful for years to come.

Chapter Nine

Putting it all together: incorporating video into the inbound marketing funnel

You're now equipped with the knowledge needed to create high-quality videos fit for purpose in your marketing, whether you're simply using your smartphone, have invested more significantly in film-making gear or are working alongside a videographer. But how do you actually incorporate your videos into your marketing system so that they prove highly effective, delivering the results you desire and drawing more fans, followers, customers and clients to your business? What kinds of videos should you be creating, how should they be shared and what purposes should they serve for both you and your viewers?

There are endless ways to use video to market your business; the method outlined in this chapter (which may well be the most important section in all of *Grow Your Business With Video*) is just one way to do it. It's not necessarily the best, and there's no guarantee that for your business in particular it will bring about the biggest return. However, I strongly believe that it is an effective strategy and one that many business owners and marketers would benefit hugely from implementing. Most of my clients have their own version of this system in play, because it continues to prove effective and is continuously being tweaked and improved over time.

One alternative to the method I'm proposing is for you to follow what most other business owners do: create and share videos that seem decent and hold the potential to be effective on the surface, but are sporadic in their objectives and do not come together to form a coherent, strategised system as a whole. In other words, they just kind of exist for the sake of it. Sure, some people get most things right – they'll provide their audience with content that's useful and valuable, or they'll successfully demonstrate the benefits of their products and services in a proficient and professional manner. But seeing as so many businesses are doing this anyway, and we know already that the online world is beyond saturated in content, you shouldn't settle for merely creating whatever video idea comes into your head – especially if its underlying message is something along the lines of "buy my stuff, right now!" – if you really want to leverage its power.

It's kind of like planning a wedding. Unless you're doing the Vegas or registry office thing, you won't have a remarkable day without some prior planning and orchestration. There are venues to book, meals to have prepared, transport to be arranged and then friends and family to invite. Each segment of the day flows into the next, with you and the attendees embarking on a specific, predetermined journey.

It's exactly the same with really effective marketing, done properly. Rather than leaving things to chance or until the last minute, you determine from the outset the path upon which your potential customer will tread. You create a system where one video performs a certain function, and then that video leads either into another film, or to another part of your marketing system, and so on. You purposefully and consistently market to your target audience over time, rather than putting all your efforts into one big, bold film, or even several films, that you simply *hope* will win over your audience there and then.

And yet, this is the way most businesses do it. They create video content designed to convert total strangers into enthusiastic customers pretty much immediately. Most if not all of their marketing material is shared with the sole intention of selling their product or service straight away, which sounds sensible enough on the surface, but is actually making a great deal of assumptions if you really think about it.

By doing this, you assume that the viewer:

- Knows who you are
- Likes your personality and what you stand for
- Trusts in what you do
- Is aligned with your values and opinions (or at least some of them)
- Has a problem relating to your product or service
- Is aware of how your product or service can help fix their problem
- Knows the details of how your product or service works
- Is financially able to buy your offering
- Is in a geographical area appropriate to your business
- Is in a buying mindset at that particular moment

That's a whole lot of assumptions. And it's safe to say that no matter how far-reaching your offerings are, and no matter how many people your business may apply to, only a very small percentage of them will tick all the boxes. Very few of your prospects will see your one video and immediately convert into paying customers. Even fewer will continue to do so over a longer period of time and become your long-term, repeat clients.

So why waste your time, money and effort trying to appeal to anyone and everyone who *might* be applicable to your offerings, or *might* be ready to buy? Wouldn't it make more sense to target a more specific group of people who are much more likely to be interested in your offerings from the very beginning, and then market to them in a way that encourages the most loyal, long-term fans and customers to come forward, like cream rising to the top? In this immensely valuable and important chapter, you'll learn how to do just that.

> Despite all this talk of a strategised system for your video content, you don't have to stick to it religiously for evermore; there's still value to be found in spontaneous, rough-and-ready videos that aren't as methodically planned out. The kind of off-the-cuff, point-of-view video content made popular by vloggers has risen in popularity mainly because it looks and feels so authentic. Ephemeral content – which expires after being "out there" for a certain amount of time – can also be very much effective even without a detailed plan behind it, so if you just want to throw something quick and easy up there for your followers to see, do it. Not every video you make from today onwards needs to be fully strategised and methodically planned out, and neither do they all need to be visual masterpieces. But hedging your bets solely on impulsive ideas isn't very business-minded, and you'll see a much greater return if you have a plan for your more "formal", purposeful content that is based around the needs, wants and problems of your potential customers. Better yet, in many cases the value of such content actually increases as time goes on, so if you're continuously reviewing, renewing, repurposing and adding more video content to your library, it won't be long before that library becomes your most valuable and powerful marketing asset – but more on that in chapter eleven.

The very best way to market your business

To create some of the most effective video content for your business, you need to follow the steps of the inbound marketing funnel. This can be quite an in-depth subject, and there are far more detailed guides available elsewhere that delve into the specifics of how it works. But to set you up for success quickly and easily, I'm going to distil it down to the basics and tailor the whole concept towards video.

Inbound marketing means that you attract potential customers towards your business by putting out content that is relevant to their interests, helpful with regard to the problems they might be facing, or simply entertaining. You draw people towards you, inviting them into your world by offering solutions, entertainment and guidance. Hence – *in*bound. The opposite is outbound marketing. This is the more traditional method of pushing your message far and wide to as many people as possible, hoping that some of them – even if just a tiny percentage – might just happen to be applicable customers. Cold calling, TV/radio commercials and printed ads in magazines are examples of outbound marketing techniques.

So rather than pushing your name out there with traditional advertisements, with inbound marketing you create content that doesn't advertise your business directly (initially, at least), but instead serves as valuable, informative and entertaining content for your viewer to consume, with your name and identity conveniently attached to it. Thus, you are still actually advertising because the content is uniquely yours, but you're doing so in a much less in-your-face way while simultaneously giving your viewer useful information, entertainment, guidance or support, which ultimately is the thing that's going to earn their trust.

As you'd expect, the return-on-investment of inbound marketing is much higher than outbound, and many businesses now prioritise their marketing budgets heavily towards it. In fact, I'd argue that outbound marketing is, for the most part, a waste of time, money and effort and isn't worth even considering. Even so, many businesses still throw bags of cash at production companies, who charge a fortune to produce TV ads partly because the fees charged by the channel-owning companies and ad agencies are so astronomical. It's all done in the hope that *someone* out there watching will go on to become a customer, and apparently plays ignorant to the fact that most of us aren't just paying less attention to adverts, but aren't watching terrestrial TV in the first place (at least not in the traditional sense). In my opinion, the kind of business owner who relies on hope rather than systems and strategies in order to attract followers, fans, customers and clients should rethink their way of doing business.

Inbound marketing is also important now more than ever because, as we've already discussed, information itself has gone from being highly valuable and sought-after, to widespread and easy to obtain. According to Eric Schmidt, former chairman of Google, 5 exabytes (equating to 5 million terabytes or 5 billion gigabytes) of data was created between the dawn of civilisation and 2003. Now, the same amount of information is created *every two days*, and the pace is quickening. With so much information available to us at a moment's notice, the problem now is that *attention* has become scarce. Would-be customers simply don't pay attention to stuff that doesn't interest them, is irrelevant, is unengaging or isn't helpful – or all of the above. This solidifies the argument that merely "putting your business out there" is not good enough anymore. Furthermore, even if you are creating video content that is purposeful, it needs to be *delivered* in the right way, depending on where each viewer is at in their own buyer's journey, in order to be effective.

So how do you make it work? What kind of content should you create? How do you package it all up? It's easier than you might think. First, you need to hop into the shoes of your ideal customer.

Find your tribe amid the strangers

Any and all of your customers begin as someone completely new and unknown. They don't have a clue who you are, where you're based, what your business does or what you offer. And, most importantly, they don't care. Why should they? You're just one of thousands of brands they encounter (and do their best to ignore) every week.

The knee-jerk reaction would be to advertise to them, sharing videos and other content that tells your audience who you are and what you do. You pitch your products and/or services to them because you know you're awesome and have a wonderful business that can help many people.

Insert "wrong buzzer" noise here. This is where the vast majority of businesses get it wrong, big time. They go all "salesy" far too early, approaching fresh-faced prospects with offers and propositions galore. Sure, you might obtain a few customers by marketing like this, but the big problem is that most prospects at this stage aren't in the frame of mind even to think about whatever it is you're trying to sell, let alone go ahead and make the purchase. They're procrastinating from work by scrolling through Facebook, or they're hopping between entertaining videos on YouTube, or they're searching for inspiration on Instagram. They're hardly in the mood to buy at all, never mind from a brand they haven't heard of. Worse, they're also trying to drown out all the other businesses that are trying to market to them in exactly the same way, and they're getting distracted by cat videos and memes.

Trying to sell to your prospect at an early stage like this essentially turns you into one of those guys waving leaflets in people's faces on your local high street. It doesn't matter what they're flogging – endangered panda adoption, the sickest new club in town or even cancer research – hardly anyone gives them the time of day, no matter how deserving of it they might be. Why? Because it's an almost-nauseating form of marketing that pays no attention to where the prospect is at *right there and then*. They're not in town to save wild animals or solve the biggest problems facing the human race, so why would they literally stop in their tracks to do so?

Thus, the name of the game at the very beginning of the inbound marketing funnel is to "meet them where they're at". Treat your viewers like the strangers they are. Yes, we want to lead them through the Know, Like, Trust process, and at this stage we're dealing with "Know", but let's go one step beyond merely proclaiming "*We're Company X and we do Y and Z*" – instead, let's dish out some really effective video content tailored to the prospect's position in the buyer's journey.

Before you create the content itself, you need to know who it's for. For the content to be most effective, it needs to be targeted at a specific group of people rather than trying to appeal to anyone and everyone. Again, this is where most businesses miss the mark, instead aiming to get as many sales from as many viewers as possible. But presumably your business itself and its offerings appeal to a particular type of person – not every single person in the world – so why would your content be any different? You should therefore identify as much about your ideal customer as possible:

- Their level of income
- Where they live
- Their profession
- Their hobbies

Then most importantly (and in relation to your business, of course):

- What problems they're facing
- Their goals and aspirations

- Their problems and pain points
- What they'd find entertaining and interesting
- What information they might benefit from knowing or being aware of
- What solutions might fix said problems and pain points

The more you know about your ideal customer, the better you can target your video content to suit them. The more relevant, enjoyable and useful that content is, the more likely the viewer will be to move through to the next stage of the funnel. Even if your product or service is designed with a large portion of the general population in mind, having a greater, more detailed understanding of what your specific audience is likely to find useful, valuable, interesting and/or entertaining means your content is much more likely to be well-received and thus serve as the vehicle that drives people towards your business.

> That's worth repeating: *your content is the vehicle that drives people towards your business.*

A good exercise is to create an "avatar", which you may have done already. This is where you make a potential client profile that is so rich in detail, you even give them a name. For example, one of my customer avatars is called Joe (we'll use him as an example as we work through the whole inbound funnel in this chapter). He's in his thirties and owns a high-end restaurant in a UK city centre, which he started from scratch. The business reaches maximum capacity once or twice a week on average, but he wants to take the next step. He doesn't necessarily want to bring in as many customers as possible seven days a week – he'd rather have his business positioned as premium and exclusive, with prices that reflect the quality of the service. He wants to attract the more affluent people who will truly appreciate the restaurant's offerings. So he needs to do two things: market his business in a way that conveys it as first class; and potentially create another arm of the business that does generate revenue on its own, but is primarily designed to bring forward the most qualified potential customers.

Once you've painted a more detailed picture of your ideal customer like this, you can brainstorm some ideas for content that you know will be super-relevant to them right from the off. Remember that at this stage you're not looking to sell, because the prospect probably isn't going to buy. Instead, you're aiming to do one or several of the following:

- **align** the prospect with your values
- **educate** them on potential solutions to their problems
- **entertain** them with light-hearted, interesting content

Creating these types of videos, and utilising them over time rather than just once, puts your business top of mind. You become recognised and valued because you're appealing to your ideal customers' interests and pain points. The word spreads naturally as viewers engage and share your content with others. Under the surface, you're attracting the kinds of people who are near-perfect matches for your business, while gently repelling those who probably wouldn't be a good fit.

At this stage, restaurant owner Joe could make videos such as:

- a behind-the-scenes look into the kitchen
- a quick and easy recipe
- an insight into a particular ingredient and its many uses
- an entertaining, engaging story relating to his restaurant experience

These types of video, which will be the very first touchpoint for many of your prospects, are perfect for sharing on social media – as traditional "organic" posts but especially as paid-for ads. In the case of the latter, most platforms (namely Facebook and YouTube) will allow you to specifically target your content towards users who match certain traits, rather than taking the old-fashioned approach of attempting to push your name far and wide. The targeting options at your fingertips are immensely powerful. You can dish out your content to people in a particular age range, who live in a certain area, who have expressed an interest in specific topics, brands, industries or businesses … the list is near endless. Once you're aware that the most successful inbound marketing campaigns are tailored to and targeted at specific groups of people, it's easy to appreciate the importance of truly knowing your ideal customers.

Oh look, a visitor

If a stranger engages in some way with your content, they become a visitor. Usually this is defined as someone taking a trip over to a domain (i.e., your website) that is more under your control than where they first saw the video. But I personally like to define visitors as those who take some form of action after viewing your content.

There are different forms of this engagement – likes, comments, shares, etc. – and it's important to know what they mean and understand their relative value. We'll make sense of video metrics such as these in the next chapter. For now, just be aware that even though the prospect has only undergone a subtle change from stranger to visitor at this stage, you need to treat them differently and thus deliver different content.

The most significant distinction is that a visitor is immediately a more qualified and higher-value prospect than a stranger, because they've effectively told you they're interested; even a simple like on a Facebook post or YouTube video subtly says "I'm listening". So rather than providing them with the same kind of content that you're aiming towards strangers, you should now *expand* upon what you've shown your visitors previously, empathising with their problems and – at the right moments – offering potential solutions.

Answer the following:

- What kinds of problems do your customers (current and potential) face?
- What could they really do with knowing that would help fix their problems?
- What content would they love to see and be likely to engage with, after viewing your align/entertain/engage videos?

For example, to better appeal to his visitors, Joe's videos targeted at strangers could be:

- More detailed how-to videos on a recipe or a cooking skill
- Q&A sessions – answering frequently asked questions about cooking or the restaurant
- A closer look at the restaurant and its staff, asking them about their favourite dishes

Notice how the focus is still very much on the prospect, but with a greater inclusion of the business – we've started to put names to faces and throw in a bit more personality. As such, viewers are more likely to remember the actual creator of the video at this stage, rather than blindly taking in the content before moving on to something else.

At this point you've probably got some video content ideas floating around for your own business. If so, then that's great – just remember that the earlier your prospect is in the funnel, the shorter your videos should be. You're still competing for attention with all the other business and personal stuff online, so your content needs to be super-succinct. Even if your video is highly relevant and of great quality, it'll only see limited success if it's too long for most people to bother watching. While it's true that "there's no such thing as too long – only too boring", you can't blame viewers for not watching your super-duper 30-minute documentary if they're riding the tube, on their lunch break or supposed to be working. But they might be more inclined to give it their full attention at a more appropriate time. That's why you need to create a range of touchpoints with your prospect, as we're talking about in this chapter, so that you don't get forgotten about.

Lead generation

This stage of the inbound marketing funnel is arguably the most important, and you've probably heard of it before. Marketo.com defines a lead as:

" *a qualified potential buyer who shows some level of interest in purchasing your product or solution* ".

At this stage, a proportion of your audience are visitors who clearly enjoy your content and are finding value in it – these are the people to focus your lead generation efforts towards. For them to become leads, they need to be separated from the rest of your audience; you filter away those who aren't interested in, don't apply to or otherwise aren't appropriate for your offerings, while conversely attracting more of the people who are most likely to go on to become customers. The best part of it is that, when done correctly, you can create a fully automated system that allows the prospect *themselves* to declare their interest. Effectively *they*, not you, put themselves in one of two buckets: "interested" or "not right now".

> This is an important point, actually – one of the biggest lessons I learnt early in business is that "no" almost never means "never". Even if you have given someone an offer and it seems like they're just plain not interested, this is to all intents and purposes a temporary, short-term decision of theirs. Neither you nor they can guarantee that they'll never reconsider doing business with you at some other time in the future, perhaps when circumstances are a little different. If you don't get a reply at all, it's especially true. Very few of my clients said "yes" to a production after a single conversation; in fact, many of them fell silent for a while and I thought they'd dropped off the face of the earth. One of them even said "no – you're too expensive". In these situations, *follow-up* cannot be overstated, because in most cases it's not that the prospect doesn't want your service or has run away with one of your competitors; it's usually just because they're so busy that you've drifted to the back of their mind. In the case of the chap who said "no", it transpired that he really meant "not right now", as a few weeks later he came back and booked a production (which went brilliantly). If you really want the business, you have to work for it. That doesn't mean bombarding prospects with emails and phone calls, which will make you look desperate and poor – a sure-fire way of damaging your positioning. What it does mean is making sure your marketing system is systemised such that it pretty much does all this for you, gently tapping your prospect on the shoulder and saying, "Hey … remember me?"

So, for a visitor to become a lead, *they* need to take action, not you. Yes, once again it's a case of you expanding upon the content your viewers have already seen and engaged with; but, crucially, when they're finished with that content, it's the viewer themselves who decides whether or not to take the next step (which is probably the most significant distinction from the traditional outbound way of just advertising to them).

Thus, an audience member becomes a lead when they "opt in" and provide you with some kind of contact information (like their email address) in exchange for the so-called next step – something provided by you that's of greater value than the content they've been exposed to so far. A prospect taking the time and effort to do this unequivocally demonstrates that you have not only their attention and interest, but also a certain amount of their trust. Our email inboxes are one of the few locations of salvation amid the other noise- and distraction-filled platforms online, and for many of us even they are cluttered with spam. So for a prospect to gladly grant you access to one of their more private digital areas is for them to effectively raise their hand and say, "I'm interested, and I trust you."

Naturally, to attain this trust you need to offer something valuable enough to be worth the risk, time and effort for the prospect to input their details. You could simply promise to provide more of what they've seen so far: entertaining, engaging content that is aligned with their values. But for many of your prospects, this won't suffice, as they can find as much entertainment as their hearts desire elsewhere online. Thus, your hidden offering gated by the prospect handing over their contact details should aim to *fix a particular problem.* Even if your previous content has been somewhat educational, you need to go one step further here and really drill down into a specific issue that your prospect might be facing, offering a potential solution.

The actual solution that you offer is called a lead magnet, and can take many forms. Many businesses (including mine) offer a free PDF e-book, cheat sheet or report – a short, simple document that addresses a specific issue – but it could also be video (either a single film or a training series), a consultation, a free trial, or something else entirely. Whether or not you use video as the format for the lead magnet itself, naturally I would advise that you use video to promote it.

Let's go back to Joe, who now knows that there's a segment of his audience who really dig what he's doing. They engage with his content and are clearly interested to know more. To generate leads from this group, he could create a high-quality, high-value educational product such as "Five Winter Warming Recipes", which runs through how to make some delicious home-cooked food that is suitable for the colder months. This could be in a written document, in a video, or (for maximum impact) both. However it's packaged up, it needs to be nothing short of excellent in all respects. The last thing you want is your prospect to get access to the lead magnet and feel underwhelmed, unsatisfied or have difficulty deciphering the information.

> You don't have to create a lead magnet to generate leads – alternatively you could provide your prospects with a compelling special offer, such as a voucher or discount code. This kind of "deal-making" with your customers can also be handy for building up reviews of your business. You see it all the time in restaurants and cafés: "Fill out a comment card and get a free latte" or "Leave a review for 20% off your next meal".

Content fuels your lead generation, so remember our quote from two previous chapters: *what your audience sees is what they think they're going to get.* All of your content needs to be representative of the quality of what's to follow, not least of all when it comes to your lead magnet. It's no good spending hours on a beautifully designed and hugely valuable cheat sheet if the videos that advertise it look cheap and nasty.

Your marketing needs to be consistently high-quality at every stage if you really want to obtain premium, expert status.

By generating a list of leads, you ascertain which of your viewers are most likely to buy in to your other offerings. And by separating them from your overall audience, you open up a hugely powerful way of marketing where your efforts will receive maximum return.

Lead nurturing

You've got a list of your most qualified potential customers … but now what? Simple – you carry on marketing to them! But unsurprisingly, you treat them differently to the strangers and visitors they once were – notice the recurring theme here?

Not only do prospects who are further into their journey require a different approach because of the level of interest they've shown up to this point, but by obtaining their contact details, you have the ability to communicate with them on a much more personal level that you have previously. The cloak of anonymity that they wore while consuming your content up to now has been lifted, and most importantly you've led them away from the noisy, distraction-filled channels like Facebook and YouTube and taken them somewhere much more quiet, private and focused, like their email inbox.

Your lead magnet, or whatever offer you exchanged for their details, shouldn't be the end of your offerings. Now is the perfect time to provide more (perhaps even your core product or service). To do that, we need to lead them from Knowing you, to Liking you. Yes, they've Trusted you with their contact details, but they could just as easily unsubscribe or even ignore your communications. The key shift here is that the relationship between you and the prospect becomes more focused on the long term, and thus much more valuable. A stranger can come and go without you even knowing, and a visitor might only appear once or twice, but the most qualified leads are in it for the long game. They feel like they Know you enough to disclose their contact details, and they might really enjoy everything they've seen from you so far, but them Liking you can *only* come as a result of communicating with them over time. Only then will they feel comfortable and ready enough to make some kind of purchase.

Again, it's like dating. You might feel comfortable enough giving someone your phone number or adding them on Facebook, but you only grow to really Like someone after a few dates and extended communication. Conversely, it usually doesn't take as long to determine if you *don't* really like someone, which is a lesson in itself …

Once your prospect becomes a lead by being open to you communicating with them on a platform like email, you truly control the conversation. You decide when to connect with them and how, rather than leaving it to the gods of social media. I'm sure you pay more attention to, and place a greater level of importance and priority on, your personal emails compared to everything else online. We all ignore spam and salesy emails, but if you're anything like me, you open those sent by friends, peers and respected experts as soon as they arrive. Your lead is no different, so that's exactly how you nurture them – by keeping it personal.

Both you and your prospect have granted each other access into your worlds – you've both invited each other into your domains. So, in a way, you've said "hello" and have the beginnings of a proper relationship. Thus, you should treat your prospect like the person they are. Even though this is another prime opportunity to market your business, speak to them as you would anyone you'd meet face-to-face. Ask them questions, talk about what's going on in the world right now, tell stories and offer advice. Yes, sell whatever else you've got to offer, but *keep it human.*

This is, once again, where a lot of business owners get it wrong. They successfully tick all the boxes leading up to lead nurturing, and then they revert back to "prim and proper professional mode". They draw a line in the sand separating the customer and the business as two distinct entities, only ever talking about their products and services. They write polished, heavily formatted emails that, as pretty as they are, fail to stand out from the typical newsletters and special offers we're so used to ignoring in our inboxes. Even if they offer good advice here and there and do try to address their prospects' problems, they do so in a way that feels detached, impersonal and probably boring as hell.

I urge you to stand out from all the other spammy, salesy emails people are so used to receiving by doing something very simple: keep the formatting to a minimum, and be yourself. Be known as a *person*, not a business. Write your emails like you would any other – simply formatted and plainly laid-out. Be professional, but down-to-earth. Be interesting, funny, insightful, useful, entertaining and knowledgeable. Become part of that handful of emails that your prospect actually looks forward to opening.

Joe might think that the first thing he should offer to leads is an invitation to his restaurant. Maybe he could even sweeten the deal with a discount or a free glass of champagne. Or maybe he's created a fully fledged video masterclass on cooking (which would make him a clever Joe indeed) – such a high-quality product would undoubtedly be near the top of Joe's list of things to offer his leads. There's nothing stopping him from doing these things, but take another moment to think about his prospect and where they're at right now. Do they really want to be sold to immediately after signing up? Not particularly. They just had to overcome a whole list of objections and convince themselves that handing over their contact details in the first place was a good idea. Selling to them too early runs the risk of putting them off and maybe even feeling bitter – after all, this isn't what they signed up for. But if they found value in his lead magnet, it's likely that they will be willing to hear more from Joe, so long as it's the right message at the right time.

As such, Joe does everything we just mentioned. He tells stories, offers advice, asks questions and promotes meaningful engagement, over a period of time. He's very open and honest, and over the course of a few days or weeks his leads grow to Like him. At least, a proportion of them will; some of them will be turned off purely by his style, opinions and/or personality. Maybe they don't agree with his preferred technique of poaching eggs, or his dislike for fast food, for example, but this is totally fine. Because Joe's a switched-on business owner, he doesn't mind if a few prospects decide to go elsewhere. By being somewhat polarising, he automatically (and effortlessly) attracts and keeps more of those who *really* like what he's got to say. They're the ones who will go on to become the most loyal customers and clients.

I haven't written the word "video" in a while, so let's come back to that …

The most common form of lead nurturing is through email marketing, and I'd strongly suggest that you set up a system that encourages strangers to become visitors to become leads in this way. But while traditional written emails can be very powerful (and boast excellent ROI for most companies), video and email are a match made in marketing heaven.

Just having the word "video" in your email subject line can increase open rates significantly, and click-through rates even more so. Emailing your prospects to let them know that you have a new video to watch retains the personal touch of a written message landing in their inbox with the irresistible eye candy of the moving image. It's easier to watch than it is to read, so you're making the whole content consumption process as effortless as possible. Everyone's different, of course – once you start tracking key video metrics (as we'll discuss in the next chapter), you'll probably find that some prospects read all of your emails but don't watch every video, or vice versa. As such, I wouldn't advise using email solely to promote your video content – mix it up and keep it as interesting as possible for as many prospects as possible.

As for what videos you should include in your emails, by all means send your prospects links to videos that are openly available to the public, such as those on your YouTube channel or Facebook page. You'll increase view counts (and thus get more value from your time and effort spent creating them), and you're adding another important touchpoint (for example, the prospects on your email list might have simply missed or scrolled past the video even if they also follow you on said platform, but now you've made them aware of it). But it's exclusive video content where you'll reap the rewards. Your leads, being more qualified than strangers and visitors, have become part of an exclusive club of sorts, so treat them accordingly. Deliver only the best, most valuable content to them via email, and make sure they know and appreciate its worth. Tell them that it's restricted and only available to them. And make sure the strangers and visitors know that, too.

Just what we've always wanted – a customer!

So what about the business of actually turning that lead into a customer? Up to this point, if you've made such offerings (and you should have), your leads might have bought lower-value products or services like training courses. But what about the core thing that you really want them to buy?

There are a great many variables here, especially between physical products and done-for-you services, so it all depends on how your business works and what it is you're offering. But regardless of the specifics, above all your lead needs to be able to *visualise* themselves using that product or service in order even to consider purchasing it. They need to know the finer details of what the thing is, and how it works. They need to overcome the many objections that their conscience is currently using as reasons to postpone the purchase. They need to know the ins and outs of not only what it does, but, most importantly, what it does *for* them.

As we discussed in chapter five, what a product or service gives someone, what they take away from it or what the actual end result is for them, is a crucial distinction from simply owning the thing itself. It's never the "thing" that someone wants – it's what it gives them or allows them to do as a result. It actually goes even further than that – it's the *feeling* that stems from having used a product or service that people really, deeply want.

This is such an important concept that it could be (and certainly is) a book on its own. But as usual, here are the basics. Sell the *benefits* of your product or service, not the features. Don't sell what it does; sell what it does *for* the user. Any business owner with any product or service on offer can reel off a list of its features, but making the switch to talk about and demonstrate the benefits of a product to the end user's state of being really separates you from the marketers who don't know how to do any better.

Joe could do the usual thing and make a video talking about all the wonderful features of his restaurant. Maybe the script would go something like this:

"We are a short walk from the city centre and offer a range of meals from various cuisines. We have seating for only 30 people and are in very high demand, so booking is essential."

Or, he could go one step beyond stepping into the shoes of his prospects and actually get into their *heads*, thinking about what it is they *really* want …

"Does the hustle and bustle of the hectic city centre on a Friday night take away the romance of a special evening with your partner? Sick of turning up at big chain restaurants just to wait 45 minutes for a table? For a select few seeking a more sophisticated dining experience, salvation lies in a quiet, enclosed area of the city centre, away from the outlandish crowds. Escape to a refined institution, revel in each other's company undisturbed, indulge in taste experiences from around the world … and feel bloody good about it."

Maybe this is a bit on the ostentatious side, but hey – if Joe wants to target the more affluent people who will gladly pay accordingly for such an exclusive experience, he'll do a good job of convincing them by appealing to their emotions like this. And if he packaged that message up into a film that not only *shows* the viewer what they'll experience, but also plays to their emotions in exactly the same way, he'll be classified as a remarkable marketer. Better yet, he could make a series of videos each focused on a particular aspect of the service. For example, one film could feature lots of abrupt, sharp cuts between a couple having a less-than-great time at a packed chain restaurant, and another enjoying real quality time with each other in his exclusive, classy establishment, to highlight the vastly different experiences. As well as that, he could educate his leads on what goes into creating such a desirable atmosphere, bringing their attention closer to the details so that they can develop a greater appreciation for it. Or, he could address some of the concerns and objections that previous customers said they had before committing to an evening at his restaurant.

The same applies if it's products you're selling – show them in as many uses and applications as possible. Yes, show them the practicalities of how it works and why it's useful, but also tell the viewer about how owning and using it themselves will make them *feel.* Land Rover could have merely listed the specifications of the 2018 Range Rover Sport – three-litre V6 engine, 600 newton metres of torque, eight-speed transmission, etc. – but they took it many steps further (quite literally) with their Dragon Challenge video series that we discussed in chapter five. A film with a message like this does a far greater job of appealing to the *feelings* their customers want to enjoy – power, dependability, safety and fun – even in a more ordinary driving scenario.

The opportunities are endless, and I find it really exciting to play around with ideas like this because it's such an enjoyable creative process. Do this for your own business and you'll be communicating with your leads in a far more meaningful way than the vast majority of your competitors, and in turn finding more customers.

The final flourish at this stage is social proof. After all, it's one thing claiming all this wonderful stuff about your products and services, but for all your viewers know, you could be talking complete tripe. The simple fix to reservations and objections is the much-sought-after testimonial. Ask your current and previous customers to answer a few questions about their experience, why they bought what they did, what it's let them do as a result, how it made them feel and what might have prevented them from buying. And – it should go without saying – get them on camera. Having written testimonials is fine, but the cynics out there might think you made them up yourself, so put a face to the name and allow your viewers to hear it from the horse's mouth, as they say. Interviewing and capturing testimonials is a big part of film-making, and over the years I've worked hard to develop a signature style for extracting the most valuable, honest accounts from whoever's in front of the camera. The most important thing is to have your testimonial-giver feel comfortable and relaxed while they're being recorded, so that their account sounds natural and thus believable.

The final stage – delight 'em

You might think that after a lead takes the plunge and becomes a customer or client, that means you're all done – no more marketing required, because we achieved what we set out to do. But to stop here would be a mistake; there are two more ways of using video to continue extracting value from your prospects.

The first is to make the most of your prospect's newly instigated status as a customer. Effectively you've gained another fan, another supporter of your brand, but only in a small, transactional way at the moment. Even if whatever they've purchased fulfils your prior promises and helps fix whatever problem the customer was facing, you risk undermining the value of that customer if you neglect them from this point on. If you fail to keep in touch, check in or merely remind them that you and your business still exist, you may be forgotten about, and you risk the customer taking their business elsewhere.

This is why it's so important not only to deliver value to your customers in the first place, but to continue to delight them after the point of purchase. You should want your customers to become more than one-time buyers – they're worth far more to you as evangelists of your brand, proper fans who can't get enough of what you deliver, who will not only buy from you again themselves but also spread the word and recommend your business to friends, family and colleagues. Maximum value from your customer is attained when they're invested in you and your business in the long term, when they become so loyal that they wouldn't even think of taking their business elsewhere. The proviso, of course, is that this works both ways; you need to be constantly delivering consistent, positive results that steadily and dependably appeal to their wants, needs or problems, so that they have little to no reason to stop doing business with you.

So, by once again meeting the prospect "where they're at", think one step beyond the purchase. What would really benefit the customer right now? What would serve as useful information or guidance relating to their purchase? What would allow them to get the most out of what they've bought? What would make them feel truly delighted, enough to tell their friends and colleagues? The goal of this kind of content is not to immediately increase your earnings, but simply to treat the customer as best you can so that they stick around for longer, and to increase the chances of them spreading the good word for you.

There are many ways video can help impress your customers. A simple "thank you" video can go a long way, so long as it comes across as genuine. There's plenty more beyond that, though, such as how-to videos or tutorials relating to their purchase, an example of how another customer of the same product has put their purchase to good use, or, if it's an experience or service that they've bought, a visual insight into what they can expect.

This leads nicely into the second way to use video to extract more value from your customers, which was taught to me by my friend and client Jon McCulloch (the Evil Bald Genius). He rightly says that there are only three ways to make more money in your business:

1. Sell to more people
2. Sell more stuff
3. Sell at higher prices

He goes on to say that most people try to do number 1 first. They concentrate their efforts on finding more people who are like their current clients, with high hopes of filling up their diaries with, and fulfilling orders to, as many different people as possible. Indeed, that's mainly what we've been focusing on throughout this chapter – the process of turning strangers into visitors into leads into customers. But while it's the first thing people jump to when they want more business, it can also be, as EBG says, costly, speculative and risky.

There remains an untapped area of potential that many business owners simply forget about – their current clients and newly found customers. Why are we so keen and enthusiastic to pursue new customers when most of us have access to a group of people who *already* Know, Like and Trust us to the extent that they've bought from us once or more in the past?

Even if you know you've delivered a truly remarkable product or service, and your customer has made it clear how happy they are with it, you should take the next (simple) step – offer them something else! If they're happy with what you've delivered so far, they should have little reason to believe that you'll fail to supply good stuff from now until forever. Thus, having more to offer to your existing customers is hugely beneficial. You don't need to start at zero again because most of the work has already been done, and the things you actually offer them can prove useful (and thus profitable) in many other ways to many other people.

If you offer a range of products and services, you could create a video that aims to upsell either an additional and/or a higher-priced option to your prospect. Ideally it will complement the original item of interest, but it could be something completely different. For example, Joe could (as we've already mentioned) offer part, or all, of his extensive 10-part video masterclass on cooking to customers of his restaurant. Not only will these videos deliver massive value and be immensely useful to those who are really interested in home cooking, but they will effortlessly serve as further touchpoints to those customers long after they leave his restaurant. Joe's business will remain top of mind and he'll be positioning himself as an expert almost completely passively. Furthermore, there's nothing stopping Joe offering his video masterclass to prospects who are at an earlier stage of the inbound marketing funnel. In fact, a comparatively cheap product may be the first thing many people buy, before the core offering of a restaurant experience, which is a loftier investment of time, effort and money with a greater number of potential objections.

Whatever communication you make with your customers after they've made a purchase, and however you market to them, do so purely with the intention of delighting them further. The skill to do this while encouraging further purchases and thus earning more revenue isn't easy to attain, but is absolutely worth honing once you understand and appreciate how valuable and important your most loyal, long-term clients are.

Chapter summary

Knowing and implementing the steps of the inbound marketing funnel, and using video as a major element within it, is hugely important if you want to create a remarkable business that is positioned as premium and high level. It's relatively simple, but it's not so easy to implement, and requires significant investments of time, money and effort (hence why most business owners simply don't do it). You'll need to treat each stage of the funnel differently, and in the pursuit of developing it you'll encounter things that work, and things that don't; you'll feel equally excited and frustrated along the way. Yes, the commitment to creating your own inbound funnel and all the content that goes alongside it can seem daunting, and you may think that you simply don't have the resources. But as is the case for many aspects of your business, developing a strategy and then *systemising* it is massively valuable and well worth the effort; you just have to be comfortable taking a more long-term view and appreciating that much of the return may well be deferred. But part of running a successful business is being different, and the fact that most marketers simply don't bother to build such valuable, powerful systems should be enough encouragement for you to do so yourself.

Action steps

1. Create videos for each stage of the inbound marketing funnel.

Rather than creating random, non-strategised content (like most business owners do), create a harmonious system or sequence of videos that will help lead your prospects through the entire funnel.

2. Create and promote a lead magnet.

Offer your prospects a valuable resource that provides a solution to some kind of problem they're probably facing, in return for their contact details.

You don't have to use this lead magnet forever, and you don't just have to use one – *done is better than perfect*, so create a "version one" and then refine and add to it if necessary.

3. Ask your past and current clients to provide video testimonials.

Add valuable social proofing to your marketing by capturing the genuine first-hand accounts of those who've bought your product or service. You could either film these yourself, or ask your customers to submit their own videos, but you'll almost certainly get better results from the former.

Chapter Ten
Tracking your videos' effectiveness

A robust, strategised video marketing system is very powerful, but taking the time and effort to create and implement one without tracking, measuring and evaluating its performance would be something of a waste. Even the most elaborate series of films, which are all designed to complement the various points of the customer journey discussed in the previous chapter, will have limited effectiveness if they simply "exist", standing unaltered and in isolation for evermore. To ensure that your content is not only generating ROI, but remains consistently on-message and is relevant to viewers in the first place, you need to do some measuring. You don't have to spend hours staring at statistics, graphs and charts (depending on the size of your business, your budget and what kind of an impact you intend to make), but it pays to be able to understand several key metrics, which, when understood properly, provide a great deal of information about how your videos are performing and thus the steps you should take to further capitalise on their success. Having this skill is the cherry on top when it comes to standing out from the other 99% of video marketers, who are, for the most part, clueless as to both their meaning and relevance.

Understanding the handful of metrics discussed in this chapter kind of brings the whole video marketing process full circle. When you set out to create and share a film of any description, you're telling a story. So long as it's underpinned with a solid Why, even the most factual, down-to-earth, "professional" video will contain at least certain elements of storytelling, such as the expression of values, opinions, anecdotes and attitudes. Fast forward all the way to looking at your videos' analytics, and the same thing happens in reverse – *they* tell their own story about how your videos are being received, the impact they're having and therefore their effectiveness.

As we've discussed, all your videos – even your more spontaneous, temporary content – should serve a purpose. In fact, they each need to serve two purposes, because they themselves serve two entities: you, and your customers. For you – the business owner, the marketer – your videos should initially be designed with *your* specific goals in mind. They need to perform a certain function in your marketing system, such as intriguing strangers, attracting people towards a special offer, educating them on a product's features, sending people to the sign-up page for your lead magnet, providing social proof through a client testimonial, et cetera, et cetera. The video – or, more accurately, the action a prospect takes as a *result* of watching the video – therefore serves you. It plays a predetermined role in your marketing, and, as such, its effectiveness can be measured by examining the actual results versus your original intentions and objectives.

At the same time, your videos obviously need to do something for the people watching them, too. It's no good creating a video that only has your goals in mind, because it will likely be seen as worthless and insignificant in the eyes of your viewers. This is how most businesses use video; the creator merely thinks of how it might best serve *them*, what content *they* really need in order to achieve their goals, rather than considering the needs, wants and problems of the members of its target audience, which ultimately determine the value of a video (or indeed any marketing material). Conversely, videos that are valuable to *both* the creator and the consumer are among the most highly sought-after assets of any marketer.

So, for each video you create, start by establishing your own goals based on the result that you want to occur as a result of a viewer watching it. For example:

" I want this video to encourage people to visit a specific page on my website, where they will have the opportunity to download my lead magnet in exchange for their email address."

With a goal like this in mind, you can then design the actual video around it. You know from the very start of the process that your video will be purposeful, built around a predetermined objective, and therefore valuable. You're immediately one step ahead of the many marketers who make all of their videos on a whim and would struggle to define their purpose beyond a vague, ambiguous term like "brand awareness". For your video to actually be effective and deliver on your objectives, you simply need to step into the shoes of one of your viewers, and determine what kind of video content they might like to see, by answering questions such as:

- What sort of video would be seen as valuable, entertaining, engaging or useful, and therefore would make the viewer pay attention in the first place?
- What would help *retain* their attention and keep them engaged?
- What might encourage them to take action relating to your goal once they've finished watching?
- Is your video likely to be shared by viewers, allowing the message to be spread organically to even more prospects?

If we stick to our example of wanting to acquire new leads via the exchange of an email address for a lead magnet, we might start by considering the lead magnet itself – what it is, what problems it helps fix and who it is designed to help – and then design appropriate video content around it.

For example, a lead magnet used by our good friend and restaurant owner Joe might be a recipe in downloadable PDF format. The idea is that home-cooking enthusiasts sign up for and download the lead magnet in exchange for their email address, following which Joe intends to build a relationship with them over time and offer subsequent products and services, such as video masterclasses, in-person cooking lessons and – his core offering – restaurant visits. Obviously the lead magnet needs to be promoted in the first place, and thus Joe opts to create a video to share on his social media channels. *His* goal is to raise awareness of the lead magnet and encourage people to obtain it, but his target audience don't care about what he wants. Thus, if his video was created with only his own objectives in mind, it would probably only see limited success because it would offer little, if any, value to the viewer. However, by also considering the wants, needs and problems of his target audience, Joe can create a video that not only serves to fulfil his objectives, but is genuinely valuable, well-received and enjoyed by his viewers. With this in mind, instead of making a simple talking-head video in which Joe essentially says, "Please download my recipe", he provides value to the viewer by giving them a taste (pun intended) of what he's offering: he shows them high-quality footage of the various ingredients of the recipe in the lead magnet being combined in the kitchen, and then images of the final, glorious end result of the dish itself. He explains that the recipe is designed for fairly experienced home cooks who are willing to invest a little time, energy and money to create the dish themselves (and thus are more likely to eventually become qualified leads for his other offerings). Finally, he explains the process of obtaining the recipe – just click the link, enter your name and email, and download immediately.

This shift in thinking is quite subtle, but has profoundly different end results compared to making videos built purely around your objectives. Such a scenario often results in the creation of boring, ineffective video that blends in with all the other substandard content online and ultimately doesn't hold much value to anyone. Designing content around both *your* objectives and those of *the viewer*, however, truly is marketing "done right" – valuable and effective for both parties.

There's nothing to stop you flipping this process around, and starting with your viewer in mind before actually considering your own objectives. In fact, it's often easier to come up with content ideas that you know will be well received by your audience regardless of how that content might actually function in your marketing system. For example, Joe might have a sudden creative surge and think of a great video idea – short-and-sweet interviews with his kitchen staff where they each speak about their favourite foods, or each tell a story about their cooking experience. Almost anyone could think of a content idea like this, but out of the millions of business owners in the world, it's only the few who really understand marketing who will be able to extract maximum value from its implementation. Joe being one of them, he decides not only to create the content but also to put it to effective use by incorporating his own appropriate goals and objectives. For example, he could encourage viewers of the interview video(s) to sign up to his emails when they've finished watching, where they'll find even more insightful, entertaining stories like those they've just seen. Or viewers could be prompted to directly engage with the video by commenting with food stories of their own. In either case, Joe is doing much more than creating video content for the sake of it, as most marketers do – he is making sure his videos are *effective* and aim to achieve a desired result.

> Asking your audience to simply engage with your content is something of a "top tip" when considering calls to action, in the way Joe might have done in our fictitious example. Comments in particular are among the most significant forms of engagement, because they take time and effort for viewers

to write and post. As such, they're a strong indicator of a potentially highly qualified lead, because they also require a degree of courage to post – the internet is a hostile place, as we've discussed, and so a prospect who shares their (positive) opinion, asks a question or otherwise openly attaches their name to your content is one who is more likely to become a fan, follower, customer or client than someone who doesn't. That being said, it's important to remember that there is always value to be found in among your silent viewers. We'll revisit this point towards the end of this chapter.

Once you've defined how your video will function and how it will prove valuable to your viewers, the next (obvious) step is to get it out there – upload, post and share the video to the appropriate platform as per your objectives. This is another "end point" for many marketers; these marketers think the job is done as soon as the video is released. But to think like this is to have the oft-sought but rarely helpful emotion of hope take you hostage once more. It's like driving without a dashboard – you *might* get where you want to go, but there's no way to tell how well the vehicle itself is performing. Unbeknown to you, it might be running less efficiently than it should, perhaps because of an oil leak that you would have been able to identify and fix if you'd had the appropriate instrumentation available. In the same way, your video *might* do exactly what you want, but no matter how successful or unsuccessful it is, you need to track and measure how your content performs not only to evaluate your efforts, but also to give you the knowledge and data to create even better, more effective content in the future.

The instruments on a car's dashboard track and measure specific metrics: fuel level, engine temperature, speed, etc. The same principle applies when evaluating the success of your videos. Here are the key figures you need to know about, what they mean and how you should be measuring them. Different platforms track different metrics, and sometimes use varying terminology – this list is a brief run-through of the most significant.

View count

How many times your video has been watched

One might assume that this is the most important metric in measuring a video's performance, but it's not; it's actually become quite a misleading statistic. Aside from anything else, a "view" means different things on different platforms, so the numbers vary wildly before you even start to analyse them. For example, at the time of writing, Facebook classes a view as three seconds of watch time, whereas a view on YouTube is counted after 30 seconds.

It's also the reason why so many marketers (myself included, in the past) find themselves disappointed at their videos' apparent lack of effectiveness. But before you lose faith because your last upload only racked up a few hundred views, consider what one of those views, no matter how long that may be, is actually worth. If you want to push your content far and wide to literally as many people as possible, you'd do well to gain a high number of views. If your video in question serves to appeal to strangers by raising awareness of your brand through being entertaining, amazing or helpful, a high view count can indeed contribute to its measure of success. But given that view count alone doesn't actually deliver a tangible end result with regard to your business's bottom line or its list of highly qualified leads, who are inherently much more valuable than strangers, why should a high number of views be your primary goal? Given what you now know about inbound marketing and the practice of tailoring your content towards specific people, marketing to them over time so that they become long-term customers and clients, why would you care about your videos simply being seen many times by many people? After all, in the end, many of those watching are unlikely to take any action. Your video might get 100,000 views … and that's it. No sign-ups, no creation of highly qualified leads, no new customers, no sales.

I'm not saying that view count is an insignificant metric or that you shouldn't care about it. It's important that your content aimed at strangers reaches plenty of people in the first place, so that a percentage of them do in fact convert into visitors and beyond. And if you're monetising your videos on YouTube, for example, view count *will* impact your bottom line. But I am suggesting that you keep it in context. Consider the other metrics in this chapter and use them *in addition* to view count to measure how effective your videos are.

Retention or average view time

How long your viewers watched your video for, on average

In other words, at what point did your viewers *stop* watching your video, and thus how engaged did your audience remain over time? An effective video will keep a viewer watching until the very end. An ineffective video will fail to deliver on its audience's expectations, even if it initially looked promising, and at some point they'll switch off and go elsewhere.

It should be clear that retention is generally a more important measurement than view count, and furthermore undermines the significance of the latter – it can be easy to see a high view count and initially feel accomplished. But the truth, of course, is that those views are rarely measured as a person watching 100% of your video. In other words, it's likely that most of those views ended long before your video reached its conclusion; many people will have scrolled away, clicked-off or pressed the stop button before you wanted them to.

Once again, though, be wary of *how* this statistic is reported. Facebook themselves say "expect to see some of your audience drop off at the beginning as people scroll through their News Feed". Indeed, looking at the retention of the average video posted to Facebook shows a graph that looks unfavourable on first sight, but the reason for its sudden, steep drop-off is primarily due to most people simply scrolling past the video. Usually they do this not because it's bad or irrelevant to them, but because they are procrastinating from doing work, can't give it their full attention right now or are looking for content with more instant gratification.

There's another layer of complexity that again depends on the platform upon which your video resides. Facebook's autoplay feature is great for getting your videos watched, even partly, by people who might not have necessarily clicked the play button themselves, but it does mean that data that would previously have been straightforward to make sense of has the potential to be interpreted incorrectly. For example, how accurate can the retention measurement be, given that some people may have come across your automatically playing video in their feed, only to put their device down and take their attention elsewhere while it continues to play?

Hence, there are both autoplay and click-to-play retention statistics – in other words, how many people watched because the video had started playing *anyway*, and how many actually made the *choice* to click. Hopefully you can see that, while similar, these two measurements tell potentially very different stories. The latter is a much stronger indicator of someone who is genuinely interested in your content.

Use the retention measurement to understand when your content is engaging to viewers, when it isn't, and how long your audience prefers to watch on average (and thus the length your videos should be).

Click-through rate (CTR)

How many people took action to see more, or see something else

CTR only applies if there's some kind of link attached to your video – a prompt delivered to the viewer that encourages them to take action, like a clickable button on a Facebook or YouTube ad. The link could in theory take the viewer anywhere on the web, but most often it'll be to a specific page on your website, another video or even a chatbot conversation, because the video is serving to advertise what's on the other side.

A prospect's decision to click on your video in the first place is significant, but them clicking through to visit the location you'd really like them to is substantially more noteworthy. It tells you a lot about both the viewer and your content. The latter has clearly been effective in resonating with the former, and thus the prospect's intrigue and interest are sufficient enough to take action in order to find out more. Unsurprisingly, CTR is perhaps the most important metric to measure on any video where a link is present and thus a specific action like this is encouraged. Essentially, a high CTR means your content is doing a good job of demonstrating the value of what's on "the other side" – those who click are intrigued, at the very least.

Which brings us nicely on to another "be careful" notice: what your prospects do *after* this point is an entirely different matter. The actions they take (or don't take) at whatever destination you've led them to should be measured independently in order to accurately measure the effectiveness of your marketing. Attaining a high CTR is one thing, but like the "quarter-inch drill bits" analogy, this isn't *really* what we want – it's a particular action taken *afterwards* that is significant, such as downloading your lead magnet or applying for a consultation.

Clearly, if plenty of people are both clicking through and then taking the subsequent action you desire, both your video and your website are performing well. But if CTR is high and post-video actions are low, something's obviously wrong on the other side. Perhaps that page of your website is broken or not optimised; maybe your sign-up form is too complicated and demands too much handing-over of personal info; or perhaps the copy itself on the page doesn't sufficiently demonstrate the value of what you're offering. If your CTR is low in the first place, it could be that your offer isn't compelling enough or the call to action in your video doesn't quite cut it – if that's the case, consider revising either, or both.

Some platforms allow you to optimise for click-throughs in a number of ways, for example changing what your video ad's clickable button says on Facebook (you can choose from "Learn More", "Download", "Sign Up" and so on) or clicking on a certain area of the video on YouTube (an "annotation", which essentially works the same way as a regular hyperlink).

Engagement

How many social interactions occur on your content

Likes, comments and shares are the most prevalent forms of engagement you'll see on your videos. Negative feedback, such as hiding your content or reporting it as inappropriate, also counts … but let's not think too much about that!

Engagement pretty much speaks for itself. A higher level of (positive) engagement means your video is relevant and considered valuable. Viewers making conscious decisions to give your content their seal of approval with upvotes, praising it through comments and sharing it with others are all the fruits of an effective video. Engagement is often, but not always, influenced by view count – naturally, a video that's attained more views is more likely to have more signs of engagement. But if you've built a loyal tribe of followers like a clever business owner, even a group on the small side will be happy to openly express their enthusiasm for your content.

There are a handful of common causes of low engagement. Your content might ultimately lack value in some way, i.e. it's not entertaining/useful/interesting/relevant etc. and so people aren't inclined to engage, or it may not have been delivered in the optimum way. The fix for the former is simple, but not necessarily easy: create better content! If you know your videos are valuable and yet you still aren't seeing much engagement, it might be that either not enough people have their eyes on it (low view count), or they're the wrong eyes (i.e. not your target audience). Finally, it could simply be that you haven't prompted your viewers to engage. This is why you'll find so many YouTubers almost spelling out what they'd like their audience to do, dropping less-than-subtle hints like "Leave a comment below" or "Don't forget to hit that Like button!". People enjoy sharing their own thoughts, opinions and stories, so consider sweetening the deal somewhat by asking them to engage accordingly.

As with all of the metrics in this chapter, how much value you, as the creator, place on engagement depends on your goals. If you do want to reach droves of people, high engagement is significant, because likes, comments and shares will naturally lead to more people viewing. However, if your real objective is to gain more sign-ups to your email list, which requires prospects to navigate away from the initial video onto your website, it should go without saying that it's CTR that you should be paying more attention to, and not engagement.

Tune your marketing like a racing car

There are as many variables in marketing as there are parts on a car. When motorsport teams are preparing their vehicles for a race weekend, a team of technicians will do their best to optimise all the component parts that go into making a rapid, efficient vehicle: tyre pressure, camber, suspension stiffness and brake balance, to name but a few. Each of these facets has an optimum setting that will deliver the greatest return – a quicker lap time. However, it's rare that a vehicle will be set up exactly the same across two different circuits. One may be in a hotter country than the other, or feature more high-speed straights and fewer low-speed corners, so the car's tuning needs to be optimised for the job at hand. There's a reason why even a prestigious discipline like Formula 1 dedicates one of the three days in a race weekend to so-called "practice", when the entire team will work together to optimise the car to do the best job it can. They'll start with a rough idea of how best to set up the vehicle, but ultimately success will come as a result of trial and error, hypothesising and implementing, testing and measuring.

The same principle applies when you're marketing your business, especially through video. Just like a racing circuit, there are countless variables that may either threaten the outcome of your efforts, or complement them. A driver may find that his car struggles to reach its top speed on the longest straight of a particular circuit – his foot is pressed to the floor, but by the time he reaches the braking point for the next corner, he's only just shifted into top gear. He relays this information to his team, who then swap out his gearbox to a more suitable one. The next time he takes the vehicle round the track, he shifts into top gear much earlier down the straight, and reaches the car's top speed faster, resulting in a quicker overall lap time. Had the team opted *not* to test their car before the actual race, they would undoubtedly find themselves at a disadvantage compared to the teams that did, and would probably place lower in the race than they'd like.

Without testing, measuring and evaluating your marketing efforts, you cannot expect your results to improve. Without looking at cold, hard data, you simply won't know if what you're doing is having any effect. Without examining the metrics discussed in this chapter, and then tweaking your videos accordingly, you're showing up to the race without testing to see if your engine will start.

Once again, most business owners don't need to become complete data geeks, perusing endless graphs, tables and charts in order to measure the effectiveness of their videos. What *all* business owners should do, however – and what most simply play ignorant to – is spend a little time looking at their dashboards. Post a video, give it some time and then check the results. Compare how it's performing against your initial goals and objectives, and then tune your marketing vehicle by making some changes that might help bring about your desired outcome. Perhaps the video could be made shorter and more succinct, or you could include a more explicit call to action, or it could be targeted at a more specific audience. The most important thing to remember when you do this is to change only*one* thing at a time; otherwise, it will be difficult to determine *why* the results are different. If a racing team brought their car back into the garage to stiffen the suspension, increase the fuel load, decrease the camber angle and change the tyres, they wouldn't be able to attribute the change in lap time to any of these factors; it could have been any or all of them. The same goes for your marketing. Making small-yet-significant changes and then comparing the results will paint a more accurate picture, allowing you to become a more effective marketer, who knows what works and what doesn't.

Despite the importance of knowing and understanding the metrics discussed in this chapter, and even if you've taken the initiative to learn about others, there's only so much that data can tell you. Numbers and statistics don't give much insight into what a viewer is thinking or how they're feeling … not yet, anyway. As such, don't forget about the aforementioned *silent viewers* – those who don't engage, don't openly express their opinions, don't sign up for all your offerings or maybe even don't watch all of your videos. Just because a prospect hasn't given much indication that they're interested in you, doesn't mean they actually aren't. On many occasions I've found myself surprised after receiving a message or an email from someone I'd never expected to be interested in my services. They'd never liked any of my posts, they weren't on my email list … as far as I was concerned, they weren't even on my radar. They enquired completely out of the blue, and many went on to become long-term clients. So if there's a certain someone on your list of people you'd love to work with who hasn't yet shown any interest, or if you're feeling a little underwhelmed at how many comments your last upload received, bear in mind that no amount of data will tell you the *whole* story. If you know you're marketing your business in the proper way, don't let low numbers reduce your momentum – consistency is key.

Finally, remember that even within the same industry, no two businesses are the same. What works for one brand might not prove so effective for another. How well a business's marketing performs isn't just down to the quality, relevance or value of the material itself, in the same way that a political party who just won an election can't attribute their success solely to one thing, such as their policy on healthcare or how many flyers they posted through letterboxes. Their success (or otherwise) is the result of a culmination of many factors that does include the effectiveness of their marketing, but also extends to perception, positioning and whether their ambassadors are seen as trustworthy. The same goes for your business – how you are perceived and thus your positioning within your industry will depend on a great many things, not just the effectiveness of your marketing.

Chapter summary

"It is a capital mistake to theorise before one has data," said Sir Arthur Conan Doyle. Setting goals before testing and measuring is the only way to know how to improve and optimise your marketing efforts. Without understanding how your videos are performing, you're driving without a dashboard. You risk wasting time and money by obliviously being on a less-than-ideal route to marketing your business; something you'd be able to see with the proper data available. Examining some basic numbers doesn't take much time or effort – on the contrary, it *saves* you both in the long run by helping to steer you in the right direction.

Action steps

1. Pick a video you've already posted and examine the data for each of the metrics discussed in this chapter.

Get to grips with how to access the information on whatever platform(s) your videos primarily reside, and become comfortable reading and understanding it.

2. Evaluate the data so that your next upload is more effective.

Are the results surprising? Did your video hit the mark? You'll probably be able to identify how you could improve your videos' effectiveness after just a brief look.

3. Set some goals for how your next upload might be more effective.

Based on what you've learnt, define a couple of targets for your next video – perhaps you'd like more people to click through to your website, so your call to action could be made more explicit or your offer could be more compelling.

Chapter Eleven
Video as an asset

It should be clear to you now that video content serving specific functions in a strategised marketing system is the absolute best use of this rich form of media. Rather than investing heavily in a single video or simply posting random content, hedging your bets on it reaching and appealing to as many people as possible, you instead take full advantage of a suite of films, each having a distinctive role targeted at specific people, that come together to form a robust structure that only ever increases in value. The inbound methodology isn't the only way to market your business, but in today's world I'd argue it's one of the best and offers massive ROI.

Sometimes, though, that ROI can be difficult, or even impossible, to determine. No one can say for sure what level of return a particular video, or even the funnel as a whole, will bring back. But part of the reason for this is that the return doesn't just mean more money landing in your bank account – video content utilised properly can deliver much more than just a bit of extra cash.

In his excellent book *24 Assets*, Daniel Priestley stresses the importance of creating resources and properties relating to your business in order to increase its value. His proposed assets span seven categories and cover everything from content to management systems, brand identity and culture. He claims that the most successful businesses tick all 24 boxes, making sure that each and every element is high-quality. The assets are broad in nature, and while they are valuable in isolation, they're designed to work harmoniously as one grand system.

Jamie Oliver serves as a great example of someone whose business is rich with these assets. Most people know him from his cooking shows on TV, but he also authors books, owns restaurants, hires quality staff and has access to funding – all of which allows him to continuously scale his business.

Building up all 24 assets alongside the everyday running of your business can be tough. It takes all three of the big investments – time, money and energy – and that's why most companies are lacking in a few areas. But those who commit fully to developing and maintaining their system of assets go on to become the most successful. I'd highly recommend reading Daniel's book to learn more.

Video is in many ways an asset in itself, and while it can be complex, time-consuming and expensive in its own right, compared to many other aspects of your business, such as managing financial accounts and hiring staff, it's quite straightforward, and yet is so powerful and valuable. It primarily resides in the category of "content", but can actually fall into (and benefit) many others too. For example, you can use video to train your team members, or help secure funding. It's such a rich, dynamic and influential form of media that it is almost infinitely reusable and repurposable. It can open up countless new opportunities for your business and, if done well, stands the all-important test of time.

Jon McCulloch, the EBG, states that "nirvana" is ticking all three of the boxes we discussed earlier – selling more stuff, to more people, at higher prices. Video can be the catalyst that allows you to do that. You can sell more stuff by creating courses and informational products that sit alongside your core offering; you can sell to more people by using video in your marketing to promote any and all of your offerings; and you can sell at higher prices because quality, consistent video content helps position you as a high-level, authoritative expert in your field.

It's easy to feel overwhelmed at the prospect of using video to its full potential, so most business owners and marketers either don't do it at all, or cut corners during the process. But that gives the minority of people who *do* buy into video's long-term value the opportunity to truly exploit it and emerge on top. And, in any case, it's not as hard to come by as many think. I don't have any facts to back this up, but I reckon if the average business owner added up all the hours they'd spent over the years creating content that was temporary, lacking in substance, offered little value to the viewer or had limited ROI, it probably wouldn't be far off the time required to create a proper inbound video marketing system – one that would not only bring a swifter, grander ROI, but would also prove valuable for longer and in many additional ways.

Towards the end of *24 Assets*, Daniel empathises with the reader and speculates that they may feel like they've been given another 24 items for their to-do list. You might have similar feelings right now, after reading this book. You might have all the desire to create and utilise awesome video, but be put off by the time it will take, the energy it may sap and the money it will cost. Or maybe you've already started but have taken your foot off the gas after not seeing the results you wanted.

In either case, I urge you to stop for a moment and imagine your business at some point in the future. In six months, a year or even a decade's time, how do you want things to look? How do you want your business to be perceived by both your current customers and complete strangers? If you want any or all of the following:

- premier positioning

- premium pricing
- world-class quality
- huge respect
- true authority
- long-lasting, prosperous partnerships and collaborations
- income extending beyond your core product or service

… then you'll need to work at it. You'll need to have a vision, set yourself targets and goals, put in the hours, and always be looking ahead. The sad truth is that out of the 80% of businesses that fail within their first 18 months, most of them do so because they simply don't play the long game.

Video is no different. Creating engaging, meaningful, valuable content that will help achieve any and all of the items in the list above requires commitment and the acceptance that long-term thinking is necessary. Remember the ingredients for video excellence:

Quality
Consistency
Engaging content
A purposeful message
A clear call to action

It's the second – consistency – that catches people out more than anything else. Countless marketers will succeed in blending together the other ingredients, but only a handful do so over the entire lifespan of their businesses.

Video is an asset. It's a tool that takes hefty investments of time, money and energy in order to be fully exploited. It's an asset like any other, and unlike any other. It's a commodity with growing importance, which can help take a business to new heights when used strategically. Its long-term value has the potential to grow exponentially, with the ability to be used and reused in a multitude of ways. It's by no means a silver bullet, and shouldn't be used in isolation no matter how impressive its quality. To bring about the best return, it needs all other aspects of the business to be optimised and working together seamlessly, like the cogs in a complex, well-oiled machine.

But more than anything else, it's the versatility of video that makes it special. It's the endless ways it can be put together and then interpreted by an audience that make it worth the effort to create. It's the fact that the majority of video creations are completely mediocre that grants it huge potential value. And it's the way it's loved by people in every corner of the world that should give you the drive to use it.

I hope that this book has instilled or reinvigorated a drive to make your business truly remarkable. I trust that you've found it useful, educational and insightful. I urge you to take advantage of the offers detailed in the next section, because they will help you implement what you've learnt. It's the implementation of effective marketing that will separate you from the herd of beige, boring businesses that aren't positioned as premium, aren't considered influential, aren't admired for their remarkable offerings and aren't revered as the best in their industry. Attaining such status is tough … is it worth it? Read the testimonials that follow the Bonuses section to find out how some of my clients have been using effective video to grow their businesses.

Then, your task is simple – go forth, get shooting, and create with purpose!

Acknowledgements

When faced with the task of writing a book, your brain instinctively flags up quite a few objections to thwart your efforts. After all, it would be much easier to ignore such a silly idea, carry on with the day-to-day running of your business and not have to deal with the stress of worrying about whether anyone in the world would even read such a thing.

But throughout it all, and indeed at the very beginning of the journey (it was his idea), Dom Hodgson was there to offer steadfast guidance and encouragement. Much more than a client, he's one of my best friends and it's a pleasure to work alongside him. This book, and indeed much of Artifact Media as a whole, wouldn't have happened without him. Thanks mate.

My family humble me with their praise and support – much more than I feel I deserve, at times. Throughout everything – from buying my first camera, to quitting my job, all the way through to turning Artifact Media into the business it is today, there's been my Mam, Dad and sister Eleanor. There's also been my better half Naomi, who is always there to turn things around with her infectiously positive attitude, no matter what I might be whinging about. I appreciate you all hugely.

The video presenters at PMT – my good friends Dagan and Gaz – thanks for consistently leaving me in tears with your wicked senses of humour. Every single shoot with you both is a joy.

Thanks also to Jon McCulloch and Vicky Fraser, whose teachings and wisdom have had a profound effect on my business.

My clients are among the most passionate, driven people I've encountered, and I'm proud to play a part in transforming their businesses. We always have fun and many of them, like Dom, are so much more to me than customers. Thanks to you all.

And thanks to you, dear reader, for picking up and engaging with this book!

Bonuses

Throughout *Grow Your Business With Video* I've encouraged you to visit **artifactmedia.co.uk/resources** to help demonstrate certain points and aid your learning process. You should definitely head there if you haven't already. The most important function of these resources, however, is to get you *implementing.*

This book, and what you've learnt from it, is only valuable if you take action. I want your business to be transformed by video. So take advantage of these free gifts, because they're going to help you do just that.

Bonus 1 – Three Video Course Bundle

Get all three video courses cited throughout this book:

- *Effective Video Fundamentals*
- *How To Be Ace On Camera*
- *Tracking Video Effectiveness*

Just submit a review of *Grow Your Business With Video* to Amazon, Audible, or wherever you purchased it from. Let us know you've done so by emailing info@artifactmedia.co.uk, and you'll get full access to this highly-useful content normally valued at £97.

Bonus 2 – 2x Video Masterclasses with Dominic Hodgson

For my good friend and client Dom Hodgson's online community, we discussed the importance of putting video to work for your business across two Masterclasses. Learn more about:

- Why to use video
- 5 steps to better video
- Quick, practical tips for filming
- The inbound marketing funnel – what videos to make, and for whom

Both available to download in video and audio formats at **artifactmedia.co.uk/resources**

Bonus 3 – Amazing Videos: When You Do and DON'T Need Them

If you got *Grow Your Business With Video* directly from me, you will have already received this training material along with your book.

If not, head to **artifactmedia.co.uk/resources** to learn something crucial – when to invest 100% in your video content, and when you shouldn't. You'll also take an over-the-shoulder look at some Artifact Media productions, and learn our signature system for consistently delivering films that work *for* the business in question for years to come.

This book, along with these resources, could radically change your business. If you implement what I suggest, your marketing (and thus the perception of your brand by your prospects and customers) could end up in an entirely different league. I hope you find lots of value in this additional material and have enjoyed this book – my first, but certainly not my last.

Alex Wardle

If you have any issues accessing the resources above, send a quick email to info@artifactmedia.co.uk and we'll sort it out.

Keep shooting!

Alex